Big Fleet Actions: Tsus
Philippine Sea

Eric Grove

E1-N043-G2

V-522-952

Used - Very Good

4542045
robert owen

S

9781854092816
28634224
Alibris
2/18/2009 3:13:16 AM

S

BIG FLEET ACTIONS

TSUSHIMA • JUTLAND • PHILIPPINE SEA

Cover illustration 'The Battle of Jutland' by Dixon. Reproduced courtesy of Blackburn Museum & Art Gallery, Museum Street, Blackburn. Prints of this work are available from Cranston Fine Arts, Torwood House, Torwoodhill Road, Rhu, Helensburgh, Scotland.

Back, bottom: The Japanese Force 'C' seen from an attacking US aircraft at the Battle of the Philippine Sea. Left to right: the cruiser *Maya* or *Chokai;* then came two destroyers; the battleship *Haruna* at top right firing at the attackers with her after 14in turrets; the carrier *Chiyoda* is obscured by smoke. (USNI)

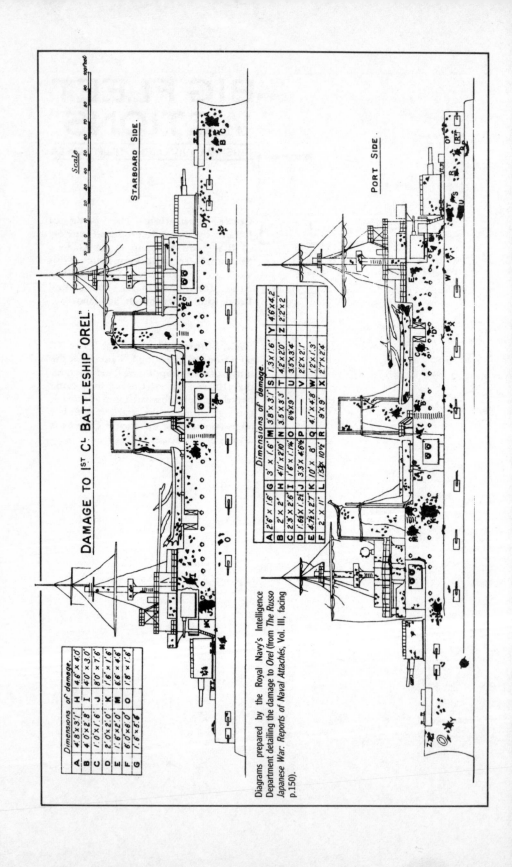

DAMAGE TO 1ST CL BATTLESHIP "OREL"

STARBOARD SIDE.

PORT SIDE.

Scale

Dimensions of damage.													
A	2'6" × 1'6"	G	3' × 1'.6"	M	3'8" × 3'.1"	S	1'.3"×1'6"	Y	4'.6"×4'.2'
B	2' × 2'	H	4'1" × 2'10'	N	3'.5"× 3'.3'	T	4'.2"×2'0"	Z	2'.2"× 2'
C	2'.3"× 2'.6'	I	1'.6" × 1'.1¾'	O	6'4"×9'	U	3'.5"×3'.4'		
D	1'.6¾×1'.2¼'	J	3'.3'× 4'.6¾'	P	—	V	2'.2"× 2'.1'		
E	4.7¾×2'.7'	K	10'× 8'	Q	4'.1"×4'.8'	W	1'.2"×1'.3'		
F	2' × 1'	L	1'.5¾× 10'½'	R	9'× 9'	X	2'.7"×2'4'		

Dimensions of damage.		
A	4'.8"× 3'.1'	H	4'.6" × 4'.0'
B	4'.0"× 2'.8'	I	4'.0'× 3'.0'
C	1'.0"× 1'.6'	J	8'.0'× 7'.6'
D	2'.0"× 2'.0'	K	1'.6"× 1'.6'
E	1'.6"× 2'.0'	M	6'.6'× 4'.6'
F	6'.0"× 6'.0'		
G	1'.6" × 1'.6'		

Diagrams prepared by the Royal Navy's Intelligence
Department detailing the damage to *Orel* (from *The Russo
Japanese War: Reports of Naval Attachés*, Vol. III, facing
p.150).

BIG FLEET ACTIONS

TSUSHIMA • JUTLAND • PHILIPPINE SEA

E R I C   G R O V E

ARMS AND
ARMOUR

Arms and Armour Press
An imprint of the Cassell Group
Wellington House, 125 Strand, London WC2R 0BB

Distributed in Australia by Capricorn Link (Australia) Pty. Ltd.,
2/13 Carrington Road, Castle Hill, NSW 2154.

This paperback edition 1995

ISBN 1–85409–281–2

Maps and diagrams by Sampleskill Ltd, West Hampstead.

Designed and edited by DAG Publications Ltd.
Designed by David Gibbons; edited by David Dorrell;
typeset by Typesetters (Birmingham) Ltd, Warley, West Midlands;
camerawork by M&E Reproductions, North Fambridge, Essex;
printed and bound in Great Britain by
Mackays of Chatham PLC, Chatham, Kent.

CONTENTS

1. **Introduction: The Fleet Action** 7

2. **The Pre-Dreadought Era: Tsushima** 10
Strategic Background 10
The Russian Forces 13
The Japanese Forces 17
Gunnery 20
Torpedoes 26
Tactics 26
The Encounter 29
Resuilts 45

3. **The Dreadnought Revolution** 47

4. **The Dreadnought Era: Jutland** 53
Strategic Background 53
The British Forces 56
The German Forces 64
Gunnery 70
Torpedoes 75
Tactics 77

Failure of Submarines and Aircraft 78
Signals Intelligence 79
The Encounter 80
Results 104

5. **The Post-Dreadnought Revolution** 106

6. **The Post-Dreadnought Era: Philippine Sea** 111
Strategic Background 111
The Japanese Forces 116
The American Forces 119
Air and Anti-Air Warfare 123
Anti-Surface Weapons 127
Tactics 128
The Encounter 130
Results 144

7. **Epilogue: The Post-War Era** 146

Notes 150
Index 153

Maps and Diagrams

The Battle of Tsushima, 27 May 1905   30

Tsushima: Formation of the Russian Fleet at 1100, 27 May 1905   32

Tsushima: Formation of the Japanese Fleet   34

British Fire Control Systems at the Battle of Jutland   73

The Battle of Jutland:
The Battlecruiser Action, 1548–1735, 31 May 1916   82

The Battle of Jutland: The Main Battle, 1735–2100, 31 May 1916   92

The Battle of the Philippine Sea:
Formation of the Japanese First Mobile Fleet, 19 June 1944   131

The Battle of the Philippine Sea:
Formation of US Task Force 58, 19 June 1944   133

The Battle of the Philippine Sea, 19–21 June 1944   135

I
INTRODUCTION:
THE FLEET ACTION

THE FLEET ACTION is the ultimate form of naval warfare. It is the clash of both sides' most powerful naval units, their 'battlefleets', to decide who commands the sea – that is, who can use the seas for communication and who cannot. As Sir Julian Corbett, the great British naval strategist, put it:

'Whatever the nature of the war in which we are engaged, whether it be limited or unlimited, permanent and general command of the sea is the condition of ultimate success. The only way of securing such command by naval means is to obtain a decision against the enemy's fleet.'[1]

Corbett was the first to point out that, despite their advantages, fleet actions were not always either desirable or necessary. Moreover, the twentieth century has seen an enormous improvement in the power of forces suitable for the 'guerre de course', the direct attack on merchant shipping. The effort devoted to the protection of that shipping, to the actual 'exercise of command' of the sea, has had to be greatly increased. Indeed, the battles to force ships through to their destinations against submarine and air opposition have sometimes been more intensive than the battles between the battlefleets which became almost too valuable to risk in combat. Nevertheless, without the cover of the battlefleets, the convoys and their escorts would have been massacred by the main fleet units of the other side.

Given the strategically fundamental nature of main fleets, it is easy to go to the extreme of making a simple attempt to 'seek out and destroy' the enemy's main fleet, the primary object of the maritime campaign. This is usually far from easy. The weaker fleet will not wish to come out and be destroyed, especially as if it remains as a 'fleet in being', it can act as a serious constraint on the strategic options of the stronger side. The twentieth century revolutions in naval warfare have made even more imperative Corbett's warnings to naval officers at the outset of that century that 'in applying the maxim of "seeking out the enemy's fleet", it should be borne in mind:

'(1) That if you seek it out with a superior force you will probably find it in a place where you cannot destroy it except at heavy cost.

'(2) That seeing the defensive is the stronger form of war than the offensive, it is prima facie better strategy to make the enemy come to you than to go to him and seek a decision on his home ground.'[2]

The two decisive fleet actions in this book, Tsushima and Philippine Sea, met these two criteria; they resulted from forcing the weaker side to mount an attack against a position already occupied by the victorious fleet. The third action, Jutland, was indecisive, being fought in a theatre that was home ground to both fleets and in a context where the weaker side had no compulsion to immolate itself for some higher strategic motive. Neither did the stronger fleet, already in command of the sea communications that mattered, have any motive to take undue risks to destroy a fleet that was sufficiently neutralized if merely contained in its harbours. Moreover, undue risk-taking was the only way the more powerful fleet might have suffered defeat. It is not surprising, therefore, that the commander of the more powerful battlefleet showed the caution that he did.

The three fleet actions that follow have been chosen not only for their strategic lessons but for their progressively changing technical contexts. They came at three qualitatively different stages in naval development. Tsushima is the greatest battle of what became known retrospectively as the 'pre-dreadnought era', the period of modern weapons directed by crude, short-range means that had changed little since the days of sailing ships. Even as it was fought, weapon ranges were being revolutionized, as much by improvements in control – the means of directing and organizing their fire – as improvements in the weapons themselves. Within a decade this revolution had changed the face of navies so that only eleven years, almost to the day, after Tsushima very different dynamics were at work at Jutland, the only occasion in the dreadnought era when two large fleets of such vessels came into violent and confused contact.

Another technical revolution was already stirring in 1916, one based around platforms able to operate in a third dimension either above or below the waves. During World War One the aeroplane and the submarine played significant roles, in the latter's case a near decisive one, in the battle to exercise command of the sea. Both began to influence the operations of main fleets also; perhaps a little more than their real technological capabilities warranted. During the inter-war period, however, the power both of the aeroplane and the submarine, especially the former, developed to a degree that more than fulfilled their threatening promise in the First World War. Indeed, aircraft became the primary striking weapons of the battlefleets of the early 1940s. The gun-armed capital ship, the primary unit of the main fleet for four centuries, became a subordinate and essentially dispensable part of the great navies of the world. The battlefleets of the late twentieth century have taken the form of aircraft-carriers, land-based strike aircraft and nuclear-powered submarines, joint capital units of the current age of naval warfare. Although their movements and encounters would not be sufficient to decide any future maritime campaign, their activities or enforced inactivity would provide the foundation on which that campaign would be built.

2
THE PRE-DREADNOUGHT
ERA: TSUSHIMA

A T ABOUT MIDNIGHT on 8/9 February 1904, Japanese
destroyers mounted a surprise torpedo attack on the Russian
Pacific Squadron anchored outside Port Arthur (now renamed
Lushun) at the end of the Liaodong peninsula. Two of the
seven Russian battleships and a cruiser were hit. The following morning
Japanese troops landed at Chemulpo (now Inchon) in Korea. The war to
decide who would be the greatest power in East Asia had begun.

The Japanese were frustrated in their attempt to inflict catastrophic
damage on the Russian fleet and, in order to safeguard the seaborne
communications of their troops in Korea, they were forced to attempt to
contain and inflict attrition upon it. Minefields were laid by both sides
that sank three battleships: one Russian and two Japanese. On 10 August
1904, with the Japanese Army mounting a siege of Port Arthur, the
Russians tried a break-out that led to an encounter with Admiral Togo's
Japanese fleet. Six Russian battleships, four cruisers and eight destroyers
faced four Japanese battleships, four armoured cruisers, ten other
cruisers, 17 destroyers and 30 torpedo-boats and torpedo-gunboats. This
Battle of the Yellow Sea was decided by two hits on the Russian flagship
Tsessarevitch which put the battleship out of control, killed Admiral
Witgeft, the Russian commander, and threw his line into confusion. Most
of the Russian fleet returned to Port Arthur and the rest was interned in
neutral ports. At the same time, three Russian armoured cruisers sortied
from Vladivostok and were defeated off the Korean port of Ulsan with
the loss of one of their number.

STRATEGIC BACKGROUND

The Russians were suffering from a problem that has afflicted their naval
strategists throughout their history: an inability to concentrate their fleet
in one overwhelming force. The Imperial Russian Navy was split into
three main squadrons: Baltic, Black Sea and Pacific. The Black Sea
Squadron was confined by treaty, but the Baltic Squadron, if sent to the

Far East, might combine with the ships already there to raise the siege of Port Arthur. During the summer of 1904 the Baltic Squadron was made combat-ready, notably the four new 13,500-ton battleships of the 'Borodino' class. The press in St Petersburg called for these vessels to be formed into a Second Pacific Squadron. This had been decided upon as early as April, but it was difficult to mobilize the ships and move them to the other side of the world speedily.

Whether to send them at all was a moot point, considering the lack of Russian bases en route and the short range and unreliability of contemporary warships, especially Russian units. The First Pacific Squadron had already made its bid for freedom on its own when Vice-Admiral Z. P. Rozhestvensky, the designated commander of the Second Pacific Squadron, hoisted his flag on 14 August. It was now clear that this fleet, if it ever went East, would have to face the full strength of the Japanese battlefleet alone, with no bases close at hand except Vladivostok, the route to which would be barred by Togo's fleet. In conference on 16 September, Rozhestvensky, an officer of considerable fighting spirit, asked to be allowed to go with what ships were available, arguing that the capabilities of the Japanese were overrated. There might indeed be a chance of arriving before the First Pacific Squadron was destroyed by the besieging troops. However, it was decided to wait until the Second Squadron could be built up to a level where it could more safely take on the Japanese on its own. Not until 15 October did the Second Pacific Squadron, the four 'Borodinos', three older battleships, six cruisers and eight destroyers, supported by eight auxiliaries, sail from Libau (now Liepaja in Latvia). Even then two cruisers, five destroyers and two auxiliaries had to be left behind to follow as best they could as an 'overtaking division'.

Over the next seven months Rozhestvensky's squadron sailed half way round the world. It was a considerable feat of leadership, seamanship and logistics. German colliers of the Hamburg-Amerika Line were contracted to supply 340,000 tons of coal to the squadron at various anchorages as it proceeded eastwards. In the North Sea the jumpy Russians opened fire on their own cruiser *Aurora* and the Hull fishing fleet, mistaking them for a Japanese torpedo flotilla. The less seaworthy older battleships, three cruisers and the destroyers passed through the Mediterranean and the Suez Canal, but Rozhestvensky himself went round the Cape with the 'Borodinos' to rendezvous at Madagascar. Problems in obtaining sheltered anchorages to coal after Dakar caused Rozhestvensky to order his ships to take on double their normal quantity of fuel by squeezing it into every available space. The strain of coaling in a hot climate coupled with the state of the coal-filled ships made the maintenance of combat efficiency all but impossible.

At the beginning of 1905 the Second Pacific Squadron concentrated in Madagascan waters. On 29 December 1904 the depressing news had been received that the First Squadron was no more, having been destroyed by Japanese siege howitzers. Port Arthur finally surrendered on 2 January 1905. Rozhestvensky now decided to make for Vladivostok as quickly as he could, but was overruled from St Petersburg. Under the influence of naval journalist Commander N. L. Klado, the Russian Government now wanted to concentrate all strength for a show-down with Togo's main Japanese fleet. Given the confinement of the Black Sea Squadron, all that could be sent to reinforce Rozhestvensky was an old ironclad of 1891 vintage, an even older armoured cruiser and three small 5,000-ton coast defence ships. Commanded by Rear Admiral N. I. Nebogatov, this grandly named Third Pacific Squadron left the Baltic in mid-February.

Rozhestvensky, who now wanted to avoid battle and get to Vladivostok as soon as possible so that his fleet could act as a 'fleet in being', was delayed at Madagascar by the need to repair his ships and to renegotiate the coaling deal with the German colliers. This allowed the 'Overtaking Division' of two badly needed fast modern cruisers, together with three of the five destroyers that he had had to leave behind, to catch up. The squadron became mutinous, however, as news came through of revolutionary disturbances back home. The trouble was put down with some severity, but Rozhestvensky was planning some insubordination of his own. In mid-March he suddenly sailed, in the hope of avoiding both Nebogatov's reinforcement, which he contemptuously referred to as a group of 'self-sinkers', and if possible the Japanese. He aimed to try to get to Vladivostok without a battle. His fleet crossed the Indian Ocean, refuelling five times at sea, an enormous achievement for coal-fired ships, but was forced to put into Camranh Bay when *Imperator Alexander III* reported itself short of coal. This gave St Petersburg the opportunity to reiterate its orders for the Second Squadron to await the Third. The concentration duly occurred on 9 May and four days later, after the 'self-sinkers' had coaled, the combined squadron steamed off to the north-east. By now there was little hope of avoiding the battle St Petersburg desired.

Admiral Togo, the Japanese Commander-in-Chief, had not been tempted to go out searching for the Russians: they had to come to him if they were to reach their base. The most likely avenue of approach was the Tsushima Straits, on the northern side of which he had chosen to place his main operating base at Mosampo Bay, Korea. Light forces were based at Takeshiki on the island of Tsushima in the middle of the Straits. The nearby Sasebo naval dockyard had helped repair the battle damage of the previous months and modify the Japanese ships in accordance with combat experience. Togo's fleet was both battle-hardened and confident. Whichever way the Russians approached, he could bar the way to Vladivostok and force them to fight. The stage was set for the show-down that St Petersburg dreamt might turn the tide of an until now disastrous war. Defeat would at least demonstrate without disgraceful loss of face that there was no alternative to peace.

THE RUSSIAN FORCES

Rozhestvensky had eleven capital ships in his fleet's battle line, but they were a mixed bag of the new and the old with the weaknesses of both. His main units were the four 'Borodino'-class battleships: *Borodino*, *Imperator Alexander III*, *Orel* and *Kniaz Suvorov*. They had been laid down between 1899 and 1901 and commissioned between November 1903 and October 1904. They were designed for a displacement of just over 13,500 tons but the tendency for all Russian battleships to become overweight during their extended periods of construction led to major increases. The 'Borodinos' were no less than 2ft deeper in draught than originally intended, which had a negative impact on fire power, protection and stability. When fully loaded with coal for their round-the-world voyage, they were approaching 17,000 tons, but the coal at least helped ballast the ships and diminish rolling. The displacement increases were due partly to improvements in officers' accommodation and partly to a tendency for Russian designers to expect too much from a ship of relatively small dimensions.

The 'Borodinos' were 397ft long overall by 76.2ft in beam. Design draught was 26ft but the actual draught with 2,450 tons of coal aboard was between 30.5 and 32.5ft. The main armament was a mixed battery of four 12in guns to penetrate the heaviest enemy armour and mounted in twin electrically traversed turrets, and twelve 6in guns well disposed in twin turrets three on each beam. The lighter guns threw out sufficient shells to have some chance of hitting at longer ranges. For anti-torpedo craft defence, there were ten 3in quick-firers along each beam but mounted too low for comfortable operation in a seaway, especially given the ships' overweight condition. The 'Borodinos', like their French-built predecessor, *Tsessarevitch*, were laid out on French lines with classic French 'tumblehome'. They were protected with the latest Krupp face-hardened cemented armour, some of it imported. There was a complete armoured belt around each ship, 7.5in thick amidships reducing to 4in maximum at the ends. This was not unduly thick by 1905 standards and the decision to narrow the belt in comparison with that of *Tsessarevitch* proved unwise, given the 'Borodinos'' problems of overloading. The belt at the waterline only rose 2ft out of the water at normal loading, and even less when extra coal was aboard, leaving the waterline unprotected.

The 12in gun turrets had 10in armour and the 6in turrets 6in armour: a thin 3in armoured belt covered the 3in anti-torpedo-boat battery. The attempt to skimp a little on armour gave no especially high speed, despite foreign fears of fast Russian battleships. There were 20 Belleville water-tube boilers and the usual reciprocating steam engines; maximum speed in normal conditions was about 17.5 knots, but less when overloaded and low in the water. The most important problem with these ships, however, was their very newness: they were still suffering from teething problems – e.g., *Orel*'s steering gave constant trouble – and their crews were never worked up to full combat readiness. The class comprised five ships, the fifth one, *Slava*, was lucky enough not to be completed until June 1905 and therefore did not sail east.

The only other modern battleship in the Second Pacific Squadron was *Osliabia*, laid down in 1895 and commissioned in 1901. Another French-type vessel, she displaced 12,683 tons, being 434.5ft long and 71.5ft in beam. She had been built with an armament designed to deliver large numbers of shells rather than a few heavy projectiles and mounted four 10in guns and eleven 6in (five on each beam and one as a bow-chaser). Given crude 1890s gunnery technique, especially in the Russian Navy, this was not a bad idea. The British Admiral Fisher had preferred a similar ship, HMS *Renown*, as his flagship in the Mediterranean in 1899–1902. The concept was, however, becoming rapidly outdated as the techniques of long-range fire were being developed. *Osliabia* carried an anti-torpedo-boat armament of twenty 3in guns and was protected by a mix of American-made Hervey face-hardened armour and some later Krupp armour. Maximum thickness was 9in on the amidships part of the 312ft belt and on the turrets, but when the ship was fully loaded the belt was completely submerged. Designed as a fast battleship, her actual performance was disappointing, with a maximum speed a little over 18 knots. Her two sisters, *Peresviet* and *Pobieda*, had both been lost at Port Arthur.

All the above five units were pre-dreadnoughts proper with armour layouts reflecting the potential of lighter, stronger materials. The other three Russian capital ships belonged to a previous obsolete generation. *Sissoi Veliki* was a transitional unit built between 1892 and 1896. She was relatively small, displacing only 10,400 tons, and was armed with two French-type turrets each mounting two 40-calibre 12in guns, but had only three 6in guns on each beam. Her nickel steel belt was of 16in maximum thickness and the turrets had 12in armour. Twelve small 3pdrs were fitted for anti-torpedo-boat protection. The lack of rapid-fire guns of sufficient size was a real weakness. *Sissoi* could make 15.7 knots when new but only at the cost of high fuel consumption for which she was notorious.

Navarin was an old 10,200-ton turret ironclad of distinctive appearance, laid down in 1889 but obsolete by the time of her completion in 1896. She was armed with two twin turrets mounting old 35-calibre 12in guns with only 80 per cent of the muzzle velocity of the 12in guns in later ships; but at least unlike many guns of their generation, they could be loaded at all angles of train. As important were the four 6in guns mounted in a central battery on each beam. Maximum belt protection was 16in of old-fashioned compound iron-steel armour with 12in of nickel-steel on the turrets and 5in of compound armour over the battery. Eight 3pdrs provided weak anti-torpedo-boat protection. *Navarin* was considered to be under-boilered with twelve old-style cylindrical boilers exhausting into two pairs of funnels, but she steamed quite well, at a price in fuel consumption. She steered badly and was very wet in a seaway, something her coal overload did little to improve.

The final major member of the Second Squadron was also of a previous generation and completely obsolete. *Admiral Nakhimov* had been completed in 1888 and was based on 1880s British concepts of second-class ironclads for distant service. An armoured cruiser rather than battleship, she displaced just over 8,500 tons and was armed with four twin 8in mountings, one fore and one aft and one on each beam. The guns were mounted on 8in armoured barbettes with 2.5in shields. Ten single 6in guns were carried in an unprotected battery, five on each beam. Reboilered and fitted with twelve 3pdr quick-firers in 1899, *Admiral Nakhimov* could make only 14 knots and her armoured belt was of compound armour only 10in thick. Slow, underarmed and under-protected, she was of little fighting value.

Little better was Admiral Nebogatov's flagship, the obsolete barbette ironclad *Imperator Nikolai I*. Of 9,672 tons, she had been completed in 1892 and modernized in an 1898–1900 refit. She mounted twin short 30-calibre 12in guns forward with two 9in and four 6in guns on each beam. Sixteen 3pdrs had been added to provide some anti-torpedo-boat potential. Her compound armour belt was 14in thick but the forward 10in armoured barbette had only a 3in partial cover and the 6in guns had no protection at all. *Nikolai I*'s relatively new Belleville boilers allowed her to steam at 15 knots, about the top speed of the Third Squadron's three small coast defence ironclads, *Admiral Ushakov, Admiral Seniavin* and *General Admiral Graf Apraksin*. Displacing almost 5,000 tons, these little ships were 286.5ft long, with a beam of 52ft. They were armed with 10in guns, a twin turret forward and a twin or (*Apraksin*) single turret aft. Secondary armament comprised four 4.7in guns plus six 3pdrs; 10in Hervey armour provided hull protection with 8in armour on the turrets. These coast defence ships were built to counter similar Swedish vessels in the Baltic and had never been intended for battle on the high seas.

Rozhestvensky was weak in support vessels. To escort his transports and provide scouts if required, he only had five cruisers, two of them old and slow. These were the 1885-vintage modernized armoured cruisers *Vladimir Monomakh* and *Dmitri Donskoi* with their maximum speeds of 15 knots, 6in compound armoured belts and armaments of 5in and 6in guns respectively; they could not really fight, sustain damage or run away. They were no longer fully rigged but their high vulnerable freeboards testified to their belonging to another age. A little more useful was *Svietlana*, a relatively new 3,727-ton ship completed in 1897 but intended primarily as a yacht for the commander of the Russian Navy. Although she had a protected deck and other armour, she carried much inflammable woodwork on board. Her speed of 21.6 knots and armament of six 6in guns, ten 3pdrs and two 15in torpedo tubes made her a useful scout. The better of the pair of first-rate modern cruisers in the Second Pacific Squadron was *Oleg*, a modern protected cruiser of 6,645 tons with a maximum speed of 23 knots. She carried twelve 6in guns in two twin and eight single mounts, a similar number of 3in, ten smaller guns and two 15in submerged torpedo tubes. Slightly older and somewhat slower was *Aurora*, the ship that twelve years later would start the October Revolution. She was a 19-knot protected cruiser armed with eight 6in guns, twenty-four 3in, eight 1pdrs and three 15in torpedo tubes.

In addition to these ships were the two 3,100-ton fast scout cruisers *Izumrud* and *Jemtchug*, enlarged destroyers capable of 24 knots. They were armed with six 4.7in guns and three 18in torpedo tubes, and were deployed with the destroyers. The latter were all new and modern ships of the 'Boiki' class, 350 tons, based on the British Yarrow design. Capable of 26 knots, they were armed with three 15in torpedo tubes, one 3in and five 3pdr guns.

To supplement his weak cruiser force, Rozhestvensky brought with him the graceful 3,285-ton despatch vessel (armed yacht) *Almaz*, armed with four 3in and eight 3pdr guns, and five armed metchantmen: the British-built *Dniepr* (9,460 tons, 19 knots, seven 6in and four 3in guns), the German-built *Kuban* (10,500 tons, 18.5 knots, light quick-firers and machine-guns), the British-built *Rion* (12,050 tons, 20 knots, eight 4.7in, eight 3in and six 3pdr guns), the British-built *Terek* (10,000 tons, 19 knots, light quick-firers and machine-guns) and the German-built *Ural* (13,600 tons, 20 knots, sixteen light quick-firers and machine-guns). *Kuban* and *Terek* had been Hamburg-Amerika Line steamers and *Ural* had formerly belonged to Norddeutscher Lloyd. There were also the armed repair ship *Kamchatka*, three transports, two of them armed, and two ocean tugs plus the hospital ships *Orel* and *Kostroma*. The last-named came with Nebogatov, as did one of the tugs.

The core of the Russian fleet was thus a battle line of five modern battleships. This was supplemented by three obsolete battleships, three small coast defence ironclads and an obsolete iron cruiser. Cruiser support was limited in both quality and quantity, with too many old and slow ships and too many armed merchantmen for a healthy, properly functioning battlefleet. The offensive and defensive destroyer force was good in quality but deficient in quantity. There was a significant number of non-combatant vessels to be shepherded. Against an efficient opponent capable of probing their weaknesses, the Russians would have serious problems, especially after a long and debilitating voyage.

THE JAPANESE FORCES

The Japanese battle line comprised four battleships and eight armoured cruisers, all modern. The battleships were all British-built and reflected the advanced nature of contemporary British warship design. Japan had started the war with six battleships but two had been mined in 1904. Togo's flagship was *Mikasa*, completed by Armstrong of Elswick in 1902. She displaced 15,200 tons and was armed with a main battery of four 12in and fourteen 6in guns; anti-torpedo armament was twenty 12pdrs. The 12in guns were of the latest British model, capable of being loaded at any angle of elevation and therefore of rapid fire – three shells every two minutes. Maximum main belt protection was 9in of Krupp cemented armour and the flat turret faces had 10in armour. Ten of the 6in guns were in a main deck box battery with 6in armour. Above were four guns in two 6in upperdeck casemates on each beam with eight of the 12pdrs between them. *Mikasa* was an exceptionally well protected and effective ship for her time.

The second Japanese battleship was *Fuji*, the first modern Japanese battleship to be built. She was smaller than the others at just over 12,500 tons. A transitional vessel, she was built at Thames Iron Works' Poplar yard between 1894 and 1897 and was fitted with old-style 18in belt armour. Her barbettes were armoured to 14in like the later ships, but her gun shields were only 6in thick. Her four 12in guns had to be trained fore and aft for loading although a limited amount of ready-use ammunition allowed firing at all angles of train. Four of the ten 6in guns were mounted in casemates at main deck level and the rest were in armoured shields on the upper deck. Her anti-torpedo armament had been strengthened to sixteen 12pdrs. Like the three other ships, *Fuji* was designed to operate at up to 18 knots.

Asahi had been completed by John Brown on the Clyde in 1900. Her good internal subdivision allowed her to survive being mined in October 1904. She displaced 15,200 tons and had a 224ft-long Hervey armoured belt of 9in maximum thickness. Her turret faces were 10in thick. Four 12in guns were carried, although the mountings were not as advanced as *Mikasa*'s: the guns had to be returned to a fixed position for loading, which reduced the rate of fire to about one round a minute. This enhanced the importance of the 6in guns, eight of which were on the main deck and six on the upper deck. Twenty 12pdrs kept torpedo-boats at bay.

Shikishima was a three-funnelled ship based on the British 'Majestic' class and built at Blackwall by Thames Iron Works between 1897 and 1900. She was the first Japanese ship to be protected with Hervey armour and she carried the more sophisticated protective system of the classical pre-dreadnought. This used a sloping armoured deck and a thinner main belt to provide more extensive protection than previously. Her armour and armament were similar to *Asahi*'s. Her sister ship *Hatsuse* had been blown up by mines during the blockade of Port Arthur in May 1904.

Faster and, given pre-dreadnought gunnery techniques, just as powerful were the Japanese armoured cruisers. With Admiral Togo's battleships in the First Division of the fleet were *Kasuga* and *Nisshin*, 7,600–7,700-ton vessels built in Italy but sold to Argentina while under construction. Argentina's war with Chile had ended before they were finished and Japan had picked them up to help match Russian strength in the Pacific. They had mixed batteries: *Kasuga* mounted one 10in gun and *Nisshin* two 8in guns forward and both ships had two 8in aft and fourteen 6in and ten 3in guns along each beam. Armour protection was 6in thick on both belt and battery and was carried over a wide area. Speed was 20 knots and the ships were typical examples of the Italian 'Nave di Battaglia', a kind of pre-dreadnought battlecruiser.

The 'Kasugas' were only 357ft long but the rest of Japan's armoured cruisers were as long as the battleships, all being over 400ft. The flagship of Vice-Admiral Kamimura's Second Division was the 9,750-ton *Idzumo*, completed by Armstrong at Elswick in 1901; her sister *Iwate* was completed in 1901. Protected by 6 to 7 inches of the latest Krupp armour, these 20.75-knot vessels mounted four 8in guns, fourteen 6in and twelve 12pdrs. The next armoured cruiser, *Adzuma*, was a French-built ship of 9,370 tons with two less 6in guns and *Yakumo* was a similar German-built 9,646-ton ship; both had been completed in 1900. The final pair, *Asama* and *Tokiwa*, had set the pattern for Japan's armoured cruisers – in all but their funnels (two instead of three) – when they were ordered from Armstrongs in 1896–1898. Both were completed in 1899 and displaced 9,700 tons with 6–7in armour and four 8in, fourteen 6in and twelve 12pdr guns. Maximum speed was originally 21.5 knots, but by 1904 this had been reduced to no more than 19; this was still safely faster than any Russian battleship. The cruisers' armament could deliver considerable weight of shot: the 8in guns could fire up to five 250lb shells per minute and the 6in up to eight 100lb shells a minute. This rapidity of fire, added to the ability to lay these guns by continuous aim, made long-range hitting easier than with a battleship's armament. In the circumstances of the time, Kamimura's Division was perhaps even more powerful than Togo's, given its superior speed and long-range striking power. It was deployed with *Idzumo* in the lead and *Iwate* bringing up the rear. *Adzuma* was second in line and *Yakumo* second from the rear. The two oldest ships were in the centre. This meant that Kamimura could turn his fast division together and retain the same fighting power.

Making up a squadron with each division of capital ships was a division of cruisers. With Togo in the First Squadron was the Third Division, with *Kasagi* and *Chitose* of almost 5,000 tons, built in the USA to British design in 1898–9 and each armed with two 8in and ten 4.7in guns; and *Otowa* and *Niitaka*, 3,000-ton ships completed only the previous year in Japan. Their respective main armaments were two 6in and six 4.7in and six 6in guns. All were capable of 20 to 22.5 knots. Supporting and slowing down Kamimura was the Fourth Division, the relatively old mid-1880s vintage British-built *Naniwa* and *Takachiho*, fitted with a modernized armament of eight 6in guns in 1903; and the newer and faster protected cruisers *Akashi* and *Tsushima*, both Japanese-built in 1894 and 1902, one armed with two 6in and six 4.7in and the other with six 6in guns. Each squadron also had a small unprotected cruiser acting as dispatch vessel.

There were five Japanese divisions of torpedo-boat destroyers:

FIRST – Composed of the four new boats of the 'Harusame' class developed in Japan from earlier Thornycroft designed TBDs. In addition, there was the ex-Russian *Akitsuki*, formerly *Rishitelny*, built at Port Arthur and captured after the Battle of the Yellow Sea. The four Japanese-built boats displaced 375 tons, were armed with two 12pdr and four 6pdr guns and two 18in torpedo tubes, and were capable of 29 knots. The ex-Russian boat was of only 240 tons and armed with one 12pdr and three 3pdr guns; she carried the same torpedo armament.

SECOND – Four 'Ikazuchi'-class boats built at Yarrow's Poplar yard in 1899: 305 tons, 31 knots, one 12pdr and five 6pdr guns, two 18in torpedo tubes.

THIRD – Two 'Murakumo'-class boats built by Thornycroft at Chiswick in 1899: 255 tons, 30 knots, one 12pdr and five 6pdr guns, two 18in torpedo tubes. *Kasumi*, built to an improved 'Ikazuchi' design by Yarrow in 1901 at 363 tons, and a normal 'Ikazuchi'.

FOURTH – Two 'Harusames' and two 'Shirakumos' built by Thornycroft in 1901–05: 342 tons, 31 knots, two 12pdr and four 6pdr guns, two 18in torpedo tubes.

FIFTH – Four 'Murakumos'.

Three divisions were attached to the First Squadron forming the First Fleet and two to the Second Squadron forming the Second Fleet. These destroyers outnumbered those of the Russians and were also of superior quality.

Such was the main fighting power of Togo's fleet. In addition, there were other units composed of virtually every other vessel in the Japanese Navy that could put to sea. The Third Squadron, commanded by Vice-Admiral Kataoka, was made up of the three 4,217-ton French-designed 'Matsushima'-class cruisers armed with single 12.6in guns and batteries of eleven or twelve 4.7in weapons built to take on the Chinese in the 1890s. He also deployed the fruits of that conflict: the former Chinese *Chin Yen* armed with four short 12in and four modern 6in guns. The rest of the squadron was made up of the old 1890 vintage 4.7in-armed small armoured cruiser *Chiyoda*, three old protected cruisers, none newer than 1896, two unprotected cruisers dating back to the 1880s, two 25-year-old gunboats, a dispatch vessel and the new 620-ton coast defence gunboat *Uji*. Twenty-seven small torpedo-boats in seven divisions were attached to the three squadrons. Three divisions of 126–203-ton First-Class boats were with the First and Second Squadrons; the rest, all Second-Class boats of 79 to 110 tons, were with the Third Squadron. All were armed with 14in torpedo tubes.

Finally, there was the Auxiliary Squadron of three torpedo-boat depot ships and seven armed merchant cruisers (AMCs). The latter, fast British-built ships of 3,800–6,400 gross registered tons and armed with two 4.7in and six 6pdr guns, were Togo's main scouting forces. Four AMCs were disposed in advanced Western Patrol stations across the entrance to the Tsushima Straits from Cheju-do to the south of the Goto Islands.

GUNNERY

The essence of pre-dreadnought gunnery was the control of each gun by its own gunlayer who aimed and fired it independently under the general direction of the ship's gunnery officers. Traditionally, guns had been laid to be fired on the roll; that is, so that they pointed directly at the target at the moment the ship came to the end of a roll. The pitch and yaw of the ship added extra uncertainties to the gunner's judgment of how the gun should be set for roll. The only real chance of scoring a hit therefore was at ranges where the target was clearly in sight and so close that minor errors did not matter. Beyond about 1,500 yards or so accuracy fell off sharply and hitting became a matter almost of pure chance. Rapidity of fire was therefore the key to effective gunnery. As a rough rule of thumb, in the same amount of time that a 12in gun could fire one shot, an 8in could fire four, a 6in 8–12 and a 3in/12pdr 16–20. This more than made up for the larger guns' inherently greater accuracy, especially as medium artillery had adequate armour penetration at normal combat ranges. A rough idea of the relative penetrating powers of Russian guns can be obtained from the following table. The figures are for thicknesses of ordinary steel penetrated at set distances.[1]

	Distances:		
Size of gun:	*1,000 yards:*	*4,000 yards:*	*12,000 yards:*
12in	21	14.9	8.4
10in	18.8	13.3	7.6
8in	17.9	10.6	4.2
6in	11.4	5.9	not pierced
4.7in	9	3.9	not pierced
3in	4.5	1.5	not pierced

The relative significance of the 8in gun with 85 per cent of the penetration and four times the rate of fire of the 12in weapon is noteworthy.

The British had pioneered a new system of gunlaying called 'Continuous Aim' in which lighter pieces of up to 6in calibre were kept on target by their layers during the entire roll of the ship using telescopic sights. This could increase effective hitting range by improving both visibility and accuracy and by allowing the quick-firing potential of the guns to be more fully exploited. It was developed by British gunnery expert Percy Scott in 1899 and improved his cruisers' hitting rate by 600 per cent. Continuous aim required equally continuous practice and had only just been adopted by the Japanese.

The Russian Navy had little opportunity to adopt continuous aim as they had only just introduced telescopic sights in their ships. Rozhestvensky's battleships were the first to get them; the 'Borodinos'' turrets had to be modified to take the sights after the fleet set sail. This work took several weeks to complete. The gun crews then had to get used to the new equipment but gunnery practice was limited by shortage of spare ammunition: only a 15–20 per cent surplus over expected battle requirements. As the fleet commander told his ships when they were anchored off Madagascar on 26 January 1905, 'We cannot afford to waste much ammunition in practice firing'. Nevertheless, he insisted, 'Great care must be taken to teach the guns' crew and all of them must be taught to use the telescopic sights'. He emphasized the need for regular aiming drills and ordered the cruiser *Jemtchug* and a guard destroyer to steam up and down to provide suitable targets. In the same signal Rozhestvensky insisted that under no circumstances was fire to be opened at ranges of more than 6,000 yards as 'not only are hits very few but it is difficult to distinguish them'.[2]

In fact, numerous aiming rifle gunnery practices had been carried out – 38 times in the battleship *Orel* between 11 November and 13 January. Those Russian crews with telescopic sights may have begun to master the skills of continuous aim but their proficiency never became very high, and nowhere near that of the Japanese. Four full-calibre shoots were carried out after the above signal with the fleet steaming at 11 knots. Some 27 rounds of 12in were fired plus 104 rounds of 6in and 152 rounds of 3in. Results were not encouraging: little attempt was made to correct for wind or range and reportedly the only hit made was on the old cruiser *Donskoi* being used to tow the target.

The Russians had only just received efficient rangefinders. The previous inferior Lugeol and Myakishev devices were supplemented by an order for 66 of the latest British Barr & Stroud 6ft base length FA3s placed in April 1904. Twenty-nine of these instruments had arrived in Russia before Rozhestvensky sailed and a further fifteen may have been sent to the fleet by one of the overtaking destroyers. The balance of the order was delivered before Nebogatov sailed and some were delivered to his squadron as they arrived. It took time to master the new instruments which in theory were accurate to 3 per cent at 6,000 yards. In practice, differences of readings in the same ship could be up to 4,000 yards!

Nebogatov was able to reduce this error to 600–800 yards by the time he joined the main fleet and his training techniques were applied to the other ships. By the time battle was joined the Russian capacity to set their sights before firing at more or less the correct range had improved significantly. Another problem for the Russians, however, was maintaining the flow of information to the guns. Only *Suvorov* had Barr & Stroud mechanical range and order indicators to do this efficiently; otherwise telephones, voice pipes, visual signals and drums had to be used – all vulnerable to the effects of high-explosive fire. Communication in Russian ships soon broke down in battle and the limited number of rangefinders was easily knocked out.

Lack of centralized control was in the circumstances much less important than the deficiencies of the individual Russian gunners. They were, as we have seen, only just beginning to enter the era of continuous aim. They also lacked combat experience and if this were not enough, they had two further disadvantages. First, they still used lanyards to fire their guns, which caused an indeterminate delay between the decision to fire the gun and its actually going off – if it went off at all, which it sometimes did not. Many Russian guns, probably most, must still have been fired on the roll: with a ship rolling 21 degrees a second in rough seas like those experienced at Tsushima and errors of 1/12th of a degree causing a complete miss at 8,000 yards, the problem of deliberate long-range hitting by the Russian ships becomes apparent. Secondly, the Russian ammunition was defective. The Russians' shells contained a relatively low proportion of explosive which was itself of the less effective pyro-oxylene type, and their ships were also still equipped with inferior cast-iron shells for up to a third of their supply. More often than not Russian shells failed to explode, and even if they did the damage was slight.

Rozhestvensky was asking a great deal from his gunnery officers and gunners when he expected them to achieve both deliberation and concentration in their fire. If action was joined at 6,000 yards, he wished his fleet to concentrate on the leading enemy ship if the two fleets were closing and on the rearmost enemy ship when pursuing. Wisely he regarded his 6in guns as his best rangefinders and if a hit was observed on the enemy, it was to be assumed for sight setting purposes that it was these guns that had done the damage. Their range and deflection were therefore to be signalled to the fleet. The Russian ships were called upon to fire deliberately. 'It is better to shoot carefully and certainly,' their commander commented, 'than for all ships simultaneously to pour out a torrent of projectiles.'[3] In this judgment the Russian admiral was almost certainly wrong: given his crude gunnery technique, a hail of shot depending on chance was probably his surest means of hitting anything.

Japanese gunnery theory and technology were several steps ahead of the Russians' and they were better able to exploit the possibilities for firing more accurately at longer ranges. Togo's fleet also had the advantages of combat experience and intensive training for its gunners. Continuous aim techniques were in use and the Japanese also had a more developed – but still crude – system of centralized fire control. The details differed from ship to ship but the general principle was that the captain decided on the object to be engaged and communicated this to the gun crews. The target's range was taken by the forward rangefinding officer and communicated via a communications officer and the conning tower to the officers in charge of the turrets and batteries. The after armament could be operated independently if required, using the after conning tower. The Japanese used a range of complementary forms of internal communication, manually worked dials, voice pipes, megaphones and even a blackboard. Several ships were, however, equipped with electrical transmitters: *Mikasa, Shikishima, Asahi, Tokiwa, Asama, Idzumo, Iwate* and *Yakumo* with Barr & Stroud equipment and *Nisshin* with Vickers.

These communications allowed the Japanese to attempt centralized fire control based on rangefinder data. Their ships were well equipped with rangefinders, up to a dozen or so on each ship; 100 Barr & Stroud FA3s had been delivered to Japan since February 1904 to supplement the 4ft 6in base length FA2s (accurate to around 4,000 yards) used previously. Even the Japanese, however, despite training and experience, found 'making the cut' of range difficult and the whole system of centralized control by rangefinder alone was fundamentally flawed. Even if the data was accurately collected, by the time it reached the guns and by the time the rounds reached the target area, it was out of date. Although some Japanese officers had developed experimental instruments similar to the British Dumaresq to work out rate of change of range, none was operational. Even if both range and rate had been accurately measured, there remained the difficulty of atmospheric conditions and actual gun velocities being different from those for which the sights were graduated and range tables calculated. Captain Pakenham, the British Naval Attache attached to the Japanese fleet, considered the Japanese fire control system more of a liability than an asset. As he wrote after the Battle of the Yellow Sea, which he had observed from the battleship *Asahi*:

'As the firing increased in rapidity its accuracy improved, and when the noise had become sufficient . . . and none had leisure to pay further attention (to transmitted range data) . . ., the system was at its best. It was at its best because it had gradually ascended through different degrees of diminishing harmfulness, until it had attained the total uselessness which was the nearest approach to perfection such a system could know. Of course, reduction of range had much to do with increased accuracy, but the coincidence of the improvement with the nullification of the method of fixing the range was at least significant.'[4]

The Japanese thus learned that the gun itself was still the best rangefinder, once brought to bear in the general vicinity of the enemy. By the time of Tsushima rangefinders were used only to start batteries off at more or less the correct range. Control orders were passed at the outset of the action and when fire ceased for any reason. This allowed communications to work more effectively and centralized control to be maintained throughout. The 6in guns were the key weapons and the officers in charge of these batteries were allowed to alter the settings of these guns on their own initiative, based on their estimates of the average performance of the battery. These ranges could then be used by the heavier guns. The fighting tops in all Japanese battleships except *Mikasa* had been cleared of small anti-torpedo-boat guns to allow their use by spotters to obtain a better view of fall of shot. This also allowed space for extra rangefinders. In *Fuji* at least there was a specially trained spotting officer in the foretop, constantly advising the ranging officer as to fall of shot. In *Mikasa*, which still seems to have retained guns in the fighting top, the gunnery officer himself spotted from the forebridge.

Japanese gunnery was good but far from perfect. A month before

Tsushima Togo carried out a firing with his division at an island at ranges of 2,500 to 3,000yds. Each battleship fired eight 12in rounds. *Shikishima* did well and scored six hits and *Mikasa* five, but *Asahi* only hit the static target three times and *Fuji* twice. The cruisers did very badly: *Kasuga* fired two 10in rounds from her single gun and scored no hits and twelve 8in shells of which only three hit. *Nisshin* fired twenty-four 8in rounds of which only six were counted as hits. The six ships' 6in guns fired 480 rounds, of which 162 were hits. Again, *Shikishima* made the best practice with 56 hits from 84 rounds. *Mikasa* only made 14 hits from 84 and *Fuji* 13 from 60. *Shikishima* had the advantage of more reliable recent ammunition, which was one reason for her excellent performance.

The poor shooting of the 6in guns was especially disappointing as they had just been fitted with improved British-made telescopic sights. The Japanese seemed to have developed continuous aim techniques and, using aiming rifles, were able to achieve good results in the constant practices carried out against targets towed by steam boats. The average number of hits in this kind of exercise had increased from 40 to 60 per cent by mid-April. 'Dotter' simulators were brought into use further to improve gunners' skills in continuous aim. Although their long-range fire might not have been all that was hoped for, this practice in continuous aim shooting, coupled with more reliable electrical ignition of the guns, meant that Japanese fire could be effective enough and distinctly superior to that of the Russians.

Based on the information received and/or on the gunlayer's own judgment, independent fire was normally the rule, although *Mikasa* experimented with deliberate salvos. There were three natures of independent fire: deliberate, ordinary and rapid, the change being signalled by bugle. On the whole the Japanese fired relatively slowly and deliberately. In *Adzuma* and *Fuji* rapid fire was never sounded during the Battle of Tsushima and ordinary fire only twice, when the range was less than 4,000 yards. On each occasion 'deliberate fire' was sounded to check fire when ranges became extended and it seemed that ammunition was being wasted. British observers were impressed by the self-discipline of the individual gunlayers who checked their fire when they could no longer clearly see the targets. Leaving so much initiative to individual gunlayers meant that it was far from certain that ships actually fired at the targets their captains intended. It also meant that, although considerable damage might be inflicted on the enemy, no real concentration of fire was possible: even the Japanese, for all their individual skill and their enterprising if premature attempts at fire control, could only peck their opponents to death rather than achieve concentrated catastrophic blows.

Japanese shells were much more effective than those of the Russians.

All were made of steel, a third of a ship's outfit being high-explosive and two thirds armour-piercing. High-explosive and armour-piercing shells were used alternately at ranges beyond 5,000 yards and all armour-piercing rounds were fired at shorter ranges. To distinguish them, AP shells were painted white and HE brown. The explosive filling was a very effective compound known as Shimose which burst at very high temperatures and produced demoralizing toxic gases. Even near misses could be effective in starting fires and creating splinter damage.

TORPEDOES

Like their guns, the torpedoes carried by the fleets at Tsushima were still at the pre-dreadnought stage of development. Torpedo performance in terms of both speed and range was about to be revolutionized by the advent of the heater to warm up the contents of the torpedo's air vessel. The best torpedoes on both sides were 18in Whiteheads. The Russians had just adopted this weapon as the Model 1904 and it had impressed British representatives at the Whitehead factory at Fiume with its accurate range of 3,000 yards at just over 24 knots carrying a 200lb warhead. Only the two new light cruisers *Izumrud* and *Jemtchug* carried this new weapon. The Russian destroyers and the rest of the fleet carried the older 15in Model 1897 and 1895 torpedoes with 100lb warheads and ranges of 2,000 and 1,000 yards respectively at 25 knots.

The older Japanese vessels carried 14in Schwartzkopf torpedoes, German copies of the Whitehead, which, with their phosphor-bronze parts, were popular with new navies given their superior ease of maintenance. This was especially true in the days before gyroscopes obviated the need for repeated running to test for deflection. The Japanese had, however, adopted the 18in Whitehead in the late 1890s because of its superior hitting power, a 220lb warhead as opposed to 132lb. The Japanese were observed by the British officers on board to be in the habit of setting both types to run out to 3,000 metres, which reduced the speed of the torpedoes to 14–15 knots. Not only could such slow-moving torpedoes be more easily avoided but the fire control solution for such long ranges was much more difficult to obtain. Having learned their lesson in combat, the Japanese began to set their torpedoes to run faster for shorter distances, 1,000 yards at 26 knots.

TACTICS

The tactical flexibility of the Russian fleet was very limited. The whole fleet had had no time to learn to work as a concentrated whole and was barely capable of the simplest manoeuvres. The battleships that sailed round the Cape had practised tactical evolutions on the outward voyage, although the ships were only dubiously manoeuvrable because of their coal overloads. There were only ten days' practice in tactical evolutions off Madagascar, although while crossing the Indian Ocean some more attempts were made to improve the situation. While at Camranh Bay Rozhestvensky, who did not trust flag signals, experimented with new methods of tactical communication – using chalk and blackboards facing fore and aft – but this did not work and was replaced by a system of numbers and figures on canvas squares. By this means the fleet could be ordered to alter course 4 or 8 points to port or starboard.

Rozhestvensky had little in the way of a complex battle plan. He intended to push on to Vladivostok, despite all opposition, after inflicting damage on the enemy in the process. Some kind of engagement was desirable if he was to achieve the mission his political masters intended, but it would be better for him to meet a detached portion of the Japanese fleet. To encourage Togo to divide his forces, Rozhestvensky sent two pairs of armed merchant cruisers in different directions. *Kuban* and *Terek* were detached from the scouting group on 22 May to show themselves off the eastern coast of Japan and *Rion* and *Dniepr* left the First Cruiser Division three days later to escort six transports, two of which had come with Nebogatov to Shanghai. The two AMCs would then threaten Japanese communications in the Yellow Sea.

Following these detachments, the cruising formation of the Russian fleet was as follows. In the lead was a scouting wedge of cruisers led by *Svietlana* followed by *Almaz* and *Ural*. This was no more than half a mile ahead of the main fleet to minimize chances of detection. *Almaz* had been transferred from the role of flagship of the Transport Division to replace *Kuban* and *Terek*. Then came two columns. To starboard were the two main Russian battle divisions, Rozhestvensky's own First Division led by *Suvorov* followed by *Alexander III*, *Borodino* and *Orel*, and then the Second Division of *Osliabia*, *Sissoi*, *Navarin* and *Admiral Nakhimov*. The Second Division's commander, Admiral Felkerzam, had died on 24 May but Rozhestvensky, fearing for its morale effects, kept the news secret and Felkerzam's flag flying from *Osliabia*. To port was Nebogatov's Third Division led by *Nikolai I*, then *Apraksin*, *Seniavin* and *Ushakov*. To the rear of this Division came the First Cruiser Division with *Oleg*, *Aurora*, *Donskoi* and *Monomakh*.

On each beam, and in effect continuing the screen begun by the scouting division, was to port *Izumrud* and the destroyers *Buini* and *Bravi* and to starboard the scout *Jemtchug* and the destroyers *Byedovi* and *Buistri*. Two of the five destroyers of the Second Destroyer Division kept station on *Oleg* and the rest escorted the transports and tugs. These sailed in single line ahead in the rear with the two hospital ships *Orel* and

Kostroma on the starboard and port quarters.

If battle threatened, as Rozhestvensky fully expected it would, on 27 May a battle line would be created on the threatened flank. If the enemy attacked from the rear, the battleships would form line abreast to starboard and the cruisers and transports would proceed ahead. Whatever the circumstances, the cruisers would operate independently, protecting the transports. The First Destroyer Division was to operate in support of the battleships, the Second the cruisers. The destroyers' role was as much taking off commanders from disabled ships as engaging in combat. The fleet was to keep formation, push on, try to sink some Japanese ships, and eventually reach Vladivostok.

Trying to stop them by a battle of annihilation was Togo's combined fleet, a very different organization from Rozhestvensky's, being a flexible formation operating either together or in separate squadrons and divisions as opportunity offered. Its higher speed also conferred upon it considerable tactical initiative. The aim was for the first division of battleships to move to cross the enemy's 'T' and concentrate as much as possible on bombarding the enemy's leading ship. The second division of armoured cruisers was to watch the enemy movements with the object of attacking from a different direction the part of the force the first division was engaging. The essential principle was to concentrate all Japan's main strength on a part of the enemy selected for destruction, catching it in a crossfire from which it could not escape. The cruisers supporting these two divisions of capital ships were to prevent Russian cruisers from interfering with the Japanese torpedo flotilla, add their weight to the main attack while not interfering with it, and finish off damaged or isolated ships after the decisive moment of the battle. The destroyers and torpedo-boats were to be held back until a good opportunity for torpedo attack presented itself, notably after the Russians' anti-torpedo-boat batteries had been destroyed by gunfire. A dispersing and fleeing enemy was to be attacked in sub-divisional units. If, however, the enemy fleet had not been destroyed, then there would be massed flotilla attacks. The Third Squadron with its torpedo-boats was not directly under Togo's command but was to act as a general reserve and make its own torpedo attacks as opportunity offered.

This was to be a decisive battle. As Sir Julian Corbett wrote in the British Admiralty's confidential Staff History of the War:

'The state of the war, the failing of the Japanese resources, and the exhaustion of their offensive energy on land demanded a crushing victory at sea to force an acceptable peace. All risks must be run to secure such a decision and there was no longer any reason why the risks should not be run . . . there was now nothing in the background for which the Japanese fleet need be husbanded. The Russians had put on the table practically every card they had available and the time had come to stake their last ship against them. It must, therefore, be a fight to the finish at such ranges as Admiral Togo regarded as most likely to lead to a decisive issue.'[1]

First, however, the enemy had to be found. Togo's advanced line of armed merchant cruisers was far from impermeable. Each ship sailed slowly to the south-west during the day and returned to its starting point during the night. The Russians came within an ace of penetrating it without being found. At 0245 in the early hours of 27 May 1905, the 6,387-ton AMC *Shinano Maru*, launched in Glasgow in 1900, was returning north-eastwards when she spotted an unidentified ship abaft her port beam. This was Rozhestvenksy's hospital ship *Orel*, fully lit in accordance with international regulations and sailing in the extreme rear of the Russian fleet's cruising order. The battle was about to begin.

THE ENCOUNTER

At 0410 *Shinano Maru* identified the vessel she had first sighted 85 minutes earlier as an enemy hospital ship and at 0445 signalled that the enemy's Second Pacific Squadron had arrived. While *Shinano Maru* made continuously updated shadowing reports, the cruisers of the Third Division steamed south-eastwards to get in touch. At 0550 they spotted the illuminated hospital ship but also saw smoke from the Japanese armed merchant cruisers to the south-west and steamed off to investigate. Not for another hour did Admiral Dewa turn his ships to find the Russians, shrouded in protective mist. Luckily for the Japanese, *Shinano Maru* regained touch at 0605 and was relieved by the cruiser *Idzumo* from Kataoka's Third Squadron.

Rozhestvensky had been unlucky not to have got by the badly deployed Japanese scouting line. His concentrated formation almost worked as an evasive strategy. Nevertheless, he *had* been ordered to fight if he was to fulfil his mission. He faced a dilemma common to later twentieth century naval commanders: he was aware that he had been spotted because of his intercepts of Japanese wireless traffic, which he was reluctant to jam because of the desire not to give a detailed confirmation of his position. There was a powerful transmitter in the AMC *Ural* that could have blacked out the Japanese shadowers' sets. He did, however, begin to redispose his forces for battle. The scouting group was first brought round to the rear in a line to help guard the transports and their place at the point of the formation was taken by *Izumrud* and *Jemtchug*. Then, as some of the veterans of the old ships of Kataoka's Third Squadron came into view on the port side, he began a battle deployment into line, moving the First and Second Divisions over to lead

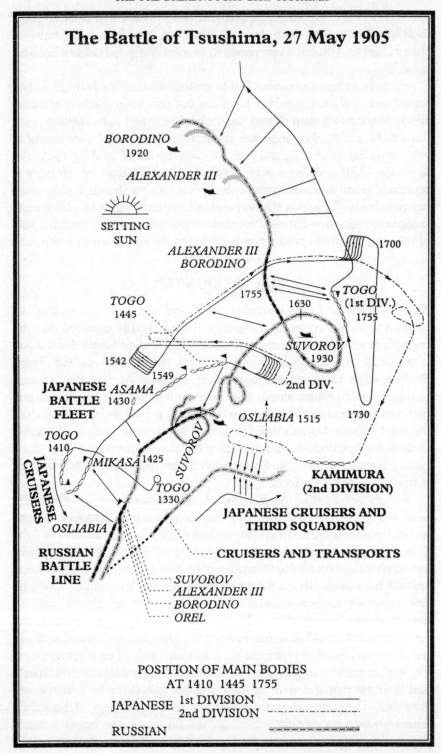

The Battle of Tsushima, 27 May 1905

BORODINO
1920

ALEXANDER III

SETTING
SUN

ALEXANDER III
BORODINO

TOGO
1445

1755

1630

TOGO
(1st DIV.)
1755

1542

1549

SUVOROV
1930

2nd DIV.

JAPANESE
BATTLE
FLEET

ASAMA
1430

1730

TOGO
1410

SUVOROV

OSLIABIA 1515

MIKASA 1425

JAPANESE
CRUISERS

TOGO
1330

KAMIMURA
(2nd DIVISION)

OSLIABIA

JAPANESE CRUISERS AND
THIRD SQUADRON

RUSSIAN
BATTLE
LINE

CRUISERS AND TRANSPORTS

SUVOROV
ALEXANDER III
BORODINO
OREL

POSITION OF MAIN BODIES
AT 1410 1445 1755

JAPANESE 1st DIVISION ———————
2nd DIVISION - - - - - - -

RUSSIAN ▬▬▬▬▬▬▬

Nebogatov. This took time, as his battleships as a group only had a 2-knot speed advantage over Nebogatov's signalled formation speed of 9 knots. By 1100 on 27 May, the fleet was finally in a battle line with the three divisions in line, the four destroyers to starboard led by the two scouts, the six auxiliaries astern and to starboard of the Third Division, with the other destroyers between and the four cruisers protecting the transports, two on each side. The scouting division brought up the rear.

At about 1100 the Japanese cruisers of the Third Division looked as if they might close to attack and came within about 8,500 yards of the Russians. This tempted some Russian ships to disobey standing orders and open fire to port, but Rozhestvensky soon stopped them with a signal not to waste ammunition. Dewa's cruisers drew out of range to rejoin the combined fleet.

Togo had sailed at 0615 that morning, passed by the northern end of Tsushima and set his two divisions of capital ships to meet the enemy fleet on its reported course. His original intention was to attack the weaker of the two reported columns; that is, the one to port. Rozhestvenksy had considered moving into line abreast about noon as he seemed to be out of sight of the Japanese, but he countermanded his orders when more enemy ships were sighted. The attempted manoeuvre had the effect of transferring his First Division to the head of the starboard Russian line ahead of the cruisers and transports, with the Second and Third Divisions in line ahead to port. This fortuitous event restored the situation to that expected by Togo. The Japanese admiral was unaware not only of the Russian fleet's formation but of its precise position as the signalled reports he had been receiving had been misleading. Rozhestvenksy then, at 1220, made a course alteration to 23 degrees to point his force at Vladivostok, and this was reported to Togo by Kataoka. He turned west to intercept and then at 1331 to south-south-west. Rather to Togo's surprise, the Russians hove into sight on his starboard bow rather than to port. The Japanese were temporarily nonplussed and turned to starboard in line to take up a more favourable attack position to cross the 'T' of the enemy's port division. At 1355 Togo hoisted his battle flag – a flag that was to be flown again 36 years later when the Pearl Harbor attack was launched. He also made a signal worthy of the occasion:

'The existence of our Imperial country rests on this one action. Every man of you must do his utmost.'[1]

Rozhestvensky was already moving his First Division back to form a single line with the rest of his capital ships. Togo moved back first to port and a course south-west by south as if to pass the Russians in the opposite direction; almost immediately, however, he went hard to port to an east-north-easterly course to attack the enemy vanguard obliquely.

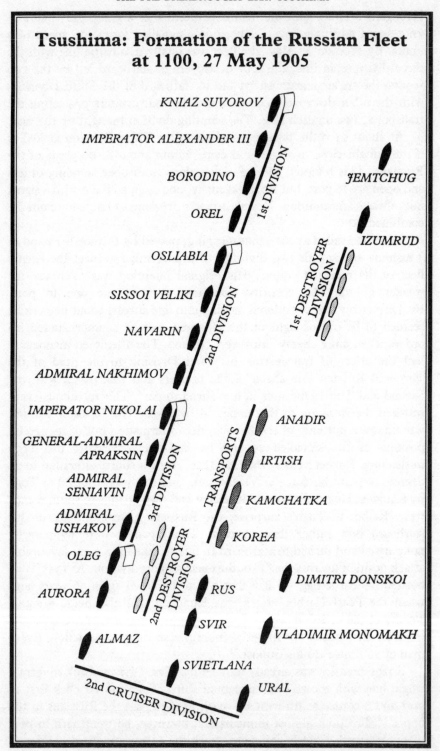

Tsushima: Formation of the Russian Fleet at 1100, 27 May 1905

This was a risky manoeuvre as the turning point was within range of the Russian ships then forming into battle line. Despite the very long range of 7,500 yards, the Russians duly opened fire and engaged each Japanese ship in turn. Togo may have made a calculation similar to Nelson's at Trafalgar: at this kind of range the Russians stood virtually no chance of hitting anything. All twelve Japanese capital ships of the First and Second Divisions turned safely, most of the waterspouts exploding harmlessly about them. The Russians' 6in guns proved their long-range potential by scoring the first hits, but at such a range and with such poor shells the effects were not serious. That they hit at all was because they seemed to have been ignoring their C-in-C's orders and fired as rapidly as they could.

The Japanese began to reply, their long-range fire proving little better at first than that of the Russians. Because of their overdependence on rangefinders, it took about ten minutes before the slow, deliberate Japanese fire found any targets. The range came down to between 5,000 and 6,000 yards with most of the Japanese concentrating on *Osliabia*, with *Mikasa* and *Asahi* firing on *Suvorov*, and *Iwate* on *Nikolai I*, at 6,200 yards. The Japanese gunners were able to maintain a devastating fire; even the 12pdrs joined in as rapid fire was ordered at 1420 with the range down to about 4,700 yards.

The Japanese shells burst with terrible effect, with blast, heat, splinters and fumes. As Rozhestvensky wrote later:

'The paint burnt with a clear flame on the steel surfaces; boats, ropes, hammocks and woodwork caught fire; cartridges in ready racks ignited; upper works and light guns were swept away; turrets jammed.'[2]

Commander Semenov on Rozhestvensky's staff was also shocked at the effect of Shimose:

'The steel plates and superstructure of the upper deck were torn to pieces and the splinters caused many casualties. Iron ladders were crumpled up into rings and guns were literally hurled from their mountings. Such havoc could never be caused by the simple impact of a shell, still less by splinters. It could only be caused by the force of the explosion . . . In addition to this was the unusual high temperature and liquid flame of the explosion which seemed to spread over everything. I actually watched a steel plate catch fire from a burst. Of course the steel plate did not burn but the paint on it did. Such practically incombustible materials as hammocks and rows of boxes drenched in water flared up for a moment. At times it was impossible to see anything with glasses owing to everything being so disturbed with the quivering of the heated air.'[3]

The 6in gunners firing by continuous aim were doing most of this damage, supplemented by the armoured cruisers' 8in guns, but occasionally a 12in shell scored a chance hit with devastating results. *Osliabia*

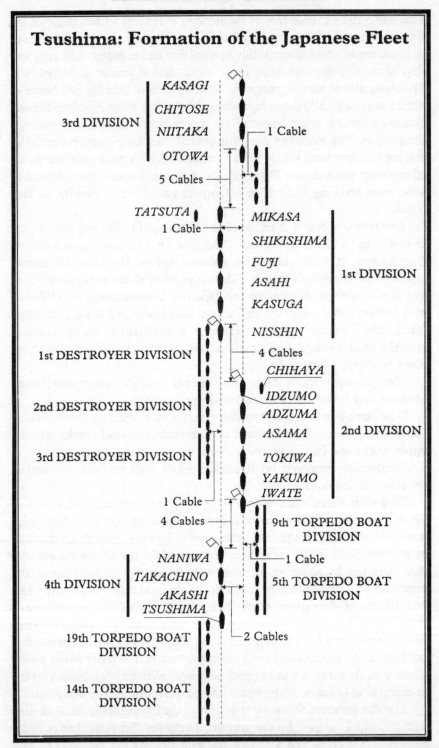

Tsushima: Formation of the Japanese Fleet

3rd DIVISION
KASAGI
CHITOSE
NIITAKA
— 1 Cable
OTOWA

5 Cables

TATSUTA
1 Cable —
MIKASA
SHIKISHIMA
FUJI
ASAHI
KASUGA
NISSHIN

1st DIVISION

1st DESTROYER DIVISION
4 Cables

CHIHAYA
IDZUMO

2nd DESTROYER DIVISION
ADZUMA
ASAMA

3rd DESTROYER DIVISION
TOKIWA
YAKUMO
IWATE

2nd DIVISION

1 Cable
4 Cables —
9th TORPEDO BOAT DIVISION

NANIWA
TAKACHINO
AKASHI
TSUSHIMA

— 1 Cable

4th DIVISION

5th TORPEDO BOAT DIVISION

19th TORPEDO BOAT DIVISION
— 2 Cables

14th TORPEDO BOAT DIVISION

was hit forward by such a shell below the waterline and began to list. A major explosion aboard, whether caused by this shell or by the general bombardment, littered her decks with killed and wounded. Burning, she listed to port with her forward 10in turret out of action.

Rozhestvensky wished to close the range to improve the effectiveness of his own artillery, but under such a pounding this would have been suicidal. He therefore ordered a change of course to starboard at 1425 to avoid the danger of having his 'T' crossed by the faster Japanese. This would have been disastrous as his leading ships would have been subjected to the withering fire of the Japanese while most of his fleet would have no chance of reply. As it was, the two fleets sailed on parallel courses north-eastwards at a range of 5,500–6,500 yards. At 1448 the Japanese reverted to more deliberate ordinary firing and concentrated on *Suvorov* and the stricken *Osliabia*. A black curtain of fumes penetrated by violent flashes covered the Russian ships and hid all but the mastheads with their blue St Andrew's cross ensigns. The Japanese battleships ceased fire and the cruisers turned their guns on to other ships.

The Russians had, in fact, replied with some effect although their fire became steadily more erratic with the impact of the murderous Japanese high-explosive. The Japanese cruiser *Asama* was unlucky enough to be hit by a 12in shell which damaged her steering and forced her to turn away to port. This exposed her to the fire of the rear of the Russian line, but significantly only the extra-rapid-firing Russian 3in small quick-firers scored any hits, causing superficial damage to the cruiser's upper works. The older Russian ships were suffering from their lack of powerful 6in batteries. A Russian 12in shell hit *Nisshin* at 1440, putting out of action her forward 8in mounting. The rearmost Japanese ship, *Iwate*, had a 6in gun knocked out by a Russian shell of similar calibre.

As the smoke cleared, the Japanese moved in again towards the Russian line. Both battleships and armoured cruisers opened rapid fire. Rozhestvensky turned to starboard to open the range once more, but not before the Japanese 12in guns had a chance of hitting. This was fatal for *Osliabia*, which suffered two more heavy hits on the waterline above the armoured belt. One hit caused another major hole and the water poured in. *Osliabia* fell out of line to starboard and stopped, listing ever more heavily to port. Her crew poured over her starboard side, many receiving injuries as they tumbled towards the water. The Russian battleship turned over, still under fire from the Second Division's armoured cruisers. The Russian destroyers picked up survivors.

Shortly after the stricken *Osliabia* staggered out of line, the flagship *Suvorov* also swerved to starboard. The hail of Japanese high-explosive had injured both the C-in-C and the flag captain, and the raging fires forced them to take refuge in the lower conning position below the shattered decks. Then the steering jammed and the ship continued to turn to starboard out of control. *Alexander III* first moved to follow the flagship but then saw that something was wrong and led the Russian fleet on the originally intended easterly course. She also began to suffer from the Japanese concentration of fire on the leading ship. *Borodino* also suffered hits and fell briefly out of line. She soon resumed station astern of *Alexander III*, but not before she, *Orel* and the sinking *Osliabia* had formed a concentrated target for the fire of the Japanese Second Division, with little chance of replying because of mutual masking of fire. The Second Division of the Russian fleet, its flagship sinking, also began to fall behind the First.

Shortly before 1500 Captain Bukhvostov of *Alexander III* turned to port as if to cross the Japanese rear. Fearing a torpedo attack, Togo turned his First Division battleships to port together. The Japanese Second Division remained locked in combat with its Russian counterpart at a range of about 3,500 yards, with both sides inflicting damage but the more effective shells of the Japanese giving them the advantage. An attempted torpedo attack by one of the 'Izumrud'-class scouts was beaten off. *Asama* was trying to rejoin the line but was prevented from doing so by Russian fire. The Second Division kept moving south-east at 17 knots as the First Division took up station again in reverse order after its turn. This effectively masked the Japanese First Division's fire but as the Japanese cruisers crossed the Russian 'T' they poured a murderous fire of 6in and 8in shells into the enemy ships. The little cruiser *Chihaya* took the opportunity of firing two 14in torpedoes at *Borodino* but at a range of over 2,700 yards these stood little chance of hitting.

The Russian change of course had, in fact, succeeded in throwing the Japanese line into confusion. As Togo's battleships and armoured cruisers switched to their port batteries and swung their main turrets to the other beam to engage the Russian First Division, Admiral Nebogatov put on full steam in the old *Imperator Nikolai I* to lead his Third Division into the gap ahead of the now leaderless Russian Second Division. The Japanese Second Division meanwhile moved away into the mist, turning eventually to the west-north-west in search of Togo's First Division.

This began the second phase of the battle. *Alexander III* had been forced to turn to starboard by the assault of the Japanese Second Division's armoured cruisers and made a complete circle, covering the damaged *Suvorov* which was still bravely firing at every available enemy ship in sight. At 1507 Togo's First Division recrossed the Russians' 'T' from starboard to port, reopening fire as it did so. *Alexander III* charged at the enemy, being deluged by Japanese shells which failed to inflict decisive material damage. As the range came down to about a mile, *Alexander III* turned away to starboard while *Borodino* and *Orel* turned away to port. *Suvorov* came under fire again, but this added little extra damage to a ship that was already crippled. *Mikasa* also tried a torpedo shot at one of the 'Borodinos' as she came within range. The Japanese First Division now moved off into the murk caused by a mixture of mist, funnel gases and gunsmoke. The Japanese turned to the south-west looking for the rest of the Russian fleet; but not finding it and fearing it would cut across his rear, Togo made two turns together to port at 1542 and 1549, reforming his line in its original order and heading north-east back towards the enemy.

The armoured cruisers of the Japanese Second Division meanwhile engaged the wrecked Russian flagship: 8in and 6in shells were poured into the stricken *Suvorov* at a range of little more than a mile. The ship 'had her masts, funnels, bridges and upper deck structures nearly all smashed to pieces by our fire at such close quarters'.[4] She seemed out of control and the persistent little *Chihaya* closed for a shorter range torpedo attack. She discharged her two port side 14in torpedoes at 1,750 yards but her forward tube misfired. At this point Nebogatov's Division brought the Japanese cruiser under fire and temporarily disabled her. Now it was the turn of the Japanese Fifth Destroyer Division, which sped across the bows of the Japanese armoured cruisers and along *Suvorov*'s port side. Despite firing at a good range, 440–875 yards, and claiming two hits, they did not in fact score any successes. *Suvorov* indeed put out such an effective barrage of 3in shells that the Japanese destroyers were driven off with the Divisional commander's boat damaged.

The Second Division's commander, Kamimura, saw Togo's turns and turned himself to starboard to take station on Togo's port bow on a north-easterly course. The Russians, led by the three battered 'Borodinos' and followed by Nebogatov and the Second Division, were just visible through the mist heading north-north-east. At 1600, as the two lines converged, both Japanese Divisions opened fire, the cruisers at 5,500 yards, the First Division at just over 7,000. The Russians had to turn north-east to avoid their 'T' being crossed yet again, which left the poor *Suvorov* alone, exposed to the guns and torpedoes of the Japanese First Division. The range steadily came down from 6,100 yards to little more than 2,000. *Mikasa* fired two torpedoes, as did *Shikishima*. Togo wished to finish off *Suvorov* although some of his other ships engaged vessels in the Russian rear.

The Russian flagship now listed heavily to port, her upper decks a complete shambles and with flames gushing through her gunports. At about 1630 'when she was being struck repeatedly, a 12in shell burst in between the decks close to the after turret for 6in guns. Explosion was accompanied by a back-rush of flame that must have projected 50ft from her side and then through the enormous rent thus made could be seen the glow of the newly ignited interior, an appearance that the immediate aggravation of the fire on board amply corroborated. The foremast had long been down. Now fell the main topmast and at the same time a considerable explosion occurred. Projectiles continued their rain and it was thought the end must have come; but though only the tip of the stern and the ragged end of the stunted mast protruded from the enveloping cloud, the *Suvorov* still maintained the unequal contest'.[5] She had been devastated by high-explosive shell, but so far catastrophic damage had not been inflicted on her watertight integrity. Pre-dreadnought gunnery was still essentially a ship-disabling rather than ship-killing mechanism.

The attempt to deliver the coup de grace on the enemy flagship prevented the Japanese from inflicting decisive damage on the rest of the Russian fleet, which, in a confused mass, began to make off to the south, into the fog at about 1630. Togo feared another attempt to slip by his rear and turned his squadron to port together to make way to the north so that he could cut them off again. This, however, only had the effect of breaking contact. Recognizing his error, Togo then came round to starboard, which took longer than expected. Somewhat desperately he ordered his flotilla to renew torpedo attacks as he got his ships into line and turned south once more at 1700. Four Japanese destroyers of the Fourth Division found *Suvorov* still bravely making way at about 10 knots. Rough seas prevented five out of the six torpedoes fired from scoring hits, but the last 18in weapon fired by *Murasame* hit *Suvorov* on the port quarter. She immediately listed a further 10 degrees. The Japanese Third Destroyer Division was about to follow up when out of the mist to the south-east came the Russian fleet returning northwards to Rozhestvenksy's rescue.

In their move south the Russian capital ships had already been able to rescue their transports and cruisers from the unwelcome attentions of the Japanese cruiser divisions and the entire Japanese Third Squadron. These had already sunk the tug *Rus*, which had been taking off the crew of the armed merchant cruiser *Ural*, damaged in a collision with another Russian ship. The Russian cruisers had been hampered in their defence by heavy seas, but the heavier Russian ships had been able to get some revenge for their previous mauling on the less powerful Japanese vessels. The cruiser *Kasagi*, already seriously holed in combat with the Russian cruisers, made off out of range. She eventually had to make for the nearest land, escorted by her sister ship *Chitose*. The older protected cruiser *Naniwa* was also badly damaged around the waterline, while *Akashi* was saved only by the defective Russian shells passing through her lightly protected hull. The Third Squadron was lucky to escape with damage to *Idzumo*, *Akitsushima* and *Matsushima*, the last-named veteran suffering disabled steering gear.

The day was saved for the Japanese by the appearance of Kamimura's armoured cruisers. This had the effect of driving the Russians north-wards again at about 1700. The rear of Togo's line on an opposite course became engaged shortly afterwards with some of the Russian battleships, the armoured cruiser *Nisshin* suffering a disabling 12in hit to one of the guns in her after 8in mounting. Togo, probably unaware of this action, held on to the south, but then at 1728 decided to turn in pursuit of the Russians disappearing into the fog to the north-east.

Their first victim was the wreck of the AMC *Ural*, into which a heavy fire was poured with all calibres. Both *Mikasa* and *Shikishima* launched torpedoes and the latter claimed a hit. The armed merchant cruiser eventually sank at 1751. The Russians had reformed their line and the badly wounded Admiral Rozhestvensky had been taken off *Suvorov* by the destroyer *Buini*. Command was then officially transferred to Nebogatov. *Borodino* now led the Russian line, followed by *Orel*, the new flagship *Imperator Nikolai I*, *Apraksin*, *Seniavin* and *Ushakov*. The damaged *Imperator Alexander III* was struggling along to the staboard of *Seniavin*. Then came *Sissoi Veliki*, *Navarin* and *Admiral Nakhimov*. The transports *Anadir*, *Irtish*, *Korea*, together with *Almaz* and *Svietlana* were in the starboard of two lines astern. To port were the cruisers *Oleg*, *Aurora*, *Donskoi*, *Monomakh*, *Jemtchug* and *Izumrud*. The Russian destroyers divided themselves between the two lines.

The Russians had the advantage of the light and at long range (6,500 yards) the Japanese fire was ineffective as much of the fall of shot was virtually invisible. As the Russians moved to port to compound further Japanese gun problems, the poor *Alexander III* became more exposed. She was ablaze and severely holed on her port side forward but somehow survived and joined the line astern of *Seniavin*, firing with her remaining armament. Russian firing remained quite good and the Japanese reported a 'very hot' engagement. The Japanese concentrated on *Borodino*, which allowed *Orel* to make relatively undisturbed practice; near misses drenched the Japanese battleships. However, at such ranges (6,000 yards) hitting was a matter of luck. *Shikishima* suffered a hit by a 3in shell on her foremast and *Mikasa* was hit by a 6in round. As the range increased, the Russians were fortunate to make two 12in hits, one on *Mikasa* and the other on *Nisshin* which demolished her last 8in gun. The Italian-built cruiser also suffered two hits with smaller calibre rounds.

The Japanese were scoring lucky hits too, however. The poor *Alexander III* could take no more. Possibly further hits created more holes in her sides: possibly the damage control crews finally lost the battle. At 1850 the Russian battleship suddenly sheered off to port, out of line. Her list to port suddenly increased and she turned over, taking 30 officers and 806 men to their doom; there were four survivors. Then, at 1920, just as the Japanese First Division was ceasing fire as it moved ahead of the Russians, *Borodino*, the main subject of Japanese attentions, blew up. She had already been set on fire astern and then *Fuji* hit her with her last 12in shot. It burst forward causing a conflagration there also. Possibly a magazine exploded as the whole ship was consumed by a massive conflagration. Still firing her 6in guns, *Borodino* suddenly capsized. Only one man was saved from her company of 855 officers and men. This was a decisive moment of the battle. As an officer in *Oleg* put it:

'The loss of the *Borodino*, which happened before our eyes, was so unexpected that we were stupified and, uncovering our heads, we gazed on the foaming grave of this heroic ship. The sun had set, and in its golden rays on the horizon from south-west to north appeared the black specks of the Japanese torpedo craft barring our passage.'[7]

In the circumstances, there seemed little point in passing on into the Japanese torpedo threat and the demoralized Russian fleet turned away to the south-east. At that moment *Suvorov* met her end. The Japanese Third Squadron, tasked with dealing with the enemy's cripples, tried to sink the flagship with their old 12.6in guns. The heavy shells added to the serious damage already inflicted. Admiral Kataoka described the scene:

'She scarcely looked like a man-of-war at all. Her interior was ablaze, and the holes in her side and gunports shot out tongues of flame. Thick volumes of black smoke rolled low on her deck, and her whole appearance was indescribably pathetic. She turned to starboard and port as if seeking to escape, while the two or three stern guns, which were all that remained to her, kept up an heroic defence.'[8]

Kataoka then ordered his Eleventh Torpedo Boat Division to attack. They were able to close to effective range, 330 yards, and fired seven torpedoes, three of which hit. One exploded a magazine and the former Russian flagship turned over as black and yellow smoke poured out of her. At 1930 she sank; all 928 men on board perished.

Togo now relied on his destroyers and torpedo-boats, abetted by the heavy seas, to inflict further damage on the wounded and demoralized Russian fleet. The Russians were confused and in no condition to mount an organized defence in the darkness, but the Japanese were also blinded by the conditions. Nebogatov managed to get his ships into some semblance of a line again and put up a hot defensive fire as the Japanese attacked on an opposite course at a range of 450–550 yards. The first wave of Japanese destroyers suffered significant damage and scored no hits. The second, the Fifth Destroyer Division, did little better and the third wave of the attack, the First Destroyer Division, quite literally ran into the Fifth, *Yugiri* ramming *Harusame*.

Nebogatov ordered his ships not to show searchlights and this compounded the Japanese problems. More divisions of both destroyers (the First) and torpedo-boats (the First, Ninth, Seventeenth and Eighteenth) attempted further attacks. One torpedo-boat suffered damage from violent manoeuvring and sank. Two more were sunk by defensive fire. In return for these tribulations, hits were scored on the old Russian armoured cruisers *Nakhimov* and *Monomakh*. Both mistook the enemy craft for Russians and allowed the Japanese to score hits; neither, however, sank immediately. The battleship *Navarin*, badly damaged by gunfire in the earlier actions and very low in the water, finally came to a standstill which allowed her to be torpedoed and damaged further. This enabled the Japanese Fourth Destroyer Division, equipped as minelayers, to inflict the coup de grace in the early hours of the following morning. They laid their mines ahead of the old wallowing ironclad which had got under way again; it ran straight into them. First one mine lifted the battleship by the stern. Then another exploded amidships on the starboard side. The distinctive old four-funnelled ship capsized, taking all but three of her crew of 674 to their deaths.

The Fourth Destroyer Division moved on to a real success that night. As they passed *Sissoi Veliki* they launched three torpedoes, one of which hit the Russian battleship aft. At first it seemed that she was not too badly damaged, but the flooding soon became serious. At 0730 the following morning, she surrendered to Japanese armed merchant cruisers, but sank just over two hours later. A similar fate overtook the two torpedoed armoured cruisers. *Nakhimov* made so much water that she had to make for Tsushima but sank as she surrendered to the Japanese destroyer *Shiranui*. The graceful old *Vladimir Monomakh*, also closing the island of Tsushima to save her crew, came across the same Japanese group and made off to the north under fire from *Shiranui*. The armed merchant cruiser *Sado Maru* took up the chase, firing at long range, and eventually after two hits *Monomakh* struck her colours. Her damage was already too great, however, and at 1430 the old Russian cruiser sank.

The last episode of the main Japanese flotilla attack was a little destroyer firefight between the Russian *Gromki* and the Japanese *Shiranui* and *Torpedo-Boat No 63*. *Gromki* had been supporting the doomed armoured cruisers but was ordered to escape northwards, pursued by *Shiranui*. The Japanese destroyer, having lost a boiler to battle damage, was falling behind but managed a 12pdr hit which slowed the Russian down. The two destroyers then traded shots at about 4,500 yards until *TB No 63* arrived. This caused *Gromki* to try a torpedo attack on *Shiranui*, but the gamble failed and she was caught between the two enemies, being progressively smashed by 12pdr and 6pdr hits. She was eventually forced to surrender but sank shortly afterwards.

On balance it had not been that successful a night for the Japanese flotillas. Four torpedo-boat divisions never found the enemy. Of the 32 torpedo-boats and 21 destroyers that did, fourteen were not able to launch any weapons. Eighty-seven torpedoes were actually fired in the entire battle, 37 by torpedo-boats and 50 by destroyers. Only four hits were scored, not counting the attacks on *Suvorov*, and only *Vladimir Monomakh* was sunk primarily by torpedo damage. The other ships had been so badly damaged by gunfire that their fate was certain anyway. The Japanese lost three boats sunk and seven badly damaged: human casualties to the flotillas totalled 32 killed and 86 wounded. One major problem was that the attack was so disorganized, with divisions of destroyers and torpedo-boats rushing in to attack at the same time in the darkness. Many collisions and near collisions took place and there was much mutual interference. All in all, there was too much enthusiasm and too little method and many of the major Russian units survived until the final denouement the following day.

Admiral Togo expected to renew a full-scale action on 28 May. At 0520 that morning ships of the Third Squadron spotted Nebogatov and the Japanese major squadrons came south to engage. Stragglers were picked off. At dawn the cruiser *Chitose* and destroyer *Ariake* sank the destroyer *Bezuprechni*. Then *Chitose* spotted *Dmitri Donskoi* and *Admiral Ushakov* but decided to join the main fleet rather than engage. Less lucky were the cruiser/yacht *Svietlana* and destroyer *Buistri* which were pursued by the new Japanese cruisers *Otowa* and *Niitaka*. The latter could make 18 knots, the Russians barely 15 because of battle damage to *Svietlana*. *Otowa* scored an initial hit on the Russian cruiser's stern and, as the range closed to almost 6,500 yards, *Niitaka*'s 6in and 12pdr guns reduced the graceful *Svietlana* to a burning wreck. *Buistri* escaped to the north pursued by *Niitaka* and the destroyer *Murakumo* which had joined the chase, while *Otowa* poured more 6in, 4.7in and 12pdr shells into *Svietlana* at ranges as low as half a mile. The Russians had agreed not to surrender and 'although there was nothing to be done the crew determined to die . . . Bathed in a shower of shell they waited for the ship to sink. The captain was killed, the commander mortally wounded; the ship gradually heeled over; most of the crew jumped into the sea. By 10.50 . . . we saw she was on the point of sinking and the *Otowa* ceased fire.'[9]

The fate of the main body of the Russian fleet was less heroic. Nebogatov still hoped to make Vladivostok but Togo's battleships and armoured cruisers hove into sight once more on a converging course. The Japanese cruiser divisions barred his retreat and it seemed to Nebogatov that the enemy 'were making a ring about us with a well defined radius which they were able to select owing to their superior speed'.[10]

At 1034 *Kasuga* fired a sighting shot and the rest of the battleships and armoured cruisers were soon in action at long range (7,500–8,750 yards). Nebogatov was told by his gunnery officer that his old guns could make no effective reply. The only ship in his surviving force with modern armament was *Orel* and she, he assessed as 'a mass of scrap iron without ammunition, spent and exhausted' after twelve 12in hits, seven 8in and at least twenty-two 6in.[11] None of Nebogatov's surviving undamaged capital ships had modern 6in batteries and the old slow-firing 12in, 10in and 9in guns stood no chance at all of hitting at such ranges. What completed Russian demoralization was the apparently undamaged state of the enemy: '. . . when at dawn we found ourselves surrounded by an iron wall of 27 large enemy ships, none showing any trace of damage both officers and men lost hope . . . they fell on their knees and cried that all was lost. That splendid array of ships, the whole Japanese fleet with no vessel missing, which was making a ring round the poor remnant left to us, who could look at it without feeling as if his soul had been torn from his body? . . . That is why at the moment of surrender no man had power to show his wit or courage'.[12]

The Russians signalled to the Japanese by flags their intention to strike their colours and lowered their ensigns to half mast. The Japanese continued to fire, however, for ten or fifteen minutes, scoring no hits at such an extended range. Nebogatov then ordered a white flag to be flown but it was not until he flew the rising sun of Japan over his St Andrew's cross ensign that Togo finally got the message. The surrender was too much for Captain Ferzen of the scout cruiser *Izumrud*, who made off to the south-east at 20 knots, easily shaking off the slower Japanese ships that gave chase. Sadly for her brave crew, the scout's machinery had suffered combat damage and she was forced to put into a badly surveyed bay to the east. She ran on to the rocks and was blown up to avoid falling into enemy hands. At 1430 *Admiral Ushakov*, which had been separated from Nebogatov's main force, hove into sight but turned away when she spotted the danger. The fast armoured cruisers *Iwate* and *Yakumo* steamed off in pursuit. They overtook the coast defence ship west of Oki island and signalled to her by flags to surrender but *Ushakov* had decided to resist and opened fire. The Japanese cruisers fired back with their much more effective quick-firing batteries and *Ushakov* eventually developed such a list she could not reply. Captain Miklukha had ordered the sea cocks opened to scuttle the ship. The Japanese closed in, firing deliberately and effectively until at 1807 the little 5,000-ton ironclad blew up, probably as a result of the heavy Japanese fire.

At 1600 that afternoon the Japanese destroyers *Kagero* and *Sazanami*, after a visit to the port of Ulsan for repairs and replenishment, spotted the Russian destroyers *Byedovi* and *Grozni*. Because of shell damage and shortage of fuel on *Buini*, the wounded Rozhestvensky had transferred earlier that day from *Buini* to *Byedovi*: *Buini* later broke down completely and was sunk by *Dmitri Donskoi*. The Japanese pair pursued the Russian destroyers and it became clear that *Byedovi* could not escape: she therefore surrendered, as her companion made off, firing at her pursuers. *Grozni* eventually reached Vladivostok. *Byedovi* was towed ignominiously back to Ulsan.

While this final act in the Rozhestvensky drama played itself out, the old Russian cruiser *Dmitri Donskoi* was meeting her fate. The Japanese tried to contact her by wireless to get Captain Lebedev to surrender and after their success against *Svietlana* the cruisers *Otowa* and *Niitaka* found the Russian ship. *Otowa* opened fire at 1900 at about 8,500 yards and *Niitaka* joined in shortly afterwards. Then the entire strength of the cruiser division of the Second Squadron, *Naniwa, Takachiho, Akashi* and *Tsushima* joined in. The storm of fire directed at about 3,000–4,000 yards prevented the unprotected gunners in *Donskoi* making a strong reply. Her upper deck, covered with survivors from *Osliabia* and *Buini*, became crowded with dead and dying. The stately old cruiser did, however, put a 6in shell into *Naniwa* when she came too close. *Donskoi*'s compound armour stood up well to the light guns of the Japanese and, with the failure of attempts by Japanese destroyers to finish her off, she remained afloat close to the rocks of Matsushima. The Russian cruiser then scuttled herself by opening her sea cocks at daylight on 29 May. Her surviving crew surrendered to the armoured cruiser *Kasuga* the following afternoon.

All the large Russian warships had now been accounted for. Of the destroyers only *Bravi* made Vladivostok. The destroyers *Blestyashtchi* and *Bodri* fled southwards. The former sank in heavy seas; the latter was towed into Shanghai where she was interned. The most important group of survivors were the protected cruisers *Oleg, Aurora* and scout cruiser *Jemtchug* commanded by Admiral Enkvist. The latter decided to make for Shanghai and the Russian colliers: he also transferred his flag to the less badly damaged *Aurora*. Enkvist now split his force, himself making for Manila and the other two ships being given liberty of action. Their engines consumed much more coal than normal because of damaged funnels, so *Oleg* and *Jemtchug* decided to make for the Philippines also, to land wounded and re-store. All three Russian cruisers were interned by the Americans and disarmed. They were later returned to the Imperial Russian Navy. *Jemtchug* was sunk in 1914 by the German cruiser *Emden*; *Oleg* was torpedoed and sunk by British *Coastal Motor Boat No 4* in the British attack on the Red Fleet at Kronstadt in 1919: and *Aurora* achieved immortality by beginning the Bolshevik Revolution in November 1917 at Petrograd (Leningrad), where she still lies.

The fate of the Transport Squadron was as follows. The graceful armed yacht *Almaz* slipped away and, hugging the Japanese coast for cover, made Vladivostok. The armed repair ship *Kamchatka* had been sunk in battle. The armed transport *Irtish* was too badly damaged to do anything else but wreck herself on the Japanese coast. The other armed transport, *Anadir*, was more fortunate. She turned back, reached Madagascar a month later and made it back to the Baltic with 300 survivors of the armed merchant cruiser *Ural*. The ammunition ship *Korea* and surviving tug *Svir* were interned in Shanghai. The two hospital ships were captured by the Japanese; one, *Kostroma*, being released, the other, *Orel*, whose spotting by the Japanese had started the battle, was retained as a prize of war.

RESULTS

Sir Julian Corbett in his confidential Staff History of the battle called Tsushima 'perhaps the most decisive and complete naval victory in history'.[1] No major Japanese unit had been seriously damaged and only three torpedo-boats sunk: 117 Japanese officers and men had been killed and 583 wounded. On the Russian side twelve major units, four destroyers and three auxiliaries had been sunk or scuttled after being disabled, and four major units and a destroyer captured. Of all Rozhestvensky's motley, but imposing, array only one armed yacht and two destroyers got through to their destination. The toll in casualties was terrible, in the worst Russian tradition: 4,830 killed, 5,907 prisoners, 1,862 interned.

All that remained to the Russians in the Far Eastern theatre of war was the armed cruiser *Rossia* and a small flotilla of torpedo craft at Vladivostok. As Corbett went on to say: 'Not once in our most successful naval wars had we obtained a command of the sea so nearly absolute as that which Japan now enjoyed . . .', nor he doubted from the perspective of 1914 would 'such an uncontrolled sway ever be won again'.[2] Japan could strike when and where she wished without fear of detection let alone interdiction. 'In short,' the master naval strategist summed up, Japan 'had absolutely secured her hold on the territorial objects of the war and she was free to open the third phase of the operations: that is she was at liberty to bring such pressure to bear as she could in order to force her enemy to recognize the conquest; and for this purpose she was free to strike wherever the Imperial Staff saw the point best suited to their resources.'[3]

In June, on American initative, negotiations were agreed between the two belligerents. In order to maintain the pressure on the Russians, the following month the Japanese Combined Fleet, which now included the captured Russian ships (although few were actually ready for service), landed troops on Sakhalin. The island was soon in Japanese hands and its future became a key issue at the peace talks organized by President Roosevelt in Portsmouth, New Hampshire. In the end the island was partitioned as part of a settlement that gave Japan what she had gone to war to achieve: mutual withdrawal from Manchuria; a free Japanese hand in Korea; Japanese control of Port Arthur and the Liaodong Peninsula.

With her financial position becoming increasingly weak and a powerful undefeated Russian army of over a million in Manchuria, this was as good a deal as the Japanese could have expected – 'a peace cleverly snatched by the Japanese at the most favourable moment'.[4]

Sea power, even after such a crushing success, could not so fundamentally affect Russia that a war indemnity could be forced upon her. Indeed, one modern historian of the war considers that, given her reinforced army in Manchuria (over a million men built up via the trans-Siberian railway and Lake Baikal), Russia was ill advised to make peace:

'. . . in view of what happened in Russia after peace was made it seems likely that the Russian Government would have been better advised to continue the war to fight at least one more battle. A victory would almost certainly have been won, thanks to the increased Russian strength and the exhaustion of Japan's resources'.[5]

Nevertheless, after the shock of the annihilation of Rozhestvensky's fleet and the clear demonstration of maritime power to wound at will demonstrated by Sakhalin – and subtly demonstrated so as to disturb without provoking too extreme a reaction – the pressure to make peace was too strong to be ignored. Total naval victory thus gave Japan overall victory in what had always been essentially a limited war.

3

THE DREADNOUGHT
REVOLUTION

E VEN AS ROZHESTVENSKY'S FLEET was sailing round
the world to its doom, the type of warfare for which it and its
opponent had been designed was rapidly becoming obsolete.
Both guns and torpedoes were beginning to acquire the ability
to hit at long ranges. Tsushima was a pre-dreadnought action fought at
long range for the available technology and technique. This, 5,000 yards
or so, now became a new base for which further range extensions took
place.

In the late 1890s the addition of gyroscopes to torpedoes had given
them sufficient directional accuracy to make them effective at over 1,000
yards. This led to experiments with longer gun ranges and in 1899 the
Royal Navy began firings at ranges up to 6,000 yards. It soon discovered
that the best way of firing at such ranges was to fire a number of guns
together in a salvo. This increased the probability of hitting by covering
a small area of ocean with shells: given correctly set sights the shells
would straddle the target.

A new technique of fire control was developed to direct salvoes on to
the target at long range. Experiments were carried out in 1903–04 in two
British battleships, *Venerable* and *Victorious*, and the practicality of long-
range fire with 12in heavy artillery proved. Leading fire control experts
like Edward Harding, a captain in the Royal Marines, were soon arguing
that given the superior effect of a 12in round on impact and the flatter
trajectory of the heavier gun – which meant that it could find the target
more rapidly – the 6in quick-firer was doomed as a major capital ship
weapon. It would be much better and simpler in this new era of fire
control, he reasoned, to move towards a main armament of heavy guns
of uniform calibre. Given the improvements in the rate of fire of 12in
guns, this seemed the obvious choice, both for battleships and armoured
cruisers.

In 1904–05, against the background of the developing Russo-Japanese
War, the British Admiralty, prodded by the energetic First Sea Lord, Sir
John Fisher, made some epochal decisions on future capital ship design.

The designs of both a new battleship and a new armoured cruiser with all big gun armament were approved by the Board of Admiralty in March 1905. Fisher preferred the cruiser but was overruled by his colleagues to the extent that the first new capital ship to be built was a battleship. Christened *Dreadnought*, she gave her name to a revolution in naval technology that made all previous vessels obsolete. Other navies were working on the same lines and speed was of the essence. The new ship was laid down on 2 October 1905 and was completed in just over a year. Displacing just over 18,000 tons, she was powered by steam turbines that gave her a speed of 21 knots compared with her predecessors' 18. Her ten 12in guns meant that she was the most powerful warship in the world. Fisher, however, regarded her as an 'old testament' ship. He followed her up with three pointedly named 'Invincible'-class armoured cruisers, faster still at over 25 knots and armed with eight 12in weapons.

Fisher's original strategy had been to move ahead rapidly with the construction of bigger and more powerful armoured cruisers. This would deal with the threat of both German battleships and French armoured cruisers. The demise of France as a rival because of the signature of the Entente in 1904 (and the demise of the Russian threat at Tsushima) left Germany as Britain's major opponent and she had few armoured cruisers. Better, therefore, to press ahead with the construction of more 'Dreadnoughts' with a few 'Invincibles' as a fast squadron. Once more Fisher was overruled and the 1906 capital ships were slightly modified versions of the battleship design. Fisher's fundamental concept, however, worked well enough. He hoped to use a technical lead to give Britain more years of naval supremacy at a more acceptable cost than that of merely outbuilding her growing number of rivals in incrementally improved vessels of 'pre-dreadnought' conception.

The German building programme, finely orchestrated because of Reichstag politics, was thrown into confusion. Germany did not lay down her first answer to *Dreadnought* until the summer of 1907 and even then these were slow reciprocating-engined ships not capable of 20 knots. Her first new model armoured cruiser, *Blücher*, laid down in the same year, was a false start with only 21cm (8.2in) main armament. *Von Der Tann*, the first real answer to *Invincible*, was not laid down until 1908; she came into service in February 1911. By the end of that year Britain had in service ten dreadnoughts of five continuously improved classes and four 'Invincibles' of two classes. New 'super dreadnoughts' with 13.5in guns were approaching completion. The Germans had seven slower dreadnought equivalents of two classes, and their single real battlecruiser (although two more of the latter were already launched). Britain was to maintain this kind of lead into the First World War.

Torpedo design did not stand still either. A revolution comparable to that of fire control occurred in the design of torpedoes. In 1904–05 both the Whitehead factory at Fiume and Armstrong Whitworth at Elswick developed heaters that produced hot gas to drive torpedo engines rather than the simple compressed air used previously. This greatly increased both speed and range. The disappointing contemporary results of torpedoes in the Russo-Japanese War stimulated the rapid adoption of the new propulsion system. A typical 18in torpedo of pre-heater design had a range of only 800 yards at its maximum speed of about 30 knots: the first heater torpedoes of the same size could travel over 2,000 yards at 34 knots and about 4,400 yards at 28 knots. By 1909 British '18in' (actually 17.7in Mk VII) torpedoes, using their newly developed simplified Hardcastle 'wet' heater system, were capable of 3,500 yards at 45 knots and 5,000 yards at 35 knots. Larger torpedoes made their appearance also with still greater speed, range and hitting power. The German 500mm (19.7in) Type G of 1906 could run for over 6,000 yards at 36 knots with double the charge (440lb) of an 18in weapon. The British Mk II 21in torpedoes, introduced in 1910, could carry a 400lb charge 5,000 yards at 35 knots.

These greatly enhanced torpedo ranges made longer gunnery ranges imperative for survival, not just for offensive advantage. The lessons of the Russo-Japanese War were ambiguous, but the dominant consensus was that they had confirmed the logic of the 'dreadnought' revolution; big guns had demonstrated their decisive superiority for the infliction of catastrophic damage on a ship's structure. Attempts were therefore made to improve further the techniques and technologies of fire control. New longer base length rangefinders were adopted, capable of accurate measurement at 10,000 yards, and early analogue computer systems were developed to solve the problem of working out the precise area of sea in which the enemy ship would be when the salvo arrived. This was a not inconsiderable mathematical problem, with both firing platform and target manoeuvring at 20 knots or more.

Thanks to Professor Jon Sumida, it is now well known that the Royal Navy turned down the privately developed Pollen fire control computer system, preferring instead the inferior ideas of Admiral Sir Frederic Dreyer, whose fire control systems (which in their more advanced versions bowdlerized Pollen's concepts) could not cope with a rate of change of range that was itself changing.[1] Nevertheless, without computer assistance but with the help of instruments to plot the change of range (dumaresqs), range clocks to grind out changes of rate and 9ft rangefinders, British capital ships could by 1912 engage in experimental firing practices at 14,000 yards. In 1913 the British battlecruiser force, equipped with new 13.5in-armed 'Lion'-class equivalents of the 'super dreadnoughts', was experimenting with 12,000-yard ranges under expected tactical conditions of high speeds and sharp turns.

The other independent development to make long-range firing more practical was Sir Percy Scott's development of director firing, the operation in normal circumstances of the ship's armament by one man aloft in a mast. This did away with the inevitable extra uncertainties involved in trying to co-ordinate the actions of individual gunlayers with their own judgments of range and bearing. In November 1912 the super dreadnought *Thunderer*, fitted for director firing, achieved six times the hits of her sister ship, *Orion*, using older independent methods.

Within a decade of Tsushima, therefore, naval warfare had been transformed. Then fleets of mixed armament had pecked at each other with light guns at ranges rarely greater than 2½ miles, waiting for the effect of the hail of high-explosive and resulting fire, or a highly uncertain shot with a heavy gun, actually to sink an opponent. Torpedoes were only effective at very close ranges and even then with little reliability. After the revolution, navies traded potentially catastrophic blows with heavy shells at ranges of at least 5 miles, often much more. The new capital ships were supported by a new generation of smaller craft too, fast light cruisers with speeds of up to 28 knots, and large 30- to 35-knot, 1,000-ton, ocean-going destroyers armed with the new large heater torpedoes.

Naval warfare was also becoming three-dimensional. Submarines had become practical enough to be procured by the world's major navies in the early years of the twentieth century, the breakthrough being reliable internal combustion engines for use on the surface coupled with battery-electric drive submerged. Britain laid down her first submarine in 1901. Germany, with little spare money in the naval estimates for such experimentation, did not have *U1* in service until 1906. Early submarines were small and slow and could not work directly with the increasingly fast ships of the main fleet. They could, however, work as a kind of mobile mine both in coast defence and in more open sea areas, laying traps for unwary surface units. Their contemporary utility tended to be confused with their potential, but there could be no doubt that the possibility of attack by submarine torpedo-boats (as well as more conventional platforms for the new torpedoes) and the threat of mines, did cause a significant change in the handling of battle fleets. Closing enemy coasts became too dangerous. In December 1912 the Admiralty bleakly reported that: 'the enemy's submarine, in conjunction with the destroyer, has made an efficient blockade impossible'.[2] Not only would fleets have to wait out of range of submarine attack: once battle was joined the threat of underwater attack, from the long-range torpedo delivered by the invisible submarine, or even the mine dropped in front of the advancing squadrons as at Tsushima, would weigh heavily on British fleet commanders in the coming war. The battle fleet was no longer quite as supreme in the ocean as it had been. It had to be handled with more care and circumspection.

If fleets were to be handled more cautiously, then finding the enemy was more important than ever, either to engage him or avoid him. The conquest of the air in the early years of the twentieth century promised to help here. The Germans had a technological advantage, having perfected the world's first long-range aircraft, the Zeppelin airship, but again the Navy proved reluctant to risk scarce resources on a new and untried device. The first naval airship was lost in an accident and by the outbreak of war in 1914 only one was in service. Nevertheless, the Germans did have the potential to build rapidly as good a maritime air reconnaissance capability for their fleet as any available anywhere.

The British recognized the importance of airships but sadly could not build rigids that would fly. Naval Airship Number 1 was an expensive failure and the smaller non-rigids, although at least able to fly, were no real substitutes. With support from the First Lord of the Admiralty, Winston Churchill, enthusiasts for aeroplanes were given their head in the Royal Navy after 1911 and by 1914 the Royal Naval Air Service was the largest naval air arm in the world, with over 100 aircraft. Sadly, however, these machines could be used for little more than coastal patrol or operations ashore. The Royal Navy subsequently developed the aircraft-carrier so that it could use its aeroplanes with the fleet. It would take time, however, to develop fully workable designs.

Despite the advent of new torpedoes, submarines and aircraft, the gun-armed capital ship was still the supreme arbiter of sea power in 1914. Its guns still far outranged torpedoes in effective reach and its screens of fast, newly developed light cruisers and larger, more seaworthy destroyers could do much to keep hostile torpedo craft at bay. Nevertheless, given that its activities would be much more circumscribed than ever before, the role of the dreadnought battle fleet would be much more that of a fleet in being than a decisive instrument of victory. On the stronger side, from protected distant blockading bases, the fleet would cover shipping in the wider oceans. On the weaker side, the fleet would stay in port, forcing the enemy to remain on guard and preventing him from allocating his full forces to the direct protection of shipping. This would be especially important when, much to everyone's surprise, the submarine soon proved its worth as the most effective commerce raider in the history of naval warfare. In 1917, with an undefeated Grand Fleet, Britain stared defeat by the U-boats in the face. Until then, however, Germany had from time to time attempted to direct her naval operations against Britain's Grand Fleet, trying to use U-boats to inflict attrition on its superior strength and attempting to outmanoeuvre it and defeat it in detail. One such attempt led to the largest fleet action of the dreadnought

era and one of the major events of twentieth century naval history, the
Battle of Jutland, 31 May 1916.

4
THE DREADNOUGHT ERA: JUTLAND

GERMANY LOST the pre-1914 naval race with Britain and was therefore faced with the tactical challenge of how to wear down the British Grand Fleet, or otherwise neutralize its power. Kaiser Wilhelm II, who saw the High Sea Fleet as his own private warship collection, forbade taking any more risks after an attempted battlecruiser raid on the British coast went disastrously wrong in January 1915 with the loss of the armoured cruiser *Blücher* in the Battle of the Dogger Bank. Only a signalling fiasco in the British Battlecruiser Force prevented the German First Scouting Group from being overwhelmed by its stronger opponent. Germany next tried an unrestricted U-boat blockade of Britain which gave remarkably good results – until American pressure forced Germany to limit the activities of her submarines once more.

STRATEGIC BACKGROUND

By early 1916, therefore, Germany was forced to reassess her maritime strategy. She decided on a more aggressive policy with both her main fleet and her submarines. The terminally ill fleet commander, Admiral Pohl, was replaced in February by Vice-Admiral Reinhard Scheer, with authorization from the Kaiser to take more risks. The options remained restricted, however, to raids on the British coast and other offensive moves in the hope of bringing on a battle between Germany's full fleet strength and a detached portion of the Grand Fleet. Thus might British strength be worn down to that of the High Sea Fleet and a full-scale fleet encounter become practical. The fatal flaw in Scheer's reasoning was that surprising the Grand Fleet was much more difficult than he thought. Thanks to the feats of the cryptanalysts in Room 40 at the Admiralty, the British had prior warning of many of Scheer's intentions. Intelligence often remained sketchy, and the Admiralty War Staff did not help by not handling the decrypted information properly; nevertheless, it meant that Scheer was at a major disadvantage. Only if his enemy made a series of mistakes would he stand a chance of achieving his objectives.

On 25 April 1916, Scheer mounted a large–scale raid on Lowestoft and Yarmouth. Tipped off by cryptanalysis, the Admiralty ordered the entire British fleet to sea in its three groups, the main body based at Scapa Flow under Admiral Sir John Jellicoe, the battlecruisers based at Rosyth under Admiral Sir David Beatty, and the Harwich Force of cruisers and destroyers commanded by Commodore Reginald Tyrwhitt. Tyrwhitt sighted the German scouting groups, which had already been weakened when the battlecruiser *Seydlitz* hit a mine and had been forced to pull out. Tyrwhitt was in some danger of being destroyed in detail but Rear Admiral Friedrich Bödicker, commander of the Second Scouting Group and in overall charge of the advanced German squadrons in the absence of the ill Vice-Admiral Franz Hipper, turned prematurely back to support his main fleet. Scheer, fearing an engagement with the full force of the enemy, then turned for home, shadowed by the Harwich Force. Beatty was still 130 miles away and Jellicoe 300.

Not that the British fleet commander, Sir John Jellicoe, was any less cautious. He was determined not to be drawn into battle too close to the enemy's submarine- and mine-infested coast, and, as the German fleet refused to come out into open sea, two seaplane-carrier raids were mounted in March and early May to encourage Scheer to sail to his doom. These were no more successful than the German foray.

Scheer analyzed the errors of April and decided that a major problem was that he had sent the Scouting Group against the wrong target. Sunderland, 200 miles to the north, would offer better rewards. Beatty would be encouraged south and engaged before Jellicoe would have time to come up in support. Scheer also integrated U-boats into his plan. The attempt to restart a less restricted submarine offensive against merchant shipping at the end of February 1916 led to the sinking of the ferry *Sussex* and the real threat of war with the USA. On 24 April the U-boats were restricted once more to debilitating prize regulations. It seemed to Scheer that they would be of more use in the North Sea as part of the fleet battle. Angry at what he regarded as the pusillanimous attitude of his politicians, the German fleet commander now integrated his submarines into his plans. A two-boat submarine ambush was laid for Jellicoe in the Pentland Firth and no fewer than eight U-boats lay in wait for Beatty in the Firth of Forth, one being ordered to penetrate the Firth itself. Three U-boat minelayers laid mines off the Firth of Forth, the Moray Firth and the Orkney Islands. One U-boat was off Peterhead and two off the Humber with two more off the Dutch island of Terschelling. Scheer also hoped that Zeppelin reconnaissance would give him a better picture of British movements so that he could avoid being trapped by superior forces. Scheer originally planned to execute his operation on 17 May 1916, but it was delayed because repairs to the battlecruiser *Seydlitz* took longer than expected. The final planned date was the 29th, but that day proved too windy for the German Navy's Zeppelins.

Scheer was now in deep trouble. His U-boats were within two days of the end of their endurance: they would have to withdraw on 1 June. If the U-boat ambush plan was to work, he had to take the High Sea Fleet to sea by the 31st. Yet without air reconnaissance the risks of closing the British coast were too great. A compromise plan was therefore substituted at the last minute. The scouting groups of battlecruisers and light cruisers would sail into the Skagerrak as if to attack British shipping, with the battleships in support 60 miles astern. This would draw Jellicoe and Beatty over the U-boats. Beatty might even be lured too far ahead of Jellicoe. If danger threatened, the High Sea Fleet could turn back to the Jade out of danger. The changed plans were signalled on the 30th, but changed again shortly before Hipper sailed in the early hours of 31 May. He was now authorized to go as far as Norway if required in order to 'trail his coat' in as obvious a manner as possible.

Actually the British knew something was afoot. At noon on 30 May radio intelligence revealed probable movements by the High Sea Fleet early the following morning. An important signal had been overheard, although not in all its details. At 1740, therefore, Jellicoe was ordered to concentrate his fleet in the 'Long Forties', 100 miles east of Aberdeen. The British sailors, frustrated by their enforced wait for an enemy that would apparently never appear, cheered at the orders to move. By 2230 on 30 May – 2½ hours before Scheer was due to sail on his supposedly secret mission in support of Hipper's decoy – Jellicoe's super-dread-nought flagship, HMS *Iron Duke*, was at sea leading one of the largest concentrations of naval power the world has ever seen.

Jellicoe's aim was to destroy the High Sea Fleet if he could do so without undue risk to the Grand Fleet. The latter was already in control of the world's oceans outside the North Sea. Its distant blockade kept German surface warships from interdicting the merchant shipping vital to the survival of both the United Kingdom and the whole Allied cause. True, the existence of the High Sea Fleet prevented more units being diverted to protect that trade from the submarine offensive. Destroying the German battlefleet would allow British strength to be diverted from their boring North Sea watch to a number of other causes with strategic potential. Perhaps the flank of the Western Front might even be turned: perhaps Germany's Baltic trade might be interdicted. Yet such operations would still be risky against German coast defences, whether the High Sea Fleet existed or not.

The strategic results of a crushing victory over the High Sea Fleet might therefore be limited merely to releasing destroyers for anti-submarine work. American political pressure had seemed an effective enough weapon against that. Moreover, Jellicoe could lose the war easily enough, 'in an afternoon', as the saying went. The loss of the Grand Fleet would be an unparalleled disaster. Britain would starve, and the Allied cause with her, as the victorious unopposed German surface ships imposed a blockade more quick and effective than the already effective enough guerrilla warfare of the German U-boats. This could probably be done within the prize rules and without an American declaration of war. With little to gain and everything to lose, caution was the primary quality expected of any competent British Grand Fleet commander.

As for Scheer, his primary aim had to be to keep his fleet in being. Fighting to the end against overwhelming odds would be a quixotic gesture at best. If he met lighter enemy forces (up to and including Beatty's battlecruiser fleet), he would try to sink them. If he met Jellicoe's main fleet, he would try to get away. Scheer was not seeking a show-down. His ships were far more valuable to Germany in tying down superior British warship strength. Jellicoe was seeking a show-down, but only in the most favourable conditions; conditions that were less than likely to arise. These were not the optimum circumstances for a decisive battle.

THE BRITISH FORCES

Jellicoe's Grand Fleet was the most powerful in the world. Already *Dreadnought* herself was considered obsolete and was refitting for service with the pre-dreadnoughts of the Third Battle Squadron guarding the Channel at Sheerness. Under Jellicoe's own command were three Battle Squadrons of dreadnoughts and super-dreadnoughts:

Second Battle Squadron (van squadron)
FIRST DIVISION: *King George V, Ajax, Centurion, Erin.* The three surviving members of the second class of super-dreadnoughts completed in 1912–13: 23,000 tons load displacement and armed with ten 13.5in guns in five twin turrets. The fourth ship of the class, *Audacious*, had been lost to a mine in October 1914 and been replaced by the rather similar *Erin* (22,780 tons) completed in August 1914 and seized from the Turks at the outbreak of war. *Erin* had a heavier secondary battery than the others, sixteen 6in rather than sixteen 4in, but her armoured belt was thinner and shallower and she had less coal capacity.
SECOND DIVISION: *Orion, Monarch, Conqueror, Thunderer.* The four first super-dreadnoughts completed in 1912: 22,200 tons load displacement and armed with 13.5in guns in five twin turrets and a secondary battery of sixteen 4in guns.

Fourth Battle Squadron (centre squadron)

THIRD DIVISION: *Iron Duke, Royal Oak, Superb, Canada.* A mixed bag of ships led by the fleet flagship, a 25,000-ton super-dreadnought completed in March 1914 and armed with five twin 13.5in turrets; unlike previous British super-dreadnoughts, the secondary battery in this class was increased in calibre to 6in (twelve guns). *Royal Oak* was a brand-new (completed May 1916) member of the 28,000-ton 'Revenge' class, armed with eight 15in guns, the most powerful naval weapons in the world. *Superb* was a contrast, being a member of the first production batch of 'Dreadnoughts' after the prototype and completed in May 1909. The pace of progress was shown by her displacement of 18,800 tons and armament, ten 12in guns in five twin turrets. The final member of this group was HMS *Canada,* a 28,000-ton super-dreadnought armed with five twin 14in turrets, purchased from Chile in September 1914 and completed at Armstrong's on the Tyne a year later.

FOURTH DIVISION: *Benbow, Bellerophon, Temeraire, Vanguard. Benbow* was a sister of *Iron Duke,* completed in October 1914. The other three were dreadnoughts of the first and second production batches and all armed with ten 12in guns, one twin turret forward, one on each beam amidships and two on the centre-line aft. *Bellerophon* and *Temeraire* were sisters of *Superb,* 18,000 tons, completed in 1909. *Vanguard,* 19,560 tons, was completed in 1910 and had higher velocity Mk XII 12in guns.

First Battle Squadron (rear squadron).

SIXTH DIVISION: *Marlborough, Revenge, Hercules, Agincourt.* A powerful squadron led by an 'Iron Duke'-class ship completed in June 1914 and containing another 15in gun ship, *Revenge,* completed the previous March. The other pair were both late 12in gun ships, the 20,225-ton *Hercules* built under the controversial 1909 programme, completed in 1911 and armed with the usual ten main guns and sixteen 4in, and the unique *Agincourt* laid down for Brazil, purchased by Turkey and seized by the British on completion in August 1914. She displaced 27,500 tons and was a very long ship, 671.5ft overall. She was armed with no fewer than fourteen 12in guns in seven twin turrets; it was said of her that when she fired broadsides it looked as if she had been blown up.

FIFTH DIVISION: *Colossus, Collingwood, Neptune, St. Vincent.* The rearmost division of Jellicoe's line consisted of dreadnoughts all armed with ten 12in guns. *Colossus* was the sister of *Vanguard* and completed in 1909 and *Collingwood,* another class member, completed in 1910. *Neptune* was a unique 19,680-ton ship built with staggered amidships turrets to allow cross deck firing. She was completed at the beginning of 1911.

In all, Jellicoe had twenty-four battleships, two with 15in guns, one with 14in, eleven with 13.5in and ten with 12in. Adding to his capital ship strength was the Third Battle Cruiser Squadron. This was composed of the three original 'Invincibles', *Invincible, Indomitable* and *Inflexible*. They had been sent from Rosyth to Scapa Flow for gunnery practice on 22 May and were scheduled to return on the very day the fleet sailed. They replaced a fast battle squadron, the Fifth, that had been transferred to Beatty's command in exchange. The 17,373-ton 'Invincibles', completed in 1908–09, were becoming obsolescent, being relatively slow (25 knots) compared with later battlecruisers. Their 6–7in turret and belt protection could also be penetrated more easily than the battleships' 10–12in armour at long range.

However, the 'Invincibles' were at least ships of the current generation. Unwisely the British maintained two squadrons of pre-dreadnought armoured cruisers with the main fleet. The ships were of the last three classes of such vessels built for the Royal Navy, none laid down earlier than 1903, but all now completely obsolete. The First Cruiser Squadron was made up of the last 'pre-Invincibles' built for the Royal Navy. *Defence* had been laid down in February 1905 – before the first three battlecruisers – but was completed a month before *Invincible* and after her two sisters, in February 1909. A large 'Minotaur'-class ship of 14,600 tons, she was armed with two twin 9.2in turrets and ten single 7.5in. Armour protection was actually marginally better than that of the 'Invincibles' on the turrets, but hull protection was nowhere more than 6in. With her triple-expansion engines, *Defence* gained nothing over a 1916 battleship in terms of speed (23 knots) and was woefully under-protected and under-gunned for long-range engagements. *Warrior* was name ship of the previous 13,550-ton class, armed with six 9.2in and 7.5in guns, all in single turrets. She was an excellent armoured cruiser both as a seaboat and a gun platform but also obsolescent on her completion. The rest of the squadron was made up of the sisters *Duke of Edinburgh* and *Black Prince*, both completed in 1906 and armed with six 9.2in single mountings and ten 6in. Also good vessels at the time of their inception in the 1902 programme, these ships were regarded as being weak in the era of scientific gunnery that had undermined the 6in quick-firer as the ultimate long-range weapon. Their low-mounted 6in batteries, excellent in avoiding direct fire at 2,000 yards, could not be worked in rough weather.

The Second Cruiser Squadron included *Defence*'s two sister ships, *Minotaur* and *Shannon*, both completed in 1908, and two 'Warriors', *Cochrane* and *Natal*, both commissioned in 1907. These large and vulnerable ships were death-traps in a dreadnought fleet action. Their length, high forecastles and four large funnels made them excellent aiming points and their thin 1½in deck armour offered no protection against plunging fire. British light cruisers were faster and harder to hit and could cope on their own against their German counterparts. The armoured cruisers' secondary duty of reconnaissance and keeping touch with the enemy battlefleet should also have been superfluous if the real 'armoured cruiser' force – i.e., the Battlecruiser Fleet – did its job properly. Possibly the presence of the two cruiser squadrons led both Jellicoe and Beatty into thinking that the former had his own 'organic' armoured cruiser force, releasing the BCF to become engaged as a primarily fighting force, a fast capital ship squadron.

There are signs of this in Grand Fleet Battle Orders:

'The duty of our cruisers is . . . in the event of the enemy's advanced forces becoming engaged with our battlecruiser fleet, to push on and gain touch with the enemy's battlefleet. The latter may be considered a most important duty in order that the Commander-in-Chief may receive accurate information before the battlefleets sight one another.'[1]

Jellicoe would have been better served if the First and Second Cruiser Squadrons had been swapped for the modern light cruisers remaining on foreign stations, where the old armoured ships would have been of more use. As is was, Jellicoe had only a single squadron of light cruisers, the Fourth, with representatives of the first four classes of small (4,000-ton) fast light cruisers designed specially for work with the new dreadnought fleet. *Calliope, Constance, Caroline, Royalist* and *Comus* had speeds of 28.5 to 29.5 knots and were armed with two 6in and eight (*Royalist* six) 4in guns. The mixed calibres were not to prove satisfactory for fire control purposes and 4in guns had a tendency to jam; but in general these were good ships, heavily armed and protected against light shell fire by 3–4in belts and 1in deck armour. Churchill had called the concept the 'light armoured cruiser'. Earlier ships, *Royalist, Caroline* and *Comus* carried four 21in above-water torpedo tubes; these were reduced to two in *Champion* and *Constance*, which had submerged tubes.

Six older light cruisers were also attached to the fleet, primarily to relay visual signals between members of the battlefleet – an index of the mismatch of the command and control and more physical capabilities of the dreadnought-era battlefleet. *Active, Bellona* and *Blanche* were 'scouts', earlier attempts to produce in 1907–11 the proper light cruiser for fleet work in the new era. Of 3,300–3,440 tons with 1in deck armour, a maximum speed of 25 knots and an armament of 4in guns (six in *Boadicea* and *Bellona* and ten in *Active*), they proved less than adequate for combat service in the front line, hence their relegation to communications duties. The other two ships were brand-new vessels not fully worked up: *Canterbury*, a sister ship of *Constance*, and *Chester*, a

5,200-ton ship laid down by Cammell Laird for Greece and armed with ten non-standard 5.5in guns.

Another new, but fully operational, 4,320-ton 'light armoured cruiser', *Castor*, completed at the end of 1915, acted as flagship for Jellicoe's three destroyer flotillas. Each of these was led by a Captain (D) in a large flotilla leader of about 1,500 tons, a new type conceived in 1913 partly due to the failure of the 'scout' concept and the need to concentrate the 'light armoured cruisers' on the fleet scouting role. HMS *Tipperary* was a large 1,610-ton vessel ordered for Chile. She mounted six 4in guns and two twin 21in torpedo tubes and could make 31 knots. Her sister, *Broke* (with single tubes), was also a member of the flotilla. The rest was made up of seventeen 'boats', a term still used for destroyers but becoming increasingly inappropriate as they increased in size. Sixteen were of the 'K' class, all launched in 1912-13. Of just over 1,000 tons, they could make 29 knots and mounted three 4in guns and two single 21in torpedo tubes. The odd vessel out was *Ophelia*, a new 'Repeat M'-class vessel of 1,025 tons armed with three 4in guns and four (two twin) 21in torpedo tubes; she could make 34 knots.

The 11th Flotilla consisted entirely of these faster ships and was led by *Castor* herself. The 11th also included the leader *Kempenfelt*, one of the Admiralty's own designed ships, 1,440 tons, with four 4in guns, two twin 21in torpedo tubes and with the high speed of 34.5 knots, comparable to the latest destroyers. The other 'boats' of the flotilla were all new 'Repeat Ms', fourteen in all. Eight were to the basic three-funnelled Admiralty design, three were 'Thornycroft Specials' with different-shaped funnels and higher freeboard, and three were 'Yarrow Specials' with two funnels. Both the 'Special' classes could make 35 knots.

The 12th Flotilla was led by *Faulknor*, a sister of *Broke*, and also contained *Marksman*, a sister of *Kempenfelt*. The latter had the speed of the rest of the flotilla, another collection of fourteen 'Repeat Ms', all Admiralty designs except *Munster*, a 'Thornycroft Special'. The 'M' class were fine little ships, fast and sturdy and with a good contemporary armament.

Attached to the fleet flagship to carry dispatches and to allow the C-in-C to move his flag in action was HMS *Oak*, one of a special 'Firedrake' group of the 'I' class. Launched in 1912 this small 778-ton boat was armed with two 4in and two 12pdr guns and two single 21in torpedo tubes. This group of three had been built for speed and could make 32 knots, a useful attribute for *Oak*'s special service. Another destroyer-type ship attached to the fleet was the destroyer minelayer *Abdiel*, a converted 'Lightfoot'-class leader with stowage for 80 mines instead of the torpedoes and after pair of guns.

Finally, and a portent of things to come, was the 'fleet carrier' *Campania*, a converted Cunarder of 1893 acquired in 1914 from a scrapyard as a possible armed merchant cruiser. The RNAS were in need of a large fast vessel for operations with the Grand Fleet and were allowed to acquire this rather dubious property. *Campania* was progressively modified and by May 1916 had a 200ft-long flying-off deck carried back from the bow between a split for the funnels. This allowed her to carry Short 184 reconnaissance seaplanes as well as Sopwith float fighters; at this time her complement was three Shorts and seven Sopwiths. She also carried a Caquot kite balloon for short-range observation. *Campania*'s old engines made keeping up with the fleet a strain but on 30 May she failed entirely to receive the signal to leave with the rest of the fleet. When she identified the error she set off in pursuit but Jellicoe, worried that the unescorted and vulnerable carrier of indeterminate speed would be torpedoed, ordered her back to Scapa. The C-in-C thus faced a possible fleet action with no opportunity to use his own air reconnaissance to find enemy submarines or minelayers, or to use fighters to interfere with the enemy's aerial activities.

Most of Jellicoe's fleet left from Scapa, although the super-dread-noughts of the vanguard Second Battle Squadron and four of the 11th DF's destroyers were based further south in the Cromarty Firth. They sailed simultaneously to rendezvous with the C-in-C and take station at noon the following day. Further south still at Rosyth, to guard against German battlecruiser forays, was Vice-Admiral Beatty's Battle Cruiser Fleet, the autonomous reconnaissance and mobile striking arm of the whole Grand Fleet.

Beatty flew his flag in the magnificent, 26,270-ton, 700ft-long battlecruiser *Lion*, laid down in 1909 and completed in mid-1912 as a counterpart to the 'Orion'-class super-dreadnoughts. With 42 boilers compared with the battleships' 18 and 70,000shp compared with 27,000, *Lion* could make 27 knots. Maximum armour protection on belt, barbettes and turret was 9in, insufficient to protect against 12in shells, which made the ships somewhat vulnerable given their lack of superior fire control over their opponents. *Lion*'s protection had been penetrated at the Dogger Bank when she was struck by sixteen 11in and 12in shells. Her engine room had been flooded and she had had to be towed home. Nevertheless, these ships were capable of taking numerous hits by heavy shells and surviving: other factors had to be added to their thin protection to produce a formula for catastrophe.

Lion's sister, *Princess Royal*, led the First Battle Cruiser Squadron. She had made over 28 knots on speed trials in 1913 but her engines had never been the same afterwards. Next came *Queen Mary*, 500 tons larger than the two original 'Splendid Cats', with more power (75,000shp) and rearranged armour. All these ships were armed with eight 13.5in guns on the centre-line; two turrets forward, one aft and one in 'Q' position amidships. Similarly armed was the further modernized HMS *Tiger* of 28,430 tons, capable of 28 knots with no less than 85,000shp. She carried a secondary armament of twelve 6in guns against the other ships' sixteen 4in.

In support of these powerful 'super Invincibles' were two older generation battlecruisers, *New Zealand* and *Indefatigable,* forming the Second Battle Cruiser Squadron. These were incremental developments of the original 'Invincibles' with the same armament, albeit staggered for cross deck fire as in the battleship *Neptune. Indefatigable* had problems making her designed speed of 25 knots and *New Zealand* had 1,000 more horsepower (44,000) to allow this. In fact she once made almost 27 knots on trials. *New Zealand* also had rearranged armour with a thickened belt at the expense of armour at bow and stern. Maximum armour thickness, however, remained 6in on the belt and 7in on the barbettes and turrets. *New Zealand* had been in collision with her Australian sister, HMAS *Australia* the normal flagship of the Second BCS in April 1916, and had been repaired: *Australia* was still in dockyard hands.

Normally the Third BCS of 'Invincibles' would have been with Beatty but instead he had the much more powerful addition of the Grand Fleet's Fifth Battle Squadron. This consisted of the finest battleships of their age, and possibly of the entire battleship era, the 'Queen Elizabeths'. The name ship was in refit at Rosyth, so only four ships were available: *Barham, Valiant, Warspite* and *Malaya.* These new vessels, completed between February 1915 and February 1916, were the first British super-dreadnoughts to carry 15in guns, eight in four twin turrets. This increased the weight of broadside, while allowing more space to be given to boilers, 24 as opposed to 18 in the 'Iron Dukes'. Such steam-generation capacity, combined with 56,000shp turbines and oil firing, gave a potential maximum speed of 24 knots, effectively the same performance as an 'Invincible' in normal conditions. A 'QE', however, was a much better protected platform, armoured to 13in on the belt and turret faces. Such a balanced combination of fighting power, protection and speed could only be obtained by increasing size to 28,000 tons load. The Fifth Battle Squadron was a powerful asset to any commander and Beatty was lucky to have it with him at the end of May. The secondary batteries of these ships comprised fourteen 6in guns, seven on each beam amidships.

Beatty also had the three premier squadrons of light cruisers, the First, Second and Third. The First was composed of three of the 'light armoured cruisers', three 3,750-ton 'Arethusas' (two 6in, six 4in guns), *Galatea, Phaeton* and *Inconstant,* and a 4,219-ton 'Caroline', *Cordelia* (two 6in, eight 4in guns). All had been completed during 1914–15. The

Second LCS was made up of 5,400-ton 'Towns', a modern light cruiser series laid down between 1909 and 1912 with world-wide duties in mind as well as operations in the North Sea. Belt protection was 2in of armour on top of 1in of normal plating. They were well armed with eight single 6in guns in *Southampton* and *Dublin* and nine 6in in *Birmingham* and *Nottingham*. Maximum speed was 25.5 knots. The Third LCS contained *Falmouth* and *Yarmouth* (sisters of *Birmingham*) and *Gloucester*, one of the original 4,800-ton 'Bristol' class completed in 1910 and armed with two 6in and six 4in guns. *Gloucester* was only armoured on the deck like an old protected cruiser. The final member of the squadron was *Birkenhead*, the fully worked-up 5.5in armed former Greek sister of HMS *Chester* and armoured like the later British 'Towns'.

Beatty had three destroyer flotillas. The First, led by the 3,440-ton 25-knot 'scout' cruiser *Fearless* (sister of the Grand Fleet's *Active*), was composed of relatively slow pre-war destroyers of the 'I' class, built under the 1910 programme. Five of the nine boats were standard Admiralty 'I's with a maximum speed of 27 knots; two, *Acheron* and *Ariel*, were the original pair of 'Thornycroft Specials' capable of 29 knots; *Attack* and *Beaver* were respectively a 'Yarrow Special' and a 'Parsons Special' with similar performance to the Admiralty boats. Armament was two single 4in guns and two single 12pdrs plus two single 21in torpedo tubes on the centre-line.

Combined into one operational force were the Ninth and Tenth Flotillas, normally with the Harwich Force, with eight boats between them. The four ships of the Ninth Flotilla were 1,000-ton 'L'-class vessels of immediate pre-war design (*Liberty* a two-funnelled 'Yarrow Special'): one, *Ladybird*, acted as leader. Armament of these vessels comprised three 4in guns and two twin 21in torpedo tubes. The Tenth was made up of two of the original 'M's launched in late 1914 and *Termagent* and *Turbulent*, 1,098-ton boats with five 4in guns and four 21in torpedo tubes. These had been projected as a private venture by Hawthorn Leslie, possibly with Turkey in mind, but were ordered for the Admiralty in November 1914. *Turbulent* was brand-new, having been completed only in May.

The final flotilla, the Thirteenth, was led by the light cruiser *Champion*, completed the previous year and armed with two 6in and eight 4in guns and a pair of 21in torpedo tubes; she could make 29 knots. The 13th was composed of new 'Repeat M'-class boats, nine of Admiralty design and one a 'Yarrow Special'. Beatty's flotillas were not strong. The 1st Flotilla was reduced in strength as part of it (the leader *Botha* and four 'I'-class destroyers) was attached to the Grand Fleet and left behind on the 30th. It was, in any case, too slow to be comfortable operating with fast ships like battlecruisers. The combined 9th and 10th Flotillas were an ad hoc force containing a brand-new ship and the 13th also suffered from inexperience with its new vessels. The oldest had been launched in November 1915 and four of the ships of the flotilla were so new (having been completed only at the end of May) that they had to be left behind, along with two others. What should have been Beatty's most powerful flotilla was, therefore, reduced in strength by almost 40 per cent.

At least, however, Beatty had his air support. The small (2,500-ton) converted cross-Channel steamer *Engadine* sailed with the Battle Cruiser Fleet as its seaplane-carrier. She carried four seaplanes, a mix of Short 184 reconnaissance aircraft and Sopwith fighters which had to be hoisted over the side to be launched. She could, therefore, only operate in calm conditions. She had, in fact, never been designed for main fleet work, having been originally converted to form part of a seaplane striking force where stopping to 'spot' her strike on the water was not a problem as it was in a rapid sea battle, moving over the horizon at over 30mph.

The British battlefleet, in its two component parts under Jellicoe and Beatty, was a mighty force. Its capital ships combined speed with enormous firepower, the mix required for its basically offensive tactical role, destroying an enemy trying to get away as efficiently as possible. Some of the capital ships' weaknesses were the other side of the coin to their strengths: especially deficient protection, which had been sacrificed to both speed and gunpower. The 'pre-Invincible' armoured cruisers were out of place, but the 'Towns' and 'light armoured cruisers' were good ships, fast, well protected and with superior firepower to the opposition. The only problem with the ships with mixed batteries was the difficulty in long-range fire of distinguishing fall of shot. British destroyers were intended to protect the battlefleet rather than engage in offensive torpedo work, and this was reflected in their heavy gun armament. Older destroyers were rather slow, however, given the speed of battlecruisers, and the replacement and reorganization programme with new flotillas created its own weaknesses, both in the combat-worthiness of partially trained ships' crews and the ability of flotillas to co-operate tactically. It was unfortunate that such an air-minded service as the Royal Navy had not more air-capable ships by May 1916, to get aircraft to sea with the fleet. This was a reflection, at least in part, of the RNAS's tendency to see itself as a general-purpose air force of whose roles and missions fleet work was only a small and difficult fraction.

THE GERMAN FORCES

The High Sea Fleet was a much weaker force than the Grand Fleet. The British policy of naval innovation had worked extremely effectively and the German Navy had not yet got a single super-dreadnought into service.

1. The core of the Russian Second Pacific Squadron were the four new battleships of the *Borodino* class. This is the first ship of the class to be completed, *Imperator Alexander III*, laid down at the Baltic Works in July 1899, launched on 3 August 1901 and commissioned in November 1903. Impressive enough in appearance, they suffered from being overweight; when fully loaded, their armour belts were largely submerged, a problem compounded by the heavy seas encountered on 27 May 1905. This lost them most of the advantages of their waterline protection. Three were sunk at Tsushima and the fourth captured by the Japanese.

2. Leading the Second Division of Rozhestvensky's fleet, and still flying the flag of the late Admiral von Felkerzam, was *Osliabia*. Laid down in 1895 and commissioned in 1901, she was built to exploit the rapid-firing qualities of smaller guns; her fore and aft turrets mounted 10in weapons to supplement her 6in QF guns. When fully loaded, her armour belt was completely submerged, which made her vulnerable.

3. The second ship of the Second Division was *Sissoi Veliki*, a relatively small battleship of obsolete design protected with thick nickel steel plates rather than face-hardened armour. She was also deficient in numbers of 6in guns, having only three per side.

4. Another obsolete battleship in the Russian Second Division was *Navarin*, distinctive with her four funnels. She was laid down in 1889, launched in October 1896 and commissioned in 1896. Her armament was a mix of old type 35-calibre 12in and 6in guns and her old-fashioned low freeboard made her wet in rough seas; insufficient boiler power resulted in heavy fuel consumption.

5. *Imperator Nikolai I* was Admiral Nebogatov's flagship of the 'First Independent Squadron of Ships of the Pacific Ocean' that became the Third Pacific Squadron and the Third Division of Rozhestvensky's fleet. She was an old-fashioned barbette ironclad, laid down in 1885 and commissioned in 1893. She had been reboilered in 1898–1900 when her anti-torpedo armament was also modernized.

6. Totally out of their element in the Third Division were the three coast defence ships of the *Admiral Ushakov* class, built especially for Baltic operations – that they reached the Far East at all was a considerable feat of seamanship.

7. A famous and lucky ship, the Russian protected cruiser *Aurora* was only two years old at the time of Tsushima. Of 6,700 tons, she was armed with eight modern 6in guns but was relatively slow, with a top speed of 19 knots. She had a two-inch protected deck.

8. Rozhestvensky's finest modern cruiser was the 6,645-ton *Oleg*, commissioned the previous year. She mounted twelve 6in guns in twin turrets fore and aft and in casemates and upper-deck sponsons on each beam. The turrets had five-inch armour and the protective deck was 1.3–3.3 inches thick. 23,000hp engines gave a maximum speed of 23 knots.

9. An artist's impression of the Russian destroyer *Buini* making off from the doomed flagship *Suvorov* after having just received on board the wounded fleet commander Admiral Rozhestvensky, suffering from a fractured skull. The Russian destroyers were modern 350-ton boats based on British Yarrow designs. Standing by larger ships to transfer senior officers in case of damage was an important role for destroyers in both the pre-dreadnought and dreadnought eras.

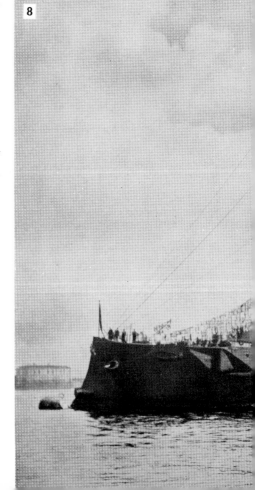

10

"OREL."

DAMAGE TO PORT SIDE.

10. *Orel* was badly knocked about by Japanese fire as can be seen by these photographs taken of the captured ship a few days after the battle. Note the shattered gun in the forward 12in turret.

11. A large hole six feet square forward of *Orel*'s starboard midships 6in turret. The heavy shell (8in or 12in) exploded on entering. The fore funnel was badly perforated by splinters from this hit.

12. A painting of the surrender of Admiral Nebogatov and the main body of survivors of the Russian Fleet the day after the battle of Tsushima. On the left is the flagship *Imperator Nikolai I* and on the right the last surviving *Borodino, Orel.* To starboard of *Nikolai* is one of the coast defence ships, *Apraksin* and the two-funnelled ship in the centre is her sister, Admiral Seniavin. The three-funnelled ships to port of the two-funnelled Russian coast defence ship are the Japanese armoured cruisers *Idzumo* (Vice-Admiral Kamimura's flagship) and her sister *Iwate* with the two-funnelled armoured cruisers *Asama* and *Tokiwa* in the right background. Heeling in the foreground is a two-funnelled Japanese destroyer of the *Murakumo* class, built in England by Thornycroft at Chiswick.

13. The Japanese flagship was the 15,140-ton *Mikasa*, one of the best battleships of her generation, built by Armstrong at Elswick between 1899 and 1902. This view was taken shortly after completion, when she was only mounting four 6in guns in casemates on the upper deck. *Mikasa*'s distinctive and well-protected box-battery for six 6in guns per side was on the deck below. The box-armour protected the 6in gunners from rounds penetrating from the other side of the ship. The 12in guns fore and aft were in the latest rapid-firing mountings, capable of being loaded at any angle of elevation or train. *Mikasa* seems to have retained 47mm guns in her fighting tops during the battle of Tsushima, with gunnery spotting from the forebridge.

14. Second in the Japanese line was *Shikishima*, a 14,850-ton ship laid down at Thames Ironworks, Blackwall, in 1897 and completed at the beginning of 1900, when this picture was taken. Still to be mounted are the four 6in guns each side in the casemates on the main deck and the similar weapons mounted amidships on the deck above. She was protected with Harvey armour and was based on the British *Majestic* Class.

15. Last battleship in Togo's line was the *Asahi* of 15,200 tons, laid down by John Brown in August 1898 and completed in July 1901. She was similar to the *Shikishima* except for rearranged boiler rooms. Like the other Japanese battleships, she seems to have gone out to Japan without her lower eight 6in casemates mounted, although all six guns per side are fitted on the deck above. The 12in guns fore and aft had to be returned to a fixed position to be loaded, which reduced the rate of fire.

16. Leading the Second Division as Admiral Kamimura's flagship was the fine armoured cruiser *Idzumo*, as long as *Mikasa* but not so broad in the beam. This both reduced displacement to 9,750 tons and allowed engines of slightly less power than the battleship's to give almost three knots extra speed. Like *Mikasa*, *Idzumo* and her sister *Iwate* were built by Armstrongs at Elswick, having been laid down in 1898 and completed in 1900 and 1901 respectively. The cruisers had the latest Krupp armour and were well armed, with rapid-firing guns, four 8in and fourteen 6in.

17. Second in Kamimura's line was the 9,307-ton *Adzuma*, built in France between 1898 and 1900 and here seen as new. She carried four 8in and twelve 6in guns as a main battery and was protected with Krupp armour. Like the other Japanese armoured cruisers, the maximum thickness of her main belt was six inches, and the upper belt five inches; barbettes and turrets had six-inch armour.

18. A fine 1923 view of the armoured cruisers *Asama* and *Yakumo*. These were third and fifth in Kamimura's line with *Asama*'s sister ship *Tokiwa* between them. *Asama* was an Armstrong ship, laid down in 1896 and completed in 1899. She had Harvey armour and was armed with four

8in and fourteen 6in guns. *Asama* was a fast ship, being capable of 21.5 knots.

19. A typical Japanese protected cruiser was the American-built *Chitose* of the Third Division, the cruisers that led the Japanese line. She had been completed in 1899 by the Union Iron Works in San Francisco and displaced 4,760 tons. Armament was an 8in gun fore and aft and ten 4.7in quick-firers. As half Togo's organic scouting force, both *Chitose* and her sister, the Third Division flagship *Kasagi*, played significant roles in the Battle of Tsushima, and both were damaged in action, *Kasuga* seriously.

19

20. The flagship of the High Sea Fleet throughout the war was *Friedrich der Grosse*, one of the five 24,330-ton *Kaiser* class battleships, armed with ten 12in guns. Four of the five were at Jutland. The picture shows the entire class lined up after the surrender of the German fleet in 1918.

21. *Indefatigable* shortly after 1602. The pall of smoke caused by the destruction of the after part of the ship is just visible to the right. The wreck is about to suffer a second explosion forward. There were only two survivors; 1,017 officers and men lost their lives.

22. HMS *Lion* in action against the German battlecruisers with her guns trained to port. She received at 1600 a hit on 'Q' turret amidships. The shell, a semi-armour piercing explosive round from the German battlecruiser flagship *Lützow*, penetrated the right corner of the left gun port and exploded, blowing part of the roof off the turret. The catastrophic loss of the ship was probably only prevented by the unpopular precautionary measures taken by the battlecruiser's Chief Gunner, A. C. Grant.

23. At 1628 burning cables caused a major cordite explosion below the damaged 'Q' turret of *Lion*. The ship would probably have blown up if the magazines had not already been flooded. Note how the funnel gases of ships travelling at full speed created murky conditions and added to the problems both of commanders and of fire-control officers.

24. *Lion*'s 'Q' turret after the battle. Everyone in the turret, manned by Royal Marines, was killed or wounded by the shell hit and the turret commander, Major Harvey, was awarded a posthumous Victoria Cross for sending a man to the bridge to report the dangerous situation despite fatal burns. The wrecked turret had to be removed to get the battlecruiser flagship back into action as quickly as possible.

25. Vital support was provided to Beatty's battlecruisers by Evan Thomas's Fifth Battle Squadron of magnificent 15-in-gunned, 27,500-ton fast battleships of the *Queen Elizabeth* class, temporarily deployed at Rosyth to replace the Third Battle Cruiser Squadron away at Scapa Flow for gunnery practice. Tactical coordination between 5th BS and the BCF left much to be desired because of Beatty's strange failure to brief Evan Thomas about Battle Cruiser Fleet tactical doctrine with its greater emphasis on initiative. This is *Warspite* at Scapa Flow in 1916 with older

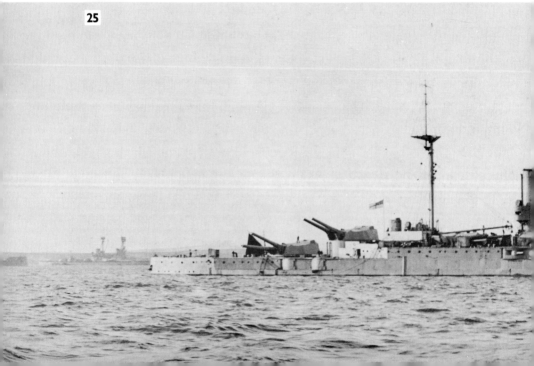

26

first generation dreadnoughts on the left. Note also the size of the old armoured cruisers on the right; they made excellent targets. *Warspite* herself was quite seriously damaged at Jutland as a result of a steering failure that forced her premature withdrawal.

26. Vulnerable anachronisms were the Grand Fleet's pre-dreadnought era armoured cruisers, which suffered heavy casualties. Flagship of the First Cruiser Squadron was *Defence*, which was handled with more enthusiasm than prudence by the squadron commander, Rear-Admiral Sir Robert Arbuthnot. The cruiser's 6–8in armour was no match for 12in Dreadnought salvoes and the bulky hull with four smoke-belching funnels was an excellent aiming point. Her 9.2in and 7.5in guns could make little effective reply. *Defence* was hit aft, causing an explosion in the after magazine that ripped through all the magazines to the forward mounting. She disappeared in half a minute and all 903 men on board perished.

27. *Chester* was a brand new light cruiser built originally for Greece and not yet fully worked up. On 31 May 1916 she was deployed with the Grand Fleet for communications duties but found herself at 1740 embroiled with the powerful light cruisers of the German Second Scouting Group. She was smothered with 5.9in shells and was only able to get off a single salvo with her 5.5in guns before her fire-control communications were destroyed and her guns' crews killed or wounded. Among the latter was Boy First Class Cornwell who was given a posthumous VC for sticking to his post at the forward mounting, seen on the left of the picture. *Chester* was only able to escape destruction thanks to the skill of her Captain, R. N. Lawson, whose manoeuvres threw the Germans off their aim. Evidence of the cruiser's seventeen hits is clear. Note the greater effects of shells striking above the armoured belt.

28. The largest of *Chester*'s scars was a hole on the port side amidships. The picture clearly shows the armoured belt, two inches thick on one-inch plates, that protected the waterline of the ship. This armour played an important role in the survival of British light cruisers. *Chester* was hit four times on her belt, but the only effect was a slight reduction in speed.

29. The surviving members of the Third Battle Cruiser Squadron eventually took up their station astern of the Battle Cruiser Fleet when the latter turned through 360 degrees at 1900. *Inflexible* and *Indomitable* are seen from *New Zealand*.

30. The centre of the British battle line was made up of the Fourth Battle Squadron. The rearmost ships of its leading Third Division were *Superb* and *Canada*, here seen hotly engaged with the High Sea Fleet with 12in and 14in guns respectively. *Superb* was an older ship, completed in 1909; *Canada* had been built for Chile and commissioned into the Royal Navy in September 1915.

30

32

33

31. A well known view, but it demonstrates the sailing order of the High Sea Fleet as it returned home after two Battle Turn Aways. In the lead is the battleship *Westfalen* followed by *Nassau, Rhineland* and *Posen* of the Second Division of the First Squadron. These were at best semi-Dreadnought ships with reciprocating engines; their main asset was their excellent protection, made possible by an increase in beam, in turn made possible by the widening of the Kiel Canal. The old pre-Dreadnoughts in the background of this peace-time view are distinctly slimmer and proved death traps for their crews when hit; like the British armoured cruisers they should never have been deployed at a Dreadnought engagement.

32. The day after the battle a disappointed Grand Fleet returned home. This picture, another of Midshipman Burgess's collection, shows the 778-ton *Acheron* destroyers of the First Flotilla screening the battlecruisers. These small boats were rather slow for operations with the Grand Fleet's fast vanguard, being capable of only 28 knots. They were armed with a 4in gun fore and aft, a 12pdr on each beam and two 21in torpedoes on the centreline. In the murk is a battleship of the Fifth Battle Squadron.

33. The most seriously damaged battleship in the Grand Fleet was *Marlborough*, sister ship of *Iron Duke* and flagship of the First Battle Squadron. At 1854 she was torpedoed on the starboard side near the forward boiler room by the brave German light cruiser *Wiesbaden*. She was forced to reduce speed at 2000 and at 0225 Vice Admiral Burney transferred his flag to *Revenge*. *Marlborough* made for Rosyth, but her flooding became serious and she had to take refuge in the Humber, where she is seen in this view. On her way back she had been attacked unsuccessfully by *U-46*. Her flooding was successfully reduced and on 6 June she left for the Tyne for repairs in a floating dock. She rejoined the fleet on 29 July.

34 and 35. The German battleship *König* after the battle; note the damage to the after funnel. She had been hit ten times by one 15in and nine 13.5in shells. *König*'s three sizes of gun are clearly visible: 12in, 5.9in and 3.5in. The extent of the damage is shown by the other photograph of the results of one of the hits; the source was probably a 13.5in round from the British flagship *Iron Duke*, which scored seven hits on the German ship.

36. The stricken battlecruiser *Seydlitz* two weeks after the battle, having been pumped out. Her forward 11in turret has had the guns removed to lessen the weight in the forward part of the ship. She had taken in more than 5,000 tons of water.

37. The effect of the 21in torpedo, probably fired from HMS *Turbulent*, that struck *Seydlitz* ahead of the port boiler room bulkhead.

38. In all, *Seydlitz* was hit 22 times by heavy shells; here are hits 18 and 21 on the after part of the ship.

39. Admiral Raymond A. Spruance, Commander of the US Fifth Fleet and victor of the Philippine Sea. A quiet and thoughtful man, Spruance took no risks and based his strategy on that of Togo at Tsushima. By exploiting the power of the defensive he was able both to destroy the Japanese carrier-based air force at little loss to his own forces and safeguard the American landings on the Marianas. Spruance was a surface-ship officer who had risen to fame at Midway when he had been a surprising choice to replace Admiral Halsey in command of the latter's carrier group (Halsey having been ill). Then Spruance had used the aviation expertise on his staff to help achieve a crushing victory in which four enemy carriers were sunk. At Philippine Sea his performance was more controversial. (USNI)

40. A thoughtful Vice Admiral Marc A. Mitscher, commander of Task Force 58, on board his flagship, the carrier *Lexington* during the 'Turkey Shoot' on 19 June 1944. An aviator, Mitscher did not always agree with his fleet commander, but the two made an excellent and complementary team. (USNI)

41. This forward view of the Japanese carrier *Junyo* emphasizes the rather strange oriental appearance of the converted liner. She carried 51 aircraft. The canted funnel was also a feature of the flagship *Taiho*. Despite her vulnerability, *Junyo* survived the war; her sister *Hiyo*, however, was one of the casualties at the Philippine Sea. (USNI)

42. The third member of 'B' Force was the converted submarine depot ship *Ryuho*, seen here after the war. A slow ship, as a light carrier she carried 27 Zeros and 6 'Jills'. Her rather old-fashioned flush-deck design was typical of smaller Japanese carriers. (USNI)

43. Oldest of the USN fleet carriers at Philippine Sea was the *Enterprise*, veteran of almost every major carrier battle. This is her flight deck and Air Group 10. Note VF(N) F4U-2 Corsair night fighters (also used by day), VF-10's Hellcat day fighters, VB-10's old Dauntless dive-bombers and, far aft, VT-10's Avenger torpedo-bombers. In all, *Enterprise* carried 69 aircraft. (USNI)

44. On the evening of 15 June, American carriers came under attack from Yokosuka P1Y 'Frances' torpedo-

bombers flying from Yap. The land-based strike aircraft stood little chance against the American fighters and anti-aircraft guns. (USNI)

45. A view aboard *Yorktown* as her fighters rise to destroy the approaching enemy. Note the crude but effective means of giving the pilot last-minute information as to the incoming raid. Note also the radar on the after 5in gun director. (USNI)

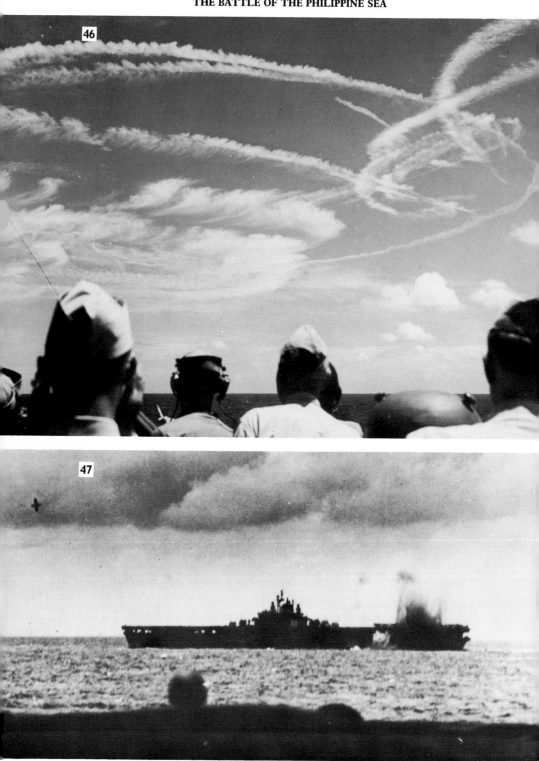

48

46. The novel appearance of a modern fleet action. The crew of the cruiser *Birmingham* observe the condensation trails that marked the tracks of the 'Marianas Turkey Shoot'. (USNI)

47. Only a few of the Japanese attackers got through. Around 1200, *Bunker Hill* was near missed aft by a 'Judy' dive-bomber that caused some damage.

48. *Enterprise* escorted by a *Fletcher* Class destroyer under attack. (USNI)

49. By the time Raid 4 arrived, Task Group 58.2 had reversed course. The attacking 'Judy' can be seen at the top of the picture. The three bombs it dropped on the *Bunker Hill* blew one of the fleet carrier's fighters into the water. The 'Judy' has not much longer to live: but the inexperienced pilot does not seem to have pressed home a proper dive-bombing attack that might have stood some chance of scoring actual hits. (USNI)

49

50. A triumphant Lieutenant (JG) Vraciu graphically illustrates his score of six 'Judys' to his shipmates in the flagship *Lexington*. (USNI)

51. The 'Turkeys' sometimes shot back. Here, on board *Essex*, a wounded fighter pilot from VF-15 is helped from his Hellcat. (USNI)

52. An Avenger search aircraft puts down on the flagship *Lexington*. Poor air searching was one of the key American weaknesses in this battle. Note the heavy AA armament of this *Essex* class carrier: 40mm guns in the foreground, then twin 5in dual-purpose, then a serried rank of 20mm on the starboard side and a pair of 5in singles on the port quarter. (USNI)

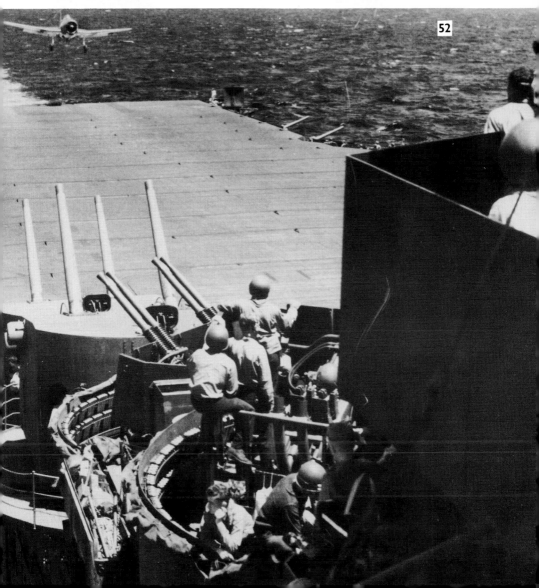

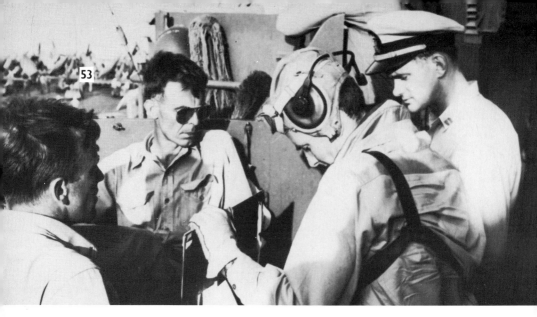

53. At 1200 on the 20th, the commanding officer of *Lexington*'s Air Group, Commander Ernest M. Snowden, led a search of Hellcat fighter-bombers looking for the Japanese fleet. He did not find the enemy, as he is reporting back here. (USNI)

54. The Japanese carrier *Zuikaku*, by now Ozawa's flagship, under attack. She was hit several times by Helldivers and came close to abandonment but, in a rare success for Japanese damage control, was saved. Note the

manoeuvres of the fleet carrier and the escorting destroyers. (USNI)

55. The American striking force comprised both dive-bombers, mainly Helldivers as seen in the foreground and Avenger torpedo aircraft, as seen in the background. Unfortunately, most of the Avengers were carrying bombs, which decisively weakened the ship-killing potential of the US counter-strike. (USNI)

56. *Chiyoda* is visible in this view with a battleship, probably *Kongo*, in the foreground. (USNI)

57. US fleet submarines inflicted the main damage on Japanese carriers in the Battle of the Philippine Sea. They later played an important role in picking up downed pilots. This rescue picture was taken from an aircraft from *Lexington*. (USNI)

The first German battleship with guns bigger than 12in, the 15in-gun *Bayern*, was still a month from completion. The first 13.8in-gun battlecruiser, *Mackensen*, would not be launched for almost a year and would never be commissioned. Germany had only four classes of all-big-gun battleship and it was arguable if the first two of these were more than semi-dreadnoughts, given their reciprocating engines and resultant slow speed (around 20 knots). The two classes of real turbine-powered dreadnoughts were, however, both excellent designs.

These formed the leading squadron of the High Sea Fleet, the Third. This in turn comprised two divisions, the 5th and 6th. The 5th Division was Germany's latest battleship class, *König, Grosser Kurfürst, Kronprinz* and *Markgraf* (respectively 'King', 'Great Elector', 'Crown Prince' and 'Margrave'). The 'Königs' displaced 25,390 tons and their twelve coal-fired and three oil-fired boilers and fifteen turbines of 31,000shp gave high speed, 21 knots at normal power, up to 24 knots in extremis. Main armament was ten 12in 50-calibre guns in five centre-line turrets, two forward, two aft and one amidships. There was a secondary battery of seven 5.9in guns on each beam. Belt armour was 14in maximum thickness with 12in on the turrets. The ships were quite new, having all been completed in the first year of the war.

The 6th Division comprised three members of the 'Kaiser' class: *Kaiser, Kaiserin* and *Prinzregent Luitpold* ('Emperor', 'Empress' and 'Prince Regent Leopold'). The first 'Kaiser', *Friedrich der Grosse* ('Frederick the Great') was Admiral Scheer's flagship and normally took up position astern of this division. The 'Kaisers' were fine 24,330-ton ships completed between December 1912 and December 1913. They were armed with ten 12in guns with one twin turret forward, one on each beam but staggered to allow broadside fire on restricted arcs, and two aft; secondary armament was seven 5.9in guns on each beam. Belt armour was 14in maximum once more with 12in maximum protection on the turrets. Sixteen coal-fired boilers (with tar oil sprays) and 31,000shp turbines gave 21 knots (22.4–23.4 knots on trials). *Prinzregent Luitpold* had reduced power as she was to have been fitted with a supplementary diesel engine. This never appeared but even on two sets of turbines rather than three she was able to make 21.7 knots on trials. A fifth member of the class, *König Albert*, was absent with condenser trouble; given Scheer's lack of proper dreadnoughts this was a serious blow.

Astern of the flagship came the slower all-big-gun battleships of the First Squadron, all, like previous German battleships, named after provinces of the Empire, another element of continuity with the pre-dreadnought era. The squadron was also divided into class-based divisions, the 1st with the four battleships of the 'Helgoland' class, *Ostfriesland, Thuringen, Helgoland* and *Oldenburg*, and the 2nd with the four ships of the 'Nassau' class, *Posen, Rheinland, Nassau* and *Westfalen*. The three-funnelled 'Helgolands', laid down in 1908, each displaced 22,440 tons and their fifteen boilers (coal-fired with tar oil sprays) and four-cylinder triple-expansion engines could drive them at just over 20 knots (*Oldenburg* made 21.3 knots on trials). They were armed with six twin turrets mounting 50-calibre 12in weapons, one forward and one aft and two on each beam, giving a broadside of eight guns in a somewhat uneconomical fashion. The main armament layout of the 'Nassaus' was the same, although the guns were 45-calibre 11in weapons. The 'Nassaus' were much shorter than their successors, almost 480ft overall (the 'Helgolands' were almost 550ft long); the 'Nassaus' consequently displaced only 18,570 tons. Twelve boilers and three-shaft three-cylinder reciprocating engine arrangements gave a normal maximum of 19.5 knots. Belt armour on both classes was 12in between barbettes and turret armour was 11in. Both classes carried powerful secondary batteries of 5.9in guns, twelve on the 'Nassaus' and fourteen on the 'Helgolands'.

The heavy secondary armaments of these ships reflected greater continuity with the pre-dreadnought past than existed in the United Kingdom, and this was symbolized even more dramatically by the presence of the Second Squadron composed of two divisions, each of three totally obsolete pre-dreadnought battleships. Rear Admiral Mauve and his subordinate officers had prevailed upon Scheer, a former Second Squadron officer, to allow the pre-dreadnoughts to sail with the High Sea Fleet and Scheer had let his heart rule his head. The Squadron consisted of the five 13,993-ton ships of the 'Deutschland' class, laid down between 1903 and 1905 and completed in 1906-08, and one of the previous 14,167-ton 'Braunschweigs', *Hessen,* laid down in 1902 and completed in 1905. The ships were armed with heavy batteries of relatively light guns built for the close-range fighting of the Tsushima era. Each carried two twin 11in turrets, mounted fore and aft, and their former main batteries of rapid firing 6.7in guns in single mountings, seven on each side. Armour protection was far from good with maximum belt thicknesses of 9.5in and 6.75in armour on the 7.5in gun battery. The 11in gun turrets were, however, armoured to a similar thickness. The crews dubbed the Second Squadron 'Five-Minute Ships': the enemy it was said would spend four minutes laughing and another minute to sink them. Their fighting value in the new era of long-range fire control was very limited, but the most serious drawback of these ships was their maximum speed. Three-shaft triple-expansion engines gave maximum speeds of 18.5 knots (18.25 for *Hessen*). This lowered the speed of Scheer's entire fleet to a pre-dreadnought pace. The two divisions of the Second Squadron were the 3rd, *Deutschland, Pommern* and *Schlesien*; and the 4th, *Schleswig-Holstein, Hessen* and *Hannover*. The last named was the flagship of Admiral

Lichtenfels, who was potentially the lead ship of the entire High Sea Fleet if it reversed direction together as it was trained to do.

Scheer's battle line was weak both in quality and quantity, but his final squadron of capital ships, the First Scouting Group of 'armoured cruisers' under Vice-Admiral Franz Hipper, was a very different proposition. The five battlecruisers that made up this force were excellent combinations of speed, firepower and protection. The key to their design was the general adoption of Schutz-Thornycroft small-tube boilers which, at a cost in reliability, allowed smaller powerplants to deliver high outputs. The latest German battlecruisers devoted less than 3,000 tons to main machinery; British battlecruisers 4,500 tons or more. Engine volume was also less, requiring less armour to protect it. Valuable displacement could thus be devoted to levels of protection greater than those possible in British battlecruisers.

No ship demonstrated the excellence of German battlecruiser design better than the two 'Derfflinger'-class ships, *Lützow*, Hipper's flagship, and *Derfflinger* herself. *Lützow* was a new ship, having been in commission for a couple of months. She displaced 26,318 tons and her fourteen coal-fired and four oil-fired boilers and four sets of steam turbines drove her at 26.5 knots – when they worked. Machinery problems had delayed *Lützow*'s entry into service. She was armed with four twin 12in turrets on the centre-line and a secondary battery of fourteen 5.9in guns. Armour was up to British battleship standards with a belt 12in in maximum thickness and 10.7in turret armour. *Derfflinger* was very similar except that she displaced slightly less, 26,180 tons, had two fewer 5.9in guns and could be distinguished by different forefunnel and foremast design. She had better engines and had been in service since November 1914. Both 'Derfflingers' were the finest battlecruisers in the world.

Next came *Seydlitz* of 24,594 tons and armed with ten 11in guns, one twin turret forward, two staggered turrets on each beam amidships and two superfiring turrets aft. Again belt armour was 12in in maximum thickness: turret armour was 10in. Twenty-seven boilers and four-shaft turbines gave 26.5 knots maximum speed (she attained over 28 knots on pre-war trials). She had been built under the 1910-11 programme and had been completed in August 1913.

Similar to but slightly smaller than *Seydlitz* was the 22,616-ton *Moltke* with similar armament (including twelve 5.9in guns). She had rather thinner armour, 10.7in maximum on the belt and 9in on the turrets. Laid down in 1908 and completed in 1912, she had 24 boilers and four-shaft turbines enabling her to make 25.5 knots. *Moltke*'s sister, *Goeben*, had escaped to Turkey in 1914 and become that navy's *Yavuz*.

Last ship in line was the 19,064-ton *Von Der Tann* armed with eight

45-calibre 11in guns. She lacked her later sister's superfiring aft turret. Laid down in 1908 and completed in 1911, she had 10in belt armour and 9in turret armour. Although she was forced up to over 27 knots on her trials, her normal maximum speed was just under 25 knots. *Von Der Tann* was an excellent ship, her main armament being fully capable of penetrating the armour of British 'Invincibles', and she had much better protection. This was the battle of quality versus quantity. By the time *Von Der Tann* was completed Britain had all three 'Invincibles' in commission and *Indefatigable* was almost ready. By May 1916 Beatty still outnumbered Hipper almost two-to-one but, given the excellence of the German battlecruisers, the British were fortunate that the four 'Queen Elizabeths' were with the BCF to redress the qualitative balance.

Operating with Hipper was the Second Scouting Group of fast light cruisers. Like the First, this was composed of a small number of relatively powerful ships. Germany had pioneered the dreadnought-era light cruiser for both fleet work and deployment on distant stations. Unfortunately, however, because of Tirpitz's mistaken ideas, they were inadequately armed, staying with the 4.1in gun until far too late. This contributed to heavy losses in the early part of the war. From December 1914 the Germans began to commission light cruisers armed with 5.9in guns, the first being *Elbing* and *Pillau*, originally laid down at Danzig for Russia. These 27.5-knot ships lacked armoured belts, but their powerful armament of eight 5.9in guns disposed in single mounts on each beam made up for a lot. Three-inch deck armour was fitted. With them were *Frankfurt* and *Wiesbaden*, 5,180-ton ships laid down under the 1912 programme. These also mounted eight 5.9in weapons and had a 2.25in armoured belt as well as an armoured deck of similar thickness. These four ships had the advantage of a single-calibre main armament of heavy guns compared with the latest British cruisers.

With the German battleships was the Fourth Scouting Group of obsolescent light cruisers of the first German generation. These transitional ships were slow and their ten 4.1in guns only gave real capability against enemy destroyers. *Stettin* and *Stuttgart* were 1907-vintage 'Königsberg'-class ships, whose two sisters had already been sunk on raiding voyages. They displaced 3,400 tons: *Stettin* had turbines and could make 24 knots, *Stuttgart* reciprocating engines which lowered her maximum speed by 1 knot. *München* and *Hamburg* were older 3,230-ton 'Bremen'-class ships of 1904-05 with reciprocating engines and speeds of 23 knots; their protective deck armour was 3in thick. *Hamburg* was the flagship of the High Sea Fleet's U-boats but allocated to the Fourth Scouting Group for the battle. So short was Germany of light cruisers that the Fourth Scouting Group also included the two-funnelled *Frauenlob*, and old 'Gazelle'-class protected cruiser of 1903, with 2in deck armour and capable of only 21.5 knots. Again the Germans were forced by numerical weakness to use ships of the earlier generation.

Two more German light cruisers were present at Jutland, each as part of the 'Torpedo Boat Forces'. Commodore Michelsen, leading Scheer's flotillas, flew his broad pennant in the four-funnelled *Rostock*, a modern 1914, 4,900-ton ship with twelve 4.1in guns. Commodore Heinrich, in charge of the First and Second Scouting Groups' flotillas used *Regensburg* which could make 28 knots with the same armament as *Rostock*. Both cruisers had 2.25in belt and deck protection.

Before 1914 the Germans had not built actual destroyers for the Imperial Navy, although the name was used by the crews of the Hochseetorpedoboote ('High Sea Torpedo Boat') flotillas for their vessels. German design had been governed by personnel shortages which meant that the boats had to be large enough to be able to operate in the open sea with the High Sea Fleet but also small enough to be commanded by one officer. The emphasis was on torpedo attack rather than defence of the fleet from torpedo-boats, whch was left more to light cruisers. Only at the outbreak of war were destroyers proper commissioned into the German Navy when foreign boats and materials were taken over. These 'Zerstörers' (destroyers) were numbered in the same series as the torpedo-boats; the prefix denoted the builder, 'B' for Blohm & Voss, 'G' for Germaniawerft, Kiel, 'H' for Howaldtswerke, Kiel, 'S' for Schichau, Elbing, and 'V' for Vulcan, Stettin.

The destroyers proper formed the large and powerful Second Flotilla operating with Hipper. *G101*, *'102*, *'103* and *'104* had been laid down for Argentina. They displaced 1,245 tons and could make 33 knots, although with a full fuel load this was reduced to 27. They carried four 4.1in guns and six 19.7in torpedo tubes (two twins amidships and a single on each beam forward). Similarly armed were *B97*, *'98*, *'109*, *'110*, *'111* and *'112*, built to a Russian concept (*B109-112* used large turbines originally ordered for Russia). These were even bigger at 1,352 tons and could make 36.5 knots. Given the speed differentials of the two classes, they tended to operate in separate tactical groups.

Hipper also had two more standard high sea torpedo-boat flotillas of smaller vessels. The 6th had representatives of all five of the classes of oil-fired 1914 'mobilization type' boats, two 'G37s' (*G37* and *G41*), three 'V43s' (*V44*, *V45* and *V46*), one 'S49' (*S50*), one 'V67' (*V69*) and two 'G85s' (*G86* and *G87*). These displaced between 802 tons in the Schichau boats and 960 tons in the later Germanias and could make between 33.5 and 34.5 knots. They carried three 3.5in guns and six 19.7in torpedo tubes. The 9th Flotilla had similar but slightly older vessels, the 812-ton 'V25s' of the 1913 programme (*V26*, *'27*, *'28*, *'29* and *'30*), four contemporary 802-ton 'S31s' (*S33*, *'34*, *'35* and *'36*) and two wartime 'S49s' (*S51* and *S52*) of similar size. The 1913 boats were also oil-burners.

Scheer had three full torpedo-boat flotillas with two boats from another. The latter were from the First Flotilla and were both 'G37s' (*G39* and *G40*). The most powerful full flotilla was the Third with all new war programme boats, a 960-ton 'G85' (*G88*), an 822-ton 'G37' (*G42*), an 852-ton 'V43' (*V48*), two 924-ton 'V67s' (*V71* and *V73*) and two 802-ton 'S49s' (*S53* and *S54*). The other two flotillas, the Fifth and the Seventh, contained small boats built under the 1911-12 programmes on the mistaken assumption that the growing size of high sea torpedo-boats made manoeuvring with the fleet more difficult. The Fifth contained all five 'G7s' (*G7–11*) and all six 'V1s' (*V1–6*). The 'G7s' were of 564 tons and the 'V1s' 559; both mounted two 3.5in guns and four single 19.7in torpedo tubes, two on each beam forward and two amidships. Speed was 32 knots but deficient range and coal firing (1,150–1,200 miles and 17 knots compared with 1,750 miles in larger boats) meant that extra fuel had to be carried on deck. The Seventh Flotilla had eight of the 'S13s' (*S15, '16, '17, '18, '19, '20, '23* and *'24*) of 559 tons, 32.5 knots and similar armament to the other small boats and 655-ton 'V180s' of 1910, also armed with two 3.5in guns and four tubes. Both *V186* and *V189* had sailed with Scheer but *V186* had to be sent home with a break in the condenser.

The German fleet was far from strong. Although the First and Second Scouting Groups were composed of excellent ships, they were outgunned and outnumbered by Beatty's fleet. Scheer's slow and outnumbered ships were no match at all for Jellicoe's fast and well-armed dreadnoughts with their powerful escorts. Only a strategically well-founded British reluctance to take risks with the sinister dual threats of torpedoes and mines stood between the Germans and disaster. The odds were also made more even for the Germans by serious defects in British gunnery techniques that made inflicting rapid and serious damage on the enemy difficult and also resulted in British ships becoming explosive tinder boxes.

GUNNERY

British gunnery practice was fundamentally and fatally flawed in several ways. Most important, as things turned out, was the dangerous way cordite propellant was stored in order to optimize offensive power through high rate of fire. Each heavy shell was fired by four silk-covered 'quarter charges' with gunpowder igniters stitched, fully exposed, to each end. To make matters worse, British cordite propellant tended to be unstable, thanks to the weakness of Britain's chemical industry. The final and decisive step to tragedy was the tendency to fill every available space with charges from the gunhouse, through the working chambers beneath, down to the handing room where charges were put into the hoist from magazines whose doors were normally left open. Against fierce opposition from turret officers, Warrant Officer A. C. Grant, *Lion*'s Chief Gunner, introduced precautions such as keeping magazine doors closed as much as possible, having no more than one charge in the handing room at one time, and only taking charges out of their protective casings when actually required. These probably saved his ship. Shells entering the turrets or barbettes of more normally run ships would cause a catastrophic explosion as the flash ignited charges in the gunhouse or hoists and then the piles of charges in the handing room. No barrier existed to stop this explosion entering the open magazines. There were thin anti-flash doors in the hoists and in the working chambers, but these proved useless against the heat of the large quantities of burning cordite.

The next weakness of the British gunnery system was defective shells. The armour-piercing rounds used were filled with lyddite as a burster, another unstable explosive prone to going off prematurely before the round had penetrated far into the enemy ship. The fuses could not cope with oblique impacts against side armour at long range, a product of inadequate pre-war testing which had emphasized normal (i.e., 90-degree) impacts. British shells could be very effective against deck armour at very long range where high angles of impact were the rule, but shells striking side armour were often unable to inflict serious damage.

Hitting the enemy at all was also a problem. It should not have been as, in principle, British gunnery was the most advanced in the world. At its heart lay a 'fire control table' in the 'transmitting station' inside each capital ship. The idea for these instruments had come from the civilian inventor Arthur H. Pollen, but his ideas had been plagiarized and bowdlerized by Frederic Dreyer, a naval officer and close associate of both Fisher and Jellicoe (at Jutland he was Jellicoe's flag captain in *Iron Duke*). The principle of these fire control tables was that information on range and bearing of the enemy was fed from the fire control observers above. This information was plotted and used, together with information on the ship's course and speed, to set instruments that worked out the gun elevations and bearings required to hit the area of ocean into which the enemy was sailing.

The fundamental weakness of all the Dreyer Tables, of which successive marks were in use with the Grand Fleet, was that range and bearing were plotted separately in order to obtain the measurements from which the rates of change of both parameters were calculated. Pollen had supported simultaneous automatic plotting of ranges and bearings to produce a 'true course' plot that could be compared directly with the course of the firing ship. Separate plotting slowed down the calculating process, especially as Dreyer's tables used manual, as opposed to automatic, range plotting. This made it harder for Dreyer Tables to cope with very rapid changes of rate of change of range.

This problem was compounded by defective instruments. The Dreyer Table Mk I used a manually set 'dumaresq', a trigonometrical slide calculator invented by the lieutenant of the same name in 1902, to work out range and bearing rates and, sequentially, the target's course. Again this all took time. To make matters even worse, the Vickers range clock to which the dumaresq mechanically transmitted its calculated rates and which mechanically worked out the ranges to be used at given rates, could only run at a number of fixed speeds. The Mk I table just could not cope mechanically if rate of change was itself changing rapidly. The older British 12in gun ships (except *Hercules*) were fitted with this flawed device, as was the super-dreadnought *Marlborough*.

The Dreyer Table Mk II was a very different machine. It employed Pollen's Argo Clock Mk IV, an analogue computer of advanced design which mechanically took in the target's bearings and range and the firing ship's speed and course; and, with the aid of variable-speed mechanical drive, computed automatically the target's future position. It could cope with rapid rates of change of range and was only slowed down by the plotting technique used. Sadly, thanks to Dreyer's influence, only six Argo Clocks were obtained by the Royal Navy. One was fitted experimentally to the battleship *Orion*, together with an Argo mechanical range and bearing plotter for trials purposes. She thus had the best fire control system in the fleet. Mk II Dreyer Tables with Dreyer's inferior plotting apparatus were fitted to the 'King George V' class and the battlecruiser *Queen Mary*. It is significant that Jellicoe, loyal as he was to Dreyer, put his three remaining 'King George Vs' in the key position at the head of his line.

Instead of the effective Argo Clock, Dreyer had persuaded the Admiralty to adopt a plagiarized and inferior instrument co-designed by himself and an engineer called Keith Elphinstone. Both had been shown details of Pollen's Argo device and they unashamedly copied features of it in the production of a simpler, cheaper, but much less effective 'Dreyer-Elphinstone Clock'. This was combined mechanically with a dumaresq, first a manual device in the Mk II Table, then an electrical device in the Mks IV and V, to make rate calculations. The clock had a variable-speed drive but it was mechanically inaccurate and the whole table was much less able to cope with rapid changes of range and bearing than the Argo-equipped Mk II. The ranges which emerged from the table were plotted alongside the plot of observed ranges so that the clock could be adjusted accordingly. This made up for the errors to some extent – at least under peacetime battle practice conditions – but it tended to emphasize the importance of simple spotting of fall of shot as the

British Fire Control Systems at the Battle of Jutland

Battleships

Battleship	Table	Clock
Bellerophon, Temeraire, Superb	Dreyer Table Mk I	Vickers
St. Vincent, Collingwood, Vanguard	Dreyer Table Mk I	Vickers
Neptune	Dreyer Table Mk I	Vickers
Colossus	Dreyer Table Mk I	Vickers
Hercules	Dreyer Table Mk III	Dreyer/Elphinstone
Monarch, Thunderer, Conqueror	Dreyer Table Mk III	Dreyer/Elphinstone
Orion	Argo Plotting Table	Argo
King George V, Ajax, Centurion	Dreyer Table Mk II	Argo
Iron Duke, Benbow	Dreyer Table Mk I Dreyer Turret Control Table	Dreyer/Elphinstone
Marlborough	Dreyer Table Mk I Dreyer Turret Control Table	Vickers
Warspite, Barham, Valiant, Malaya	Dreyer Table MkIV* Dreyer Turret Control Table	Dreyer/Elphinstone
Royal Oak, Revenge	Dreyer Table Mk IV* Dreyer Turret Control Table	Dreyer/Elphinstone
Erin	Dreyer Table Mk I	Vickers
Canada	Dreyer Table Mk IV*	Dreyer/Elphinstone
Agincourt	Dreyer Table Mk I	Vickers

Battlecruisers

Battlecruiser	Table	Clock
Invincible, Indomitable, Inflexible	Dreyer Table Mk I	Vickers
Indefatigable, New Zealand	Dreyer Table Mk I	Vickers
Lion, Princess Royal	Dreyer Table Mk III	Dreyer/Elphinstone
Queen Mary	Dreyer Table Mk II	Argo
Tiger	Dreyer Table MK IV Dreyer Turret Control Table	Dreyer/Elphinstone

Prepared by Professor J. T. Sumida from Dreyer, Rear-Admiral F. C., Fire Control Tables , Royal Commission on Awards to Inventors, Public Record Office, T 173/204; Great Britain, Admiralty, *Handbook of Captain F. C. Dreyer s Fire Control Tables, 1918,* and *Pamphlet on the Turret Dreyer Table* (1930), Naval Library of the Ministry of Defence keystone of accurate gunnery. In all ships the fire control officer could adjust the output of the clocks according to his observations of the fall of shot. Some indeed detected the weaknesses of the non-Argo Dreyer tables and went so far as partially to dismantle them, trusting to cruder methods of spotting the guns on to the target.

All British ships did, however, have the advantage of guns fired from a single master sight in a revolving director tower on the foremast. This sight followed the target, feeding information to the fire control table which sent it, corrected if required, to training and laying pointers in the turrets. The director layer aloft waited for the ship's roll to bring the guns on and then fired them himself as a group.

Range measurements came from Barr & Stroud coincidence rangefinders. Most were 9ft base length FQ2s, although all the 15in gun battleships and *Orion* had the much superior 15ft base length FT24s. The longer base length gave excellent accuracy even at 20,000 yards, and although designed for much shorter ranges than those at which Jutland was fought, the FQ2 was still accurate enough at ranges of 10,000–12,500 yards. One of its problems was a relatively low data rate, which was insufficient to correct the inherent defects of the fire control tables. This was mitigated somewhat by fitting Argo gyroscopically stabilized mountings on the capital ships' main rangefinders. These allowed twice as many readings to be made compared with more normally mounted instruments. Vibration, however, adversely affected the effectiveness of the rangefinders in some ships; for example, in the older battlecruisers the Argo was mounted in the foretop where this was a serious problem. It was not poor rangefinding that prevented British ships seriously damaging their targets but the ineffectiveness of the shells which hit and, even more so, the inability of the fire control tables to cope with rapid changes of range and bearing.

Such rapid changes were exactly the conditions for which the Germans had trained. Their Zeiss 3-metre rangefinders were no more accurate than the British FQ2s, although they could range more easily on indistinct targets. They required highly trained and healthy operators; in fact, German rangefinding personnel were ordered to avoid both beer and women when their ships awaited orders to go to sea. The tension of action, however, could not be avoided and the accuracy of rangefinding readings deteriorated seriously when ships were under fire. The German instruments were also prone to be affected by temperature changes and vibration and they needed constant adjustment. As instruments the Germans considered them inferior to the British Barr & Strouds. Their only advantage was a relatively high data rate which allowed ships with fully operational rangefinders and suitably calm operators to keep the range, despite the lack of sophisticated fire control computers.

The Germans used an equivalent of the dumaresq calculator (the Entfernungs Unterscheids Peilschreiber) to give deflection and a range clock to compensate for rate of change. There was no plotting of range and bearings. The ranges from stereoscopic rangefinders (seven in a battlecruiser like *Derfflinger*) were 'meaned' mechanically in the fore control and passed to the transmitting station below decks, from which the correct elevation was passed mechanically by 'elevation telegraph' to the gunlayers, who then made the indicator on the sights of their guns conform to that on the telegraph. The elevation telegraph was fitted with a range clock to alter indicated elevation automatically when the range was calculated to be changing. This ran at a fixed rate, depending on the setting ordered. The gunnery officer kept his periscope sight above the heavily armoured fore control position abaft the bridge trained on the target. This sight was fitted with what the Germans called a director which automatically worked indicators in the turrets that kept all the guns trained in azimuth on the target, with whatever compensation for deflection was required. The gunlayers' main challenge was to keep the guns trained at the correct elevation by compensating for the roll of the ship. It was up to the individual gunner's skill to keep his sight trained on the enemy as the ship moved up and down. This skill required months of training and, like stereoscopic rangefinding skills, the ability went off rapidly in action. Both the fore control position and, even more so, the turret sights were prone to being obscured by water and gun and funnel smoke. The fore top was used only by spotters. The simpler German fire control system could cope significantly better with situations where rate of change and bearing were themselves changing rapidly. However, it lacked staying power in action as it placed too much reliance on the skill and training of individual gunlayers and rangefinder operators.

Whatever the defects and disadvantages in the fire control on both sides, the British had the advantage of their 13.5in and 15in guns in the super-dreadnoughts. Not only did these have better striking power (when the shells performed as designed) but their flatter trajectories increased the chances of hitting at long ranges. The guns also had a greater maximum range.

TORPEDOES

The British were the weaker side in torpedoes in terms of numbers, quality and flotilla organization. Their doctrine also did not put as much emphasis as the Germans did on torpedo attack. The British destroyers deployed in total 260 21in tubes and 275 torpedoes against 326 19.7in tubes and torpedoes in the High Sea Fleet. The British 21in Mk II had a rather smaller warhead than the German 19.7in Type G and its performance was also lower, 5,000 yards at 35 knots with a 400lb warhead against 6,560 yards at 36 knots with a 440lb head. The British flotillas were in process of reorganization and were not well trained and British doctrine, in any case, emphasized the defensive use of flotillas rather than the offensive.

Pre-heater torpedo doctrine in all navies had emphasized night attacks by flotillas, as at Tsushima, but the advent of long-range heater torpedoes seemed to make daylight flotilla attacks in co-operation with the battlefleet a practical proposition. Torpedoes could now be launched at 10,000 yards at 29 knots, a distance/speed equation which gave some chance of hitting, or at least coming close. The main aim was disruption. The lines of capital ships would become confused as the vessels manoeuvred to avoid the torpedoes and gunnery would become much more difficult. The Germans, in the weaker position, emphasized the offensive role but consensus British opinion, reflecting their numerical gunnery superiority, was to emphasize the defensive role of destroyers. Stopping enemy torpedo attacks on the battleships was the British destroyers' primary duty; mounting torpedo attacks of their own came second, unless targets of opportunity presented themselves. British destroyer commanders were ordered to engage destroyers rather than make attacks on heavy units if a decision between the two types of target was required. Doctrine was, however, changing to emphasize a more aggressive flotilla policy. Beatty differed with Jellicoe on this point and believed in an early thrust by his flotillas, both to confuse the enemy's line and engage the enemy's destroyers before they had a chance to attack. His older, slower TBDs were, in any case, less suitable for engaging enemy torpedo-boats defensively, given their inferior speed and gunpower compared with Jellicoe's newer destroyers. They would also have serious problems screening the faster battlecruisers.

The British light cruisers carried a relatively large number of torpedo tubes, 60 (with 180 torpedoes carried) against only sixteen tubes in the High Sea Fleet, but again torpedo attack was a secondary function. The primary duty of these ships was reconnaissance. German light cruisers were essentially gun-armed ships. Both sides' capital ships also had torpedoes, the British carrying a total of no fewer than 364 such weapons. The chances of effective use were, however, slight, as were those of the 76 19.7in torpedo tubes in the German heavy ships. Torpedo flats were a source of vulnerability in capital ships and giving them torpedo armament was a great mistake – the torpedo flat proved to be the Achilles heel of the otherwise well protected Germans. However, the possibility of long-range 'browning' shots, in the hope of causing course changes and confusion in the enemy's line, kept the practice alive and the Germans had even developed extra-large H-8 23.6in torpedoes with a range of

18,590 yards at 28 knots for use at dreadnought gunnery ranges. These were carried in the latest German battlecruiser, *Lützow*, two each side in submerged tubes. It was flooding in these very spaces that helped seal the doom of this ship.

TACTICS

The British tactics were set out in Grand Fleet Battle Orders developed by the rather obsessive Jellicoe, their first edition being issued to the Fleet in August 1914. By the time of Jutland they ran to some seventy pages. These over-emphasized the underwater menace from torpedoes and mines. Although a super-dreadnought had been lost to a chance mine in 1914, the Germans did not in fact place emphasis on tactical minelaying. Contrary to British belief, German capital ships did not carry mines and Scheer did not even have the new minelaying cruiser *Brummer* with him on his sortie at the end of May. *No* British dreadnought was to succumb to torpedo attack in the First World War.

In Jellicoe's defence, it must be admitted that the caution he encouraged may have had something to do with that safety record. The C-in-C was especially scared of being drawn into submarine and mine traps, and this made him very reluctant to pursue a fleeing enemy heedlessly. He was also reluctant to close the range with an enemy's fleet formation, given the torpedo hazard at ranges below 14,000–15,000 yards. Attacks by flotillas would be met by turning away from the enemy. All this militated against a rapid decisive victory.

In action the fleet's capital ships would deploy in single line ahead. The idea of divided squadrons had been tested but communications were not up to it. These still relied primarily on flags and signal lights and the mismatch of this technology with the weapon ranges and speeds now available, not to mention the sophisticated fire control equipment, is one of the most remarkable features of naval warfare of this period. Dividing the fleet in these circumstances was probably a recipe for disaster and playing into the Germans' hands with their desire to annihilate a detached portion of the Grand Fleet. The only concession to the tactical heretics was the building of the battlecruiser 'Fleet' into a fast division to deal with the enemy's similar ships, but even this force had a position in the overall line should a full-scale slogging match develop.

The battle would be fought at a range of between 18,000 and 10,000 yards but, as noted above, the perceived torpedo menace dictated staying outside 14,000 yards at the outset of the action. Possibly reflecting his knowledge of the limitations of his friend Dreyer's instruments, Jellicoe wished the battle to be fought as much as possible with the two lines of capital ships on parallel courses. Then superior gunpower would win the day. Fighting at night with capital ships was considered too dangerous, given the uncertainties involved and the greater chances of torpedo strikes. Searchlights were inadequate and no star shell was provided. Night action only became practical with the development of director firing and this had not been available long enough for its possibilities to be fully explored. Only the remnants of a clearly defeated fleet would be pursued at night by destroyers and cruisers (including battlecruisers). The British fleet was too important and powerful an instrument to be hazarded to the chances of a night encounter.

There was much sound sense in the overall British tactical approach, given the strategic importance of the Grand Fleet and its deliberately developed balance of capabilities. Yet there was a problem of lack of flexibility. The desire to maintain centralized command militated even against turning ships together. This could be done by the use of a blue pendant, but if ships did not see the signal confusion would reign. Turning in succession (using a 'compass pendant') was the preferred option. At least in such circumstances ships out of signal contact could be guided by the movements of the ships ahead.

The Germans had to possess greater tactical flexibility, given their general inferiority in numbers, speed and gunpower. Their key man-oeuvre was the Gefechtskehrwendung ('Battle Turn Away') in which the line would escape from having its 'T' crossed by superior forces, by the ships turning together and reversing their course. This would be done under cover of attacks by lighter forces, up to and including battle-cruisers, which would, if necessary, be sacrificed to save the main fleet.

Scheer's best hope if a detached portion of the British fleet could not be caught was a concentration of overwhelming gun and torpedo power on part of the enemy line, rapidly followed by withdrawal under cover of smoke. At best, however, this could only be in the nature of a spoiling action. Meeting the full strength of the Grand Fleet could be no part of Scheer's plans. He was not coming out seeking a decisive engagement. Victory for him if caught by Jellicoe would be getting away with his fleet suffering as few casualties as possible, and with the maximum damage inflicted on the enemy.

FAILURE OF SUBMARINES AND AIRCRAFT

Jutland was a good example of the classic dreadnought naval battle in that submarines and aircraft played no effective role. This was more of a disappointment to the Germans than to the British as the former had high hopes of submarine ambushes inflicting significant attrition on the Grand Fleet, and its airships both keeping Scheer out of trouble and helping him find a suitable detached British squadron to gobble up.

Sadly for Scheer, the weather prevented the launching of any airships until 1130 on 31 May. Five airships, *L9*, an 879,921-cu ft three-engined 'O' type, *L14* and *L16*, 1,126,389-cu ft four-engined 'Ps', and *L21* and *L23*, 1,359,435-cu ft four-engined 'Qs', were sent up but could not get to their patrol positions in time. In any case, the weather was hazy with a 1,000ft cloud base, and the airships could see little.

The U-boats were even more disappointing as so much had been expected of them. The warning signal that the High Sea Fleet operation was starting was received by four boats only, two of them off the Firth of Forth, *U32* and *U66*. *U32* was a 674-ton 'U31'-class boat of 1914, capable of 16 knots on the surface and 9.7 knots submerged and armed with twin 19.7in torpedo tubes at bow and stern. *U70* was a 779-ton 'UD'-type boat ordered by Austria and completed in 1915. She carried four 17.7in tubes in the bow and one in the stern, and could make 16 knots on the surface and 10.3 submerged. Ranges underwater at 5 knots were 80 miles and 115 miles respectively. Only *U32* sighted Beatty's fleet and in the early hours of the 31st attacked the cruisers *Galatea* and *Phaeton* at 1,000 yards. Both torpedoes missed and the submarine had to dive deep to avoid being rammed by *Phaeton*. Forced under, a submarine of 1916 had no chance of getting into position for another attack against fast forces. To be effective on its one pass against the enemy, a submarine of this period needed more firepower than just two tubes, especially two tubes spread between two separate targets. All *U32* could do when she returned to periscope depth was sight *Indefatigable* and *New Zealand* and report the presence of two capital ships plus cruisers and destroyers, a message that was received at 0537. *U70* saw nothing.

A sister of *U70*, *U66* received the warning signal late but at 0500 saw a British armoured cruiser, then HMS *Boadicea*, then a flotilla and finally the imposing super-dreadnought of the Second Battle Squadron. An attack on three vital ships would have been disproportionately effective had it succeeded, but *U66* had to go deep to avoid a destroyer and was unable to mount an attack. Her sighting report was received at 0648. The other boats to receive the message when first transmitted were yet another 'UD', *U67* off Terschelling, and a tiny 258-ton coastal boat, *UB22* off the Humber. Neither boat saw anything. The time of the submarine as a major fleet unit had not yet come.

SIGNALS INTELLIGENCE

The British had a priceless asset in the shape of a naval signals intelligence organization based at Room 40 in the Admiralty. Helped originally by the Russians, who had captured the code-book of the cruiser *Magdeburg* in 1914, the code-breakers maintained their insight into German naval activities. As with all code-breaking, the ability to read the signals was not constant and it took time to break into some. Indeed, after a final signal at 1741 on 30 May, Room 40 had the problem of breaking into a new cypher specially brought in for the German fleet's sortie. It did not succeed in doing so until 1840 on 31 May.

Signals received and decyphered on 29 and 30 May had indicated an important movement and Jellicoe and Beatty's orders to go to sea were the result. By the morning of the 31st it had been confirmed that the units of the German fleet had been due to leave their base in the Jade river in the early hours of that day and that, as was normally done when the High Sea Fleet put to sea, Scheer's call-sign would be changed from 'Dk' (which had gone ashore at Wilhelmshaven as a simple means of deception) to 'Ra' used by the flagship at sea.

About noon on the 31st the Director of Operations at the Admiralty, Captain Thomas Jackson, came into Room 40 to ask where 'Dk' was at that time. Jackson did not like Room 40, was suspicious of its activities and was rarely seen there. He was told simply that 'Dk' was still in the Jade. Jackson had asked the wrong question and in his subsequent signal to the Fleet gave Jellicoe and Beatty the misinformation that Scheer had postponed his operation and was still at his base. This needless error shook the faith of Jellicoe and Beatty in intelligence reports emanating from the Admiralty, with important subsequent results. For it soon became only too clear that afternoon that the High Sea Fleet, far from being off Wilhelmshaven, was at sea in full strength, a plum ripe for the picking.

Another significant failure, again caused by the Naval Staff's poor liaison with Room 40, was that Jellicoe had little inkling of his true level of superiority. Room 40 knew the exact day-to-day composition and readiness of Scheer's and Hipper's forces but no attempt was made – until after Jutland – to communicate this to the C-in-C. Jellicoe and Beatty thus had a significantly overestimated impression of the true strength of their opponents, which increased their caution even more.

THE ENCOUNTER

Misinformed by the Admiralty as to Scheer's position, Jellicoe did not rush to his rendezvous with Beatty. He stopped to examine merchant ships which delayed him still further and he allowed Beatty to get well ahead of the main body of the fleet before turning north to rendezvous with it. This, however, facilitated contact, for moving into the area to the east were the German First and Second Scouting Groups, with Scheer 50 miles astern. At 1400 the Danish steamer *N. J. Fjord* was sighted by the German destroyers *B109* and *B110*. They ordered the steamer to stop and it blew off steam. This attracted the attention of the British light cruisers *Galatea* and *Phaeton* on the left of Beatty's advanced cruiser line. These closed to investigate and misidentified the big destroyers as a pair of cruisers, which were duly reported by wireless to Beatty at 1420. Eight minutes later the targets, now correctly identified, were taken under fire at 11,000 yards. Beatty was still considering the implications of this sighting, having turned north at 1415 with his three main squadrons. At 1432, however, he decided to take action and turned his two battlecruiser squadrons to the south-east to cut off from its base whatever enemy force the two ships portended.

This led to the first British mistake. The signal was made by flags which could not be seen by the Fifth Battle Squadron, which Beatty had placed 5 miles to Beatty's rear so as not to interfere with his faster ships if a high-speed pursuit was required. He felt at this stage that the (extra) power of Rear Admiral Hugh Evan-Thomas's ships was outweighed by their inferior speed and was not too worried when the four great 'Queen Elizabeths' turned belatedly to conform to his movement at 1440. The Fifth Battle Squadron had been too far away to read the flag signals which were not, contrary to standing orders, repeated immediately by searchlight. This confusion put Evan-Thomas 10 miles behind Beatty.

Meanwhile the battle around the Danish steamer had become more intense. The nearest German light cruiser, *Elbing*, came up to support the destroyers and, having misreported them as battlecruisers, opened fire on the British cruisers at 14,000–15,000 yards. One hit was made on *Galatea* at 1436, which reported to Beatty that large amounts of smoke were visible to the east. This was the smoke of the cruisers *Frankfurt* and *Pillau* with attendant destroyers coming to relieve the engaged German ship. Hipper also turned his battlecruisers to the south-west to investigate the enemy 'battlecruisers'. *Frankfurt* made a more correct identification at 1451, reporting four British light cruisers in sight. This soon doubled to eight as the First Light Cruiser Squadron was joined by the Third, all the ships steering to the sound of the guns – but in the process depriving Beatty of much of his forward screen and hence his 'eyes'.

To clarify the situation, HMS *Engadine* was ordered at 1447 to carry out an air reconnaissance. It took time to find a suitable spot to hoist out Flight Lieutenant Rutland's Short 184 and the aircraft was not in the air until 1508. It made three sighting reports but *Engadine* was unable to communicate these either to Beatty or Evan-Thomas. The aircraft was forced to put down at 1547 and she was back on board *Engadine* by 1600. Rough weather prevented further flights, which were requested, and *Engadine* could not keep up with the main fleet. She ended up helping a disabled cruiser. As with the submarine, the time of the carrier aircraft had not yet arrived.

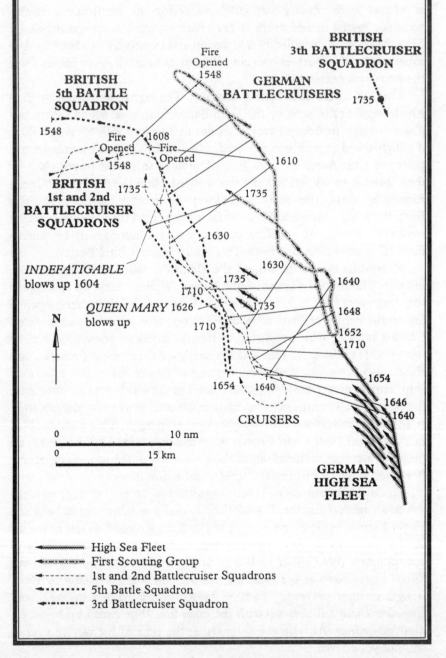

The Battle of Jutland
The Battlecruiser Action
1548 - 1735, 31 May 1916

BRITISH
3th BATTLECRUISER
SQUADRON

Fire
Opened
1548

GERMAN
BATTLECRUISERS

1735

BRITISH
5th BATTLE
SQUADRON

1548

Fire
Opened

1608
Fire
Opened

1735

1610

1548

BRITISH
1st and 2nd
BATTLECRUISER
SQUADRONS

1735

1735

1630

INDEFATIGABLE
blows up 1604

1630

1735

1640

1710

1735

QUEEN MARY 1626
blows up

1648

N

1710

1652
1710

1654

1654   1640

1646
1640

CRUISERS

| 0 | | 10 nm |

| 0 | | 15 km |

GERMAN
HIGH SEA
FLEET

High Sea Fleet
First Scouting Group
1st and 2nd Battlecruiser Squadrons
5th Battle Squadron
3rd Battlecruiser Squadron

Hipper brought his capital ships slowly round, first to the west and then to the south-west, to pursue the reported British cruisers. The British battlecruisers also turned north-westwards to intercept the German ships being drawn to the north-west by *Galatea* and her consorts. At 1520 the First Scouting Group spotted Beatty's smoke to the south-west and two minutes later *Seydlitz* spotted the topmasts of the Second BCS on Beatty's starboard bow. About ten minutes later the BCF identified its main opponents. As the two sides prepared to engage, Beatty ordered the Second BCS to prolong his own line to the rear. More or less simultaneously, Hipper turned his group in succession to starboard to run towards the south-east to draw Beatty on to the guns of the main German fleet. At 1540 Beatty ordered his battlecruisers to form a line of bearing 110°, steaming slightly to the south-east to obtain the best position with regard to funnel and gun smoke and to close the enemy.

The Germans also turned slightly to close the range more rapidly and were also on a line of bearing when they opened fire at 1548. The range had come down to 16,000 yards. The Germans had the advantage of light and wind, and all their turrets could bear. When the British opened fire at 1548–1549, only their fore turrets bore and the Second BCS could not get in range until a few minutes later still. Beatty's ships did not distribute their fire properly. Both *Lion* and *Princess Royal* shot at *Lützow*. *Queen Mary* concentrated on *Seydlitz*, *Tiger* and *New Zealand* shot at *Moltke*, and *Indefatigable* duelled with *Von Der Tann*. This should have given *Derfflinger* undisturbed target practice, but she did not exploit it, at least at this stage. *Lützow* and *Moltke*, both in receipt of fire from two ships, were the first to score. *Lützow* was firing at *Lion*, *Derfflinger* at *Princess Royal*, *Seydlitz* at *Queen Mary*, *Moltke* at *Tiger* and *Von Der Tann* at *Indefatigable*; *New Zealand* escaped attention.

The Germans were better able both to estimate the range and its rate of change. The British were firing too high, *Lion*, *Tiger* and *New Zealand* estimating the range, wrongly, at over 18,000 yards. Their first shells landed close to the screening cruisers and destroyers on the other side of the German battlecruisers. The Germans were also using all their turrets from the start. All but *Lützow* fired one gun per turret using armour-piercing capped rounds (APC). The flagship fired a different kind of four-gun salvo, first the forward turrets and then the after. *Lützow* tried one broadside with all eight guns but it fell short and only obscured the target. Her gunnery officer therefore reverted to four-gun salvoes; he chose to use semi-armour-piercing explosive ammunition, intended as much to destroy the enemy's fire control as the fabric of the British ships.

Lion's opening fire had been delayed by Beatty's being preoccupied with a signal to Jellicoe. Chatfield, the flag captain and in overall charge of the BCF's gunnery, ordered fire to be opened with all four forward guns at almost the moment the Germans opened fire. It took a few more minutes for the British ships to get their after turrets into action, which allowed the rate of fire to be increased as each turret went on to salvo firing with one gun being loaded as the other fired. Not until after 1402 were all British turrets bearing. The 13.5in ships fired armour-piercing rounds, the 12in HE shells, again to disrupt the enemy's fire control.

The best shooting in the opening phase of the action was by *Moltke*. Her target, HMS *Tiger*, barely had time to fire two salvoes with her after turrets before both were put temporarily out of action. 'Q' turret was hit on the turret roof and the concussion of the bursting shell caused considerable damage. 'X' turret's barbette was struck and the shell entered the turret from below but did not explode properly. This hit, at 13,500 yards, was about the limit of the shell's effective range. The turret was back in action in seven minutes using local laying and director training, but the training gear had been blown off bearing and the turret must have shot very wide for the next hour before the error was rectified. Poor *Tiger* was hit no fewer than nine times before 1600. Two hits pierced the side armour, the second exploded 22ft inside the ship near the after 6in shell hoist. Although two British shells were ignited, the fire did not penetrate the after 6in magazine, which was flooded as a precautionary measure.

The British flagship also got the worst of her exchange with *Lützow*. Luckily for the British, the German SAPC shells were showing some reluctance to explode, which defeated the object of using them. The first two hit forward but neither went off. The third, however, which hit at 1600, almost sank *Lion*. It struck 'Q' turret on the right corner of the left gun port, a weak point, penetrated the turret and exploded over the left-hand gun. Everyone in the turret was killed or wounded and the port roof plate was blown off. The right gun was being loaded when the shell struck and the entire turret system was fully charged with cordite. It was a dangerous situation and a sailor climbed down the trunking from 'Q' turret's working chamber to inform the magazine crew of the state of affairs. *Lion*'s Chief Gunner, Grant, was there and he ordered the magazine doors to be closed and then for the magazine to be flooded. Major Harvey of the Royal Marines, the turret commander, despite fatal burns, had meanwhile sent a messenger to the bridge to report the situation. Chatfield, therefore, himself ordered that 'Q' magazine be flooded and Stoker William Yeo was sent from the transmitting station to give the orders. It is not clear which orders actually caused the flooding but it was a timely precaution. As Grant approached the handing chamber at 1628, a major cordite explosion occurred in the turret trunking. Grant's precautions had prevented an immediate catastrophe, but fire had probably spread slowly down from the gun house via the inflammable coverings of the electric cables. At least eight full cordite charges ignited, one in the right gun loading cage that had dropped to 4ft above the working chamber, one in the left cage in the working chamber, one in the waiting positions in the working chamber, plus one in both lower turret cages, and one in both magazine hoppers in the handing room. The magazine doors were not fully flash-tight and were bulged inwards by the force of the explosion. If the magazine had not been flooded, the ship would undoubtedly have blown up.

By this time, two of Beatty's battlecruisers had already suffered this catastrophic fate. First to go was *Indefatigable*. Last in the line, she was the last to open fire and had been engaged by *Von Der Tann* for 3–4 minutes before she opened fire. She scored no hits from the forty or so 12in shells she fired. *Von Der Tann*, however, did better. After an initial hit, two 11in shells struck *Indefatigable* together at about 1602 near the after turret. At least one almost certainly penetrated the 3in armour of the barbette, causing a catastrophic cordite explosion that spread to the after magazine. This may have blown the bottom out of the after part of the ship for *Indefatigable* immediately lost control and began to sink by the stern. As she sank the ship suffered two more hits forward. One of these may have caused a catastrophic cordite fire in 'A' turret also, for half a minute later the wreck blew up and disappeared. There were only two survivors from a ship's company of 1,019.

Beatty and his staff in *Lion* took a somewhat dispassionate view of *Indefatigable*'s loss. She was after all a relatively old ship, obsolescent if not obsolete given the rapid pace of naval development. Then, however, his most effective battlecruiser suffered a similar fate. About the time *Indefatigable* sank, *Lion* had turned, in error, to starboard which caused the range to lengthen to 21,000 yards. The Germans slackened their fire as the British ships drew out of range. Evan-Thomas's Fifth Battle Squadron was now coming into action, first against German light cruisers but then from 1608 against the First Scouting Group when *Barham* fired a 15in salvo at *Von Der Tann* at 19,000 yards. Beatty therefore altered course back towards the Germans and at 1619 the range had come down to 16,000 yards between *Lion* and *Lützow*. Over the next ten minutes it was further reduced to 14,000 yards.

As the fighting flared up once more, *Lion* suffered three more hits at about 1624, two of which caused heavy casualties to the crews of the after port side 4in battery. Even before these hits, smoke from *Lion* had obscured *Princess Royal*, the next ship in line. At 1617, therefore, *Derfflinger* had shifted from *Lion* to *Queen Mary*, joining *Seydlitz* in the bombardment of this ship. *Seydlitz* had already put four 11in shells into *Queen Mary*, one of which caused an ammunition fire in the after secondary battery. After *Derfflinger* opened fire, one of her 12in shells hit *Queen Mary* at 1621, on 'Q' turret, this time to the right of the right gun. This weapon was put out of action but the left gun continued to fire. Then at 1626 two 12in shells hit forward, one of which exploded in a turret or barbette. A third shell may have hit 'Q' turret and demolished the remaining gun. There was a first explosion forward, closely followed by an even larger one as both forward magazines went up, destroying the whole fore part of the ship. As the remains of the great battlecruiser sank, the after magazine blew up also, possibly as a result of fires started by the second hit on 'Q' turret but more probably as a result of fires started by the effect of the shock of the earlier magazine explosions. There were twenty survivors; 1,266 officers and men lost their lives. Beatty was moved to remark to Chatfield: 'There seems to be something wrong with out bloody ships today.'

Until her loss *Queen Mary* had been shooting well, her Argo clock coping well with the constantly changing rates of change of range that ruined the effectiveness of the other ships' Dreyer tables. She had scored four hits on *Seydlitz*. The first, obtained in the opening minutes of the action at 1555, was just forward of the foremast and caused extensive internal damage on the battery and main decks. Two minutes later another shell hit the barbette of *Seydlitz*'s after superfiring turret. The shell burst as it penetrated, putting the turret out of action and igniting the charges in the working chamber. The fire entered the turret but the other charges there did not ignite. It also went down the trunking, but again the exposed charges there did not explode. If *Seydlitz* had been a British ship, she would undoubtedly have blown up; she was saved by her superior propellant storage and the rules adopted since the Dogger Bank limiting the number of rounds between guns and magazine. A third shell that hit *Seydlitz* underwater shortly after 1600 caused some flooding while at 1617, in *Queen Mary*'s last blow, a 12in shell exploded abaft the after 5.9in casemate, causing extensive blast and smoke damage.

Lion scored two early hits on *Lützow*, both on the forecastle. These were of little importance at the time but would become more serious later. *Princess Royal* then scored two subsequent hits, one between *Lützow*'s forward turrets and the other on the belt armour abaft the mainmast. Both burst without inflicting serious damage. *Derfflinger* escaped being hit completely, but *Tiger* succeeded in hitting *Moltke* at 1602 with an underwater hit that caused some flooding. *Tiger* later engaged *Von Der Tann*, scoring two hits at 1620 and 1623. The first hit the forward barbette and put the fore turret out of action, while the second hit close to the after barbette doing the same to the after turret. Given that the starboard wing turret began to suffer trouble from over-heated guns, the oldest German battlecruiser was soon in no condition to continue an engagement on her starboard beam. The three rearmost ships of the German line were also suffering the attention of Evan Thomas's battleships. These powerful ships shot a great deal better than Beatty's battlecruisers. There were a number of reasons for this: more constant access to the gunnery practice facilities at Scapa, longer base length rangefinders, less exposure to German fire, a flatter trajectory main armament, better visibility and, perhaps most important of all, a moderate angle of convergence and a more or less constant rate of change of range. Their latest model Dreyer tables could just about cope in these conditions.

At 1609, only a minute after opening fire for the first time, *Barham* hit *Von Der Tann* with a high-explosive shell that struck on the side 28ft forward of the stern, exploding on the armour and causing much damage from blast, splinters and vibration. The German battlecruiser's steering gear was temporarily put out of action and 1,000 tons of water entered the ship, causing it to list. Shortly afterwards, *Barham* and *Valiant* concentrated on *Moltke*, hitting her repeatedly, while *Warspite* and *Malaya* fired at *Von Der Tann* which was protected by smoke coming from her previous hits. At 1616 two 15in shells fired at 18,000 yards struck *Moltke*; the first went through the 8in side armour and burst in an outer coal bunker. A 5.9in gun was put out of action and flash passed down to the magazine, but again German safety precautions worked. The second shell hit the side forward of the stern and penetrated the plating. It did not explode but water entered through the hole. At 1623 and 1626 two more shells, fired at about 16,000 yards, exploded on the main armour belt below the waterline, causing some flooding. In all *Moltke*, like *Von Der Tann*, took in about 1,000 tons water but in general the German armour protection did its job well, even against the heavy British 15in shells.

In between the two lines of capital ships a fierce destroyer/torpedo-boat action developed as the two sides' flotillas tried to attack the other's key units and got entangled with each other. The more powerful British destroyers had the better of the action. HMS *Obdurate* was hit by two 4.1in shells from the cruiser *Regensburg* supporting the German flotillas but with little effect. Less lucky was HMS *Nomad*, hit in the engine room and brought to a standstill. The Germans, however, lost two boats, *V29* to a torpedo from *Petard* fired at 2,000 yards and set to run shallow, and *V27* hit by gunfire in the forward engine room and sunk by a sister ship after its crew had been taken off. *Nestor* and *Nicator* fired torpedoes at 6,000 yards at the German battlecruisers, which replied with their secondary armament. The Germans were forced to turn away to avoid the weapons. The Germans also launched torpedoes at Beatty's capital ships but at even longer range, 9,000 yards. The British turned to the north at 1640 before the weapons could reach their targets.

The reason for this turn was that Scheer's battlefleet had come into sight. Goodenough's Second Light Cruiser Squadron reported the presence of the battleships ahead of Beatty at 1633, three minutes after the lead German battleship, *König*, spotted the battlecruiser action coming towards her. At 1638 a complete sighting report was sent from HMS *Southampton* to Beatty, the enemy battlefleet bearing approximately 122°, course 347°. Beatty waited to see the High Sea Fleet himself before ordering reversal of course in succession to starboard. Five minutes later the four surviving British battlecruisers were all steering north-westwards. The Fifth Battle Squadron and the German battlecruisers were engaged with each other on the opposite course and just before Beatty steamed by at 1650, masking its fire, one of its battleships scored a hit on *Seydlitz*'s forecastle. Beatty was flying a flag signal to Evan-Thomas for him to turn in succession 180° to starboard. Either because the signal was late in being hauled down, or because of slow reactions in *Barham*, or both, the turn did not begin until 1654. *Barham* put her wheel over, followed at minute intervals by *Valiant* and *Warspite*. As they turned, on precisely the same area of sea, the battleships were taken under fire by a number of German battleships at about 19,000 yards.[1] The fire seemed so hot that Captain Boyle of HMS *Malaya*, the last ship of the line, turned early, cutting across *Warspite*'s stern before taking station. Actually only *Barham* was hit by a 12in shell as she turned, which put her wireless equipment out of action.

Hipper also turned northwards at 1652 while under persistent attack by the British destroyers which had not seen Beatty's recall flags. It has been called by one historian, writing between the wars, 'the most spirited destroyer attack of all history'.[2] The destroyers *Nestor* and *Nicator* dashed to about two miles of the German battlecruisers to fire torpedoes, the former at *Lützow* and the latter at *Derfflinger*. Neither made torpedo hits but the impudent little ships scored with their 4in guns against *Derfflinger*. The destroyers were engaged by the secondary batteries of the German capital ships and by the cruiser *Regensburg*. *Nestor* was disabled and forced to a standstill, being later finished off by 5.9in fire from German battleships. *Nicator* made her escape.

Petard and *Turbulent* also made torpedo attacks on *Seydlitz*, the former firing one, the latter up to three torpedoes. One of these struck the battlecruiser on the starboard side just as she turned on to her new northerly course. The tough German anti-torpedo protection allowed *Seydlitz* to maintain her speed for the time being, but a 65ft space ahead of the forward boiler room bulkhead began to fill with water. *Nerissa* fired two torpedoes at 7,000 yards at *Von Der Tann*, which missed as the battlecruiser turned; and *Moorsum* engaged the German battlefleet itself, firing pairs of torpedoes at *Grosser Kurfürst* and *Markgraf*. The British suffered from both the limited numbers of weapons fired and the Germans turning at the time of the attack. It is significant that *Turbulent*, which fired three torpedoes, scored the hit on the enemy capital ship. As a subsequent analyst put it: 'The British doctrine of firing one or two torpedoes at a time was faulty. Torpedoes evidently have better chances of hitting or influencing the course of a battle when fired together in large salvoes.'[3]

The battle now entered its second phase with Beatty's battlecruisers, supported once more by Evan-Thomas, leading Hipper and Scheer to their hoped-for doom on the guns of Jellicoe's main battlefleet. Between 1645 and 1710 the battlecruiser forces continued to engage each other, but after this it was the Fifth Battle Squadron that monopolized the Germans' attention as Beatty drew out of range. Both Hipper and Scheer took Evan-Thomas under fire but despite many shell splashes, especially around *Malaya*, the powerful 'Queen Elizabeths' had the better of the engagement as they engaged whatever targets offered themselves out of the mist and smoke. Between 1706 and 1710 three 15in rounds hit *Seydlitz*, the first making a large hole in the forecastle that let in large amounts of water and spread through previously damaged compartments. Goodenough's cruisers were also engaged by German battleships as they shadowed them to port, but no hits were scored.

At 1740 the battlecruisers were again in contact, with the sun below the clouds both dazzling the German gunners and illuminating the German ships quite clearly. This caused *Lion* grossly to underestimate the range and she began to fire at 10,000 yards. The true distance was more like 16,500 yards and *Princess Royal*, with her sights correctly set, scored a hit on *Lützow*. Despite the poor conditions, the latter scored another hit on *Lion* at 1805. The Fifth Battle Squadron also continued to pound away at the German battlecruisers. At 1755 two 15in shells each hit the battered *Seydlitz* and *Derfflinger*.

Jellicoe was now not far away. At 1605 he had sent the Third Battle Cruiser Squadron ahead to support Beatty. Its dashing and able commander, the Honourable Horace Hood, had already anticipated the order and had increased speed to 24 knots at 1600. Due to errors in estimating positions, Hood did not rendezvous with Beatty as hoped for but one of his cruisers, *Chester*, on his starboard beam, heard gunfire at 1727. She signalled to *Invincible* by searchlight and was shortly afterwards engaged by four German light cruisers of the Second Scouting Group. *Chester* was hit seventeen times and quite seriously damaged, with heavy casualties inflicted on her gun crews, including Boy First Class Jack Cornwell who was awarded a posthumous Victoria Cross for staying at his post. The German cruisers now found themselves confronted by

Hood's three capital ships which opened fire at 10,000 yards. The German ships turned away but not before *Wiesbaden* was brought to a standstill, her engines disabled. *Pillau* was also hit but was able to get away.

Hood was then attacked by German torpedo-boats and destroyers, which were themselves engaged by Hood's outnumbered escorts. The cruisers *Frankfurt* and *Regensburg* gave fire support to the German torpedo craft which included the large 'B97'-class boats. HMS *Shark* was disabled and *Acasta* damaged, but the Germans were hampered by the large waves caused by the numerous ships manoeuvring in close proximity and by their spray. The battlecruisers turned briefly to the north-east, but at 1804 were back facing due west to join with Beatty. This drew them over the tracks of the German torpedoes nearing the end of their runs and going slowly. *Invincible* had a bad moment avoiding them. She suffered jammed steering and came to a halt in clouds of steam from her safety valves. *Indomitable* was also near-missed by three torpedoes. After this near disaster, Hood reformed his ships into line ahead and moved to take station ahead of Beatty. Hood's lucky arrival had the effect of drawing the attention of the German flotillas at a crucial moment and caused such concern to Hipper that at 1759 he turned his much battered battlecruisers back to the south-west to fall back on the main German fleet. This helped mask the deployment of Jellicoe's main force and prevented the Germans crossing the 'T' of the Grand Fleet. Instead the Germans would find themselves in that unfortunate position. The mistaken identification of Hood's ships as battleships also misled the Germans into thinking that Jellicoe was further to the east than in fact he was.

As he closed the main body of the Grand Fleet, Beatty progressively altered course to starboard at 1809 and 1813 to regain contact with Hipper, cover Jellicoe's deployment and take up position at the head of the British line. As he did so, the impressive four-funnelled bulks of the armoured cruisers *Defence* and *Warrior* cut across his bows. Sir Robert Arbuthnot's First Cruiser Squadron had been scouting ahead of the battlefleet and at 1753 *Defence*, the flagship, and *Warrior*, which had been ordered to concentrate with her, opened fire on the Second Scouting Group, visible to starboard at 16,000 yards. The range was far too long for the obsolete cruisers' 9.2in guns. Shortly afterwards Arbuthnot, a single-minded martinet of an officer, spotted the crippled *Wiesbaden* and sailed to engage her. It was this manoeuvre that almost led to a collision with the battlecruisers. As Beatty's ships took evasive action, the two armoured cruisers took the hapless German light cruiser under an effective fire. They were joined by the destroyer *Onslow* commanded by Lieutenant-Commander J. C. Tovey, destined to be Home Fleet

Commander in the Second World War.

In the heat of the battlecruiser action Beatty had failed to keep Jellicoe informed of the position of the High Sea Fleet. The Grand Fleet was sailing in divisional columns of four ships arranged in numerical order from east to west. It had to deploy into line to take up battle formation. Jellicoe needed details of the enemy's course and speed to carry out a deployment in the right direction, but he did not get it. He received the first news of action at 1600, and 38 minutes later heard Goodenough's sighting report of Scheer. At 1645 Beatty sent Jellicoe a sighting report, but this had to be sent via *Princess Royal* because of damage to *Lion*'s wireless and eventually got to Jellicoe via *Benbow*. In the process it suffered mutilation and gave Jellicoe the impression that he was facing stronger forces than in fact he was. More reports had meanwhile come in, largely from Goodenough, but their usefulness was reduced by errors in *Southampton*'s estimated position. Then, from 1705, when Beatty's delayed signal arrived, there was silence for over an hour as the two fleets came inexorably closer. At 1733 *Falmouth* of Beatty's cruiser screen came within visual contact of the armoured cruiser *Black Prince*. Three minutes later she signalled 'battlecruisers engaged to the SSW of me', but this was garbled to 'enemy battlecruisers bearing south five miles' before being relayed to Jellicoe. More signals had begun to come in from Goodenough but neither Hood nor *Chester* informed Jellicoe of their activities.

At 1750 HMS *Marlborough*, on the starboard wing, reported firing on her starboard bow, and about ten minutes later that Beatty was in sight. Due to dead-reckoning errors, this was further to the west and earlier than expected. Jellicoe signalled Beatty at 1801 'Where is enemy's battlefleet?' and received the delphic reply 'Enemy battlecruisers bearing SE'. This signal strained the C-in-C's patience as it did not answer his question, and it contradicted his latest (misleading) information from Goodenough. Jellicoe repeated his signal at 1810 and at 1814 got the reply by searchlight 'Have sighted enemy's battlefleet to SSW'. No course or speed was mentioned and Jellicoe was left to make his vital decision to deploy into battle line based on guesswork – with the two fleets closing at a relative speed of 30 knots. Never was the mismatch between the speed and striking power of the early dreadnought battlefleets and their deficient command and control systems more dramatically demonstrated.

Jellicoe would have liked to have deployed on the starboard squadron, but with the enemy's position uncertain he ran the risk of exposing his ships to Scheer's flotillas and his weakest battleships to the fire of the whole German line. Even if the British 'T' was not crossed, the Grand Fleet would have to turn in an exposed position with only a fraction of its guns able to bear. Deploying to port meant that it was more likely that

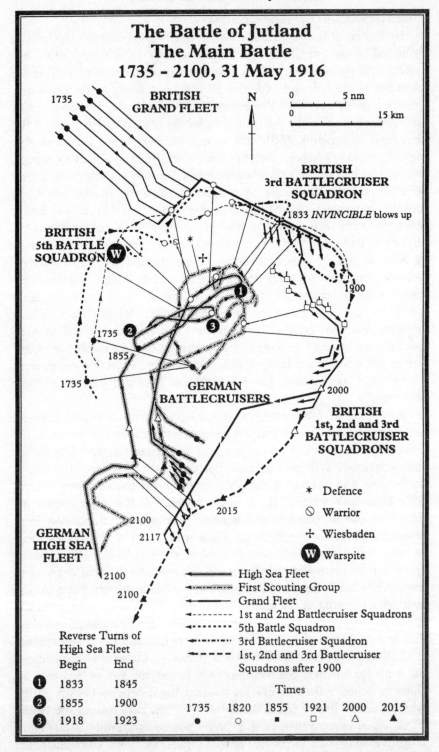

The Battle of Jutland
The Main Battle
1735 – 2100, 31 May 1916

the Germans' 'T' would be crossed by the British and that the Grand Fleet would have the benefit of the light for accurate gunnery. They would be firing out of the murk at ships silhouetted against the misty light of the setting sun. The British would also be between the High Sea Fleet and its base. The problem with such a deployment was that it delayed getting to grips with the Germans in conditions of fast-diminishing visibility. At 1815 Jellicoe duly made his crucial decision of the battle, to deploy on the port division, south-east by east. Despite subsequent criticism it was undoubtedly the correct choice.

As the fleet deployed, Arbuthnot's recklessly exposed cruisers suddenly found themselves within 8,000 yards of the German battlefleet as it loomed out of the mist to the south. 12in shells rained down on them and easily pierced the cruisers' armour. *Defence*'s aft 9.2in magazine blew up and the explosion ripped through the 7.5in magazines to the forward 9.2in ammunition. She blew up and disintegrated, sinking with all hands at 1820. Her companion, *Warrior*, was hit by twenty-one shells of various calibres but mercifully did not explode. She was probably saved by the Germans' attention being diverted by the activities of the Fifth Battle Squadron. Evan Thomas found he could not take station at the head of the British line and instead turned to port to join the rear of the line. In the process *Warspite* suffered a serious steering failure and sailed in two complete circles, coming within 10,000 yards of Scheer's line. She was hit at least thirteen times but at least it took the pressure off *Warrior*, which got away to be taken in tow by the seaplane-carrier *Engadine*. *Warrior* eventually sank 160 miles east of Aberdeen on the following morning. *Warspite* suffered another steering failure shortly after her previous adventures and she was ordered home.

Beatty was sufficiently advanced to take position at the head of the line, but to do this he had to steer across the front of the Grand Fleet, masking it with his smoke and forcing it to slow down. It also prevented Jellicoe closing the Germans as rapidly as he might have done.

Hood swung his ships to starboard at 1817 to take station ahead of Beatty. This put him on a parallel course to the First Scouting Group at a range of 9,000 yards. Hood's battlecruisers were fresh from gunnery practice at Scapa and did well against the head of Hipper's line. *Invincible* and *Inflexible* together scored eight 12in hits on *Lützow* between 1826 and 1834. Two hit below the waterline and burst near the port torpedo flat, one below the armoured belt and the other on its lower part. The large space of the flat – larger than in other ships because of the new 23.6in tubes – flooded almost immediately. Over 700 tons of water was taken in to add to that absorbed as a result of earlier hits. Flooding began to spread and the German battlecruiser flagship had to slow down to lessen the pressure on her bulkheads. Another hit on the forecastle made a dangerous hole that would let in more water as the ship settled lower. Three hits amidships (one of which failed to explode) damaged the port secondary battery. *Derfflinger* was hit twice by *Indomitable*, both by armour-piercing shells which exploded on the side armour and a third shell which exploded close alongside, causing some leakage. *Indomitable* also hit *Seydlitz*; the shell broke up, doing little damage, but her steering was temporarily impaired.

The damage to *Lützow* would eventually prove fatal but in the meantime it was the British who once more seemed to come off worse. Both *Lützow* and *Derfflinger* fired at *Invincible* and the salvoes, starting about 1,200 yards short, slowly moved closer. Hood's flagship was hit aft and then at 1834 on 'Q' turret amidships, between the guns. The turret blew up and the flash went down into the amidships magazine that fed both 'P' and 'Q' turrets. The force of this explosion seems to have touched off the other magazines and the battlecruiser blew in half, the bow and stern sections standing on the bottom for some time in grim memorial. Only six survivors were picked up by the destroyer *Badger* from the 1,027 on board. *Lützow* was the probable source of the fatal shell, a pyrrhic revenge for her own fatal wounds which caused her to drop out of line at 1837.

The two sides' battleships began to trade blows at about 1817 when *Marlborough* opened fire at 13,000 yards. The whole British line was in action by 1830. *Iron Duke* soon scored seven 13.5in hits on the battleship *König*, which was leading Scheer's battle line round to starboard to follow Hipper's battlecruisers, and *Marlborough* scored an eighth hit on the same ship. One shell hit the lower edge of the armour belt below the waterline, causing considerable flooding and destroying a secondary armament magazine. The flooding helped control the cordite fire. At about the same time the battleship *Markgraf* was also hit, probably by a 13.5in shell from *Orion*, on the port side secondary armament. A near miss shook her, which bent her port propeller shaft and caused the port engines to be immobilized. *Markgraf* had been engaging Beatty's battlecruisers, having scored two hits on *Princess Royal* at 13,000 yards at 1822. One hit the barbette armour of 'X' turret. The protection prevented an explosion but a piece of armour was driven up into the turret, killing the left-hand gun crew, and the turret was jammed because of displacement and distortion of the barbette.

As the British fleet deployed, each ship passed the wreck of *Wiesbaden* and took it under fire. The surviving members of her crew made what reply they could and succeeded in putting a torpedo into *Marlborough*, leading the tail division, at 1854. The British battleship's forward boiler room was flooded, which reduced her speed to 16–17 knots. She took avoiding action, as did *St Vincent*, to avoid further torpedoes, fired by the torpedo-boat *V48*. The British attributed the torpedoes to submarines. No other damage was inflicted at this stage on Jellicoe's battle line.

The British C-in-C still had little idea of the true situation. As he wrote later to the First Lord of the Admiralty:

'The whole situation was so difficult to grasp, as I had no real idea of what was going on and we could hardly see anything except the flashes of guns, shells falling, ships blowing up, and an occasional glimpse of an Enemy vessel.'[4]

Scheer, however, was in more serious trouble. His battlecruisers were in a bad state, with Hipper's flagship sinking, both *Derfflinger* and *Seydlitz* down at the bows because of heavy flooding, and *Von Der Tann* out of action. The only operational German battlecruiser was *Moltke*. The northern horizon was filled with a line of British ships, hidden in the murk and only visible by their gunflashes. There was only one alternative, a Gefechtskertwendung with the whole fleet sailing away from danger. This was signalled at 1833 and was covered by an attack by the Third Torpedo-Boat Flotilla. It was complete by 1845. Jellicoe could only watch perplexed as the enemy disappeared into the mist. He felt that he could not follow into the murk, given the perceived torpedo and mine threats. All he could do was to remain across Scheer's line of retreat and he turned the fleet southwards by divisions in echelon. At 1900 the battlecruisers occupied themselves in a complete 360° turn that, strangely, Beatty always insisted never took place. Its probable purpose was to close the distance between the BCF and Jellicoe.

Five minutes before Beatty's meanderings began, Scheer had once more reversed course. He later insisted that his intention was to inflict another blow on the British, but it is much more likely that this was a premature attempt to break back to Germany. It led him straight on to Jellicoe's guns. Shortly after 1900 HMS *Ajax* opened fire at 18,700 yards and then ten minutes later the other battleships engaged the advancing Germans at about 10,000 yards. Visibility for the British was as good as it was bad for the Germans and the latter suffered heavily. Scheer soon became aware of the danger and ordered his battlecruisers, now led by Captain Hartog in *Derfflinger*, to charge the British line to cover another withdrawal. A minute later he altered his orders to one to engage the enemy's leading ships, but before they saw the signal flags at 1917 the four battered German capital ships had closed to within 7,700 yards of the Grand Fleet. They suffered severely. *Derfflinger* was hit hard at 1914 by a 15in shell from *Revenge*. This penetrated the aftermost turret, killing the entire crew and starting a cordite fire which, unlike in British ships, was contained. *Revenge* scored another hit at about 1917 on the other after gun mounting, the shell penetrating the barbette and exploding under the turret. Another serious cordite fire resulted, but again it was contained. The after magazines were flooded and so much toxic gas was produced that the engine rooms could only be manned by personnel in gas masks. *Revenge* scored two more hits aft and another shell went through the German battlecruiser's forefunnel without exploding. Between 1916 and 1920 *Derfflinger* also suffered six 12in hits, five from *Colossus* and one from *Collingwood*. The tough German ship stood up well to the 12in AP rounds from *Colossus*, although considerable damage was caused to cabins by a hit aft. The shell from *Collingwood* was HE and burst in the sick-bay causing quite extensive damage to the superstructure. Three more hits were scored shortly after 1920, two with 15in from *Royal Oak* which went through the after funnel without exploding, and a 12in from *Bellerophon* which failed to penetrate the heavily armoured conning tower.

Seydlitz suffered five hits, four 12in from *Hercules* and *St Vincent* between 1914 and 1920 and a 15in from *Royal Oak* at 1927. One 12in shell hit the already disabled aft superfiring turret, while the 15in hit knocked out the right gun and the director gear in the port wing turret. *Von Der Tann* was hit once by a 15in shell.

The battlecruisers' sacrifice did not take all the pressure off the German battlefleet, the leading ships of which began once more to suffer damage. *König* was hit at 1918 and *Grosser Kurfürst* no fewer than seven times by 15in and 13.5in shells from the Fifth Battle Squadron and *Marlborough*. These caused some flooding. *Agincourt* hit *Markgraf* once and *Kaiser* twice with HE shells which did not cause much damage. *Helgoland* was hit once by a 15in shell from the Fifth Battle Squadron which caused limited flooding. The only damage inflicted in return for all this punishment was a hit by *Seydlitz* on *Colossus* which inflicted light damage.

Scheer was forced to order a battle turn away once more at 1918 and even before this manoeuvre began, the Sixth and Ninth Torpedo Boat Flotillas had already begun to charge to cover it. At 1920 Jellicoe spotted the torpedo-boats closing through the smoke and ordered the Fourth Light Cruiser Squadron to engage them. The nearer British destroyers, without waiting for orders, also moved in. At the same time Jellicoe ordered the Grand Fleet to turn away from the attack to comb the expected torpedo tracks. Some German torpedo-boats closed to 7,000–7,500 yards before firing torpedoes, being engaged by the main and secondary armaments of the British battleships. *S35* was sunk by two 13.5in shells from *Iron Duke* and *G86* was damaged by a near miss by a heavy shell. Other destroyers were hit by 6in shells, but none was disabled. The Germans used both oil smoke and 'artificial fog' to cover their retreat. The Sixth Flotilla fired eleven torpedoes and the Ninth about ten. They were moving slowly at the end of their runs by the time they reached the retreating British who were able to avoid them, despite some dangerous near misses. A third German torpedo attack was mounted by the Third Flotilla at 1923, but the British were too far away for any success. The defending cruisers and destroyers were not well placed to interfere with the German flotillas and their only success was finishing off the already disabled *V48*.

At 1935 Jellicoe began to turn back to starboard in pursuit of Scheer. The Grand Fleet was ordered to change to a more westerly course at 1940 and ten minutes later Beatty, increasingly frustrated at the situation, signalled by wireless to Jellicoe that the leading battle squadron be ordered to follow him to cut off the enemy fleet. This arrived just as Jellicoe was himself ordering a further move to a westerly course at 2000. The C-in-C thereupon signalled to *King George V* to follow Beatty but the BCF was now invisible to Admiral Jerram and his squadron and, much to Beatty's increased frustration, the battleships did not change course.

At 2023, alerted by the sounds of a light cruiser skirmish between the Third British LCS and the Fourth Scouting Group, Beatty came into contact with the German battlecruisers once more. Scheer had altered course to the south, which put the two battlecruiser forces on converging courses. The Germans were in a poor state. *Derfflinger* had her two aft turrets out of action and one of her fore turrets without director pointing gear. *Seydlitz* had also lost four guns and had another without director gear. *Von Der Tann* had got four of her guns back into action and two more on hand-working, but only *Moltke* was fully operational. Beatty had two fully operational ships, *Indomitable* and *New Zealand*. *Inflexible* had a defective 12in gun but it could be fired. *Princess Royal* had lost three main guns (one to a breakdown) and *Tiger* had one gun broken down, two restricted in rate of fire and two more on individual laying. *Lion* had lost two guns, had one gun on hand-loading and had lost the main cordite supply to a fourth. On balance the odds were in Beatty's favour.

Princess Royal opened fire at 2019 at 12,000 yards and scored two hits on *Seydlitz*. *Lion* hit *Derfflinger* forward and jammed one of her usable turrets. *New Zealand* hit *Seydlitz* three times and increased her flooding still further. The German ship made some attempt to reply but in the almost impossible gunnery conditions scored no heavy calibre hits, although one 5.9in shell hit *Lion*. The German battleships at the head of the line were also engaged and *Westfalen* was hit by splinters. In reply *Posen* hit *Princess Royal* at 2032 and staddled *Indomitable*.

The pre-dreadnoughts of the Second Squadron to the west of the main German line were also fired on by the British battlecruisers. *Princess Royal* straddled *Hannover* and damaged her with fragments. *Tiger* fired at *Hessen*, but with little effect; but *New Zealand* hit *Schleswig-Holstein* at

2032 and inflicted splinter damage on *Schlesien*. *Indomitable* put a 12in shell into *Pommern* but had to cease fire at 2033 as she could no longer spot fall of shot. The action ceased at about 2040.

Five minutes later, to the north, the cruisers *Caroline* and *Royalist* spotted German battleships to the west. They were moving to mount a torpedo attack when Jerram, worried that the ships were Beatty's battlecruisers, ordered them to stop. The two British cruisers persuaded Jerram eventually that the targets were really German and pressed home to attack, but only three torpedoes were fired at 7,600–8,000 yards, and all missed. The Commodore (F) of the Grand Fleet, with the cruiser *Castor* and the Eleventh Destroyer Flotilla, considered attacking also but as the battlefleet showed no sign of engaging (Jerram still thought the ships in question were British), he held back. Commodore Hawksley felt that it was not quite dark enough yet for a flotilla attack without battleship support.

It was, however, soon too dark for any further thought of action with the heavy ships. At 2117 Jellicoe ordered his fleet to assume night cruising order in columns abreast. At about the same time Scheer ordered his fleet into formation on course for the Horn's Reef. It took time for the German fleet to sort itself out and not until 2230 was the line in Scheer's desired order, with *Westfalen* leading the First Squadron in reverse order, followed by the flagship and the Third Squadron in reverse order and the pre-dreadnoughts of the Second Squadron in the order *Deutschland, Pommern, Schlesien, Schleswig-Holstein, Hessen* and *Hannover*. The two battered battlecruisers, *Von Der Tann* and *Defflinger*, brought up the rear. Hipper, who had boarded *Moltke* at about 2100, was leading the damaged *Seydlitz* on the port side of the main fleet but the latter ship was driven too fast and suffered more flooding that forced her to drop away from the flagship at 2230, just as *Moltke* made contact with the rear of Jellicoe's starboard column, the Second Division of the Second Battle Squadron. HMS *Thunderer* considered opening fire but did not want to reveal the Grand Fleet's position. *Moltke* also sheered off to starboard.

Although the heavy units were seeking to avoid action, the lighter forces fought a series of skirmishes throughout the night, some of which caused serious casualties. The first began when Scheer's Seventh Flotilla ran into the British Fourth Flotilla taking station astern of the Grand Fleet at about 2200. Four German boats, *S15*, *'16*, *'18* and *'24*, fired torpedoes and HMS *Garland, Contest* and *Fortune* replied with gunfire. *Garland* was near-missed. The flotillas then separated, having a further brush at 2242 when *S24* loosed off another torpedo that near-missed HMS *Unity*. At about 2213 *Castor* and the Eleventh Flotilla fought a brisk 5-minute action with the German light cruisers *Hamburg, Elbing* and

Rostock at a range of about a mile. *Castor* made three 6in hits on *Hamburg* and was hit ten times in return, but the German 4.1in shells could make little impression on her armour. HMS *Marne* was also hit but suffered little damage.

Just over a quarter of an hour later these three ships, plus the German Fourth Scouting Group, were engaged by Goodenough's Second Light Cruiser Squadron approaching from the port side. The battle lasted only three minutes but was intense, *Stettin* firing ninety-two 4.1in shells. The range was between 800 and 3,000 yards. *Stettin*, *München* and *Rostock* concentrated on HMS *Southampton* and hit her eight times with 4.1in shells. *Elbing* also engaged her and hit her twice with 5.9in rounds. A 6in gun was knocked out and serious casualties inflicted on her guns' crews, while a cordite fire was started which luckily did not reach the magazine. *Southampton* was to get her revenge, however. She fired a torpedo which hit *Frauenlob* on the port auxiliary engine compartment. The old German protected cruiser was also set on fire by gunfire as she turned over and sank; there were only nine survivors. *Southampton* avoided a torpedo fired by *München* and the cruiser forces separated. *Dublin* had been hit five times by *Elbing* with 5.9in and eight times by 4.1in. Her navigating officer was killed and her charts and wireless lost and she did not rejoin the squadron until the next day. The loss of the wireless in *Southampton* also meant that Jellicoe did not receive news of this action until 2330.

At 2245, although he was not sure of it, an escape route began to open up for Scheer as his fleet began to fall behind the Grand Fleet. At this point, judging the time to be right, he altered course to port which led him into the British flotillas guarding Jellicoe's rear and placed to deal with precisely this eventuality. Sadly, however, the night's work brought out the weaknesses of leadership and training in the British destroyer forces. No amount of individual dash and daring could make up for this, and the Germans were unimpressed by the tactical expertise of the British flotillas. Attacks were made piecemeal, with torpedoes fired at angles that were easily avoided and some of the boats were insufficiently blacked out.

The Eleventh Flotilla had got lost after its previous little battle and was probably on station astern of the German line. Thus it was that the Fourth Flotilla found the High Sea Fleet sailing across its path on a converging course. They were first mistaken for the errant Eleventh Flotilla, but at about 2330 the four-funnelled flotilla leader, HMS *Tipperary*, challenged the battleship *Westfalen*, which immediately replied with the full fire of her secondary armament. The range was about a mile. The battleship shot off 92 rounds of 5.9in and 45 of 3.5in in five minutes, turning away as she did so to avoid torpedoes. Other German ships to engage were the battleship *Nassau* next in line, the cruisers *Rostock*,

Elbing and *Hamburg*, and the torpedo-boat *S32*. The whole head of the German line turned to starboard and in the confusion *Elbing* was rammed by the battleship *Posen*.

Tipperary, the most exposed British ship, suffered badly. Her bridge and bow gun were blown away almost immediately, but she was able to fire two torpedoes from further aft. The destroyer *Spitfire* also fired torpedoes and opened fire and some of the rest of the flotilla were able to shoot as well. *Spitfire* tried to load her spare torpedo but could not do so as the necessary davit had been damaged. As she sailed round to starboard she found herself approaching *Nassau*, which was resuming her south-westerly course at the head of Scheer's line. The British destroyer could only use herself as a weapon and rammed the German battleship on her port bow. *Nassau* had desperately tried to fend off the destroyer with her forward turret, whose guns fired at maximum depression. The 11in shells passed through *Spitfire*'s bridge screens and fore funnel, but more damage was caused by gun blast than the projectiles. *Nassau*'s plating was damaged for about 50ft which cut her speed to 15 knots until it could be repaired. Miraculously *Spitfire* survived with her forward compartments flooded and was able to return to the Tyne.

The destroyers astern of *Spitfire* fired a torpedo each, but five destroyers sheered off without attacking at all with their main weapons. No hits were scored, which is not surprising given the small number of torpedoes fired. Contemporary torpedo officers overrated the power of the individual torpedo. It needed to be fired in quantity and in a tactically coherent manner to fulfil its potential. Significantly, British destroyers did better with their 4in guns. *S32* was temporarily disabled and superficial damage was inflicted on both leading German battleships. *Westfalen*'s captain was slightly wounded.

As HMS *Broke* led the flotilla to the south, she spotted the cruiser *Rostock* again on her starboard beam. The German ship opened fire when challenged and turned to allow the battleship a clear field of fire. *Rostock* was, however, torpedoed and brought to a standstill by either *Contest* or *Ambuscade*, each of which fired one torpedo. The German cruiser drifted through the German battle line and caused some confusion to the Second Squadron. *Broke* was heavily damaged by six hits from *Rostock*'s 5.9in guns and her steering jammed, causing a collision with the destroyer *Sparrowhawk*. The destroyer *Contest* piled into the stricken *Sparrowhawk*, inflicting such damage that the latter had to be abandoned. *Broke* and *Contest* were able to limp to safety.

The six survivors of the Fourth Flotilla made another attack at about 0010 on 1 June. HMS *Fortune*, the leading ship, was set afire by *Westfalen*'s secondary guns and became a target for the rest of the leading German battleships. The British destroyer fired two torpedoes which were avoided as the German ships turned away. She also hit the battleship *Oldenburg* with her 4in guns, causing significant casualties including the battleship's helmsman. A collision was narrowly avoided with the battleship's captain holding her on course himself. The destroyers *Ambuscade*, *Ardent* and *Garland* each fired a torpedo but with no success despite the range being less than 1,500 yards. *Porpoise* was hit and damaged before she could fire. At 0025 *Ardent* mounted a final attack on *Westfalen* whose well-handled secondary batteries, supported by those of *Posen* and probably other ships, pounded the British destroyer to a wreck. Her boiler blew up and she sank. The brave, but badly handled, Fourth Flotilla had shot its bolt. *Tipperary* eventually sank after some abortive attempts by German destroyers to finish her off. The German ships had been preoccupied helping their damaged cruisers and did not succeed in sinking *Broke* after a brief battle with the disabled ship. One of the German torpedo-boats, *S52*, had a brief encounter with the cruiser *Castor* but escaped.

The neighbouring flotillas showed little initiative. While the Fourth Flotilla was smashing itself against the head of the German battle line, the Thirteenth Flotilla, led by the cruiser *Champion*, actually sailed away from the action, apparently feeling that the Fourth Flotilla's engagement prevented it becoming involved. The Eleventh Flotilla did little better. After making some distant torpedo shots at German cruisers, it came under fire from German ships but held its course rather than investigating. The only support for the Fourth Flotilla came from the armoured cruiser *Black Prince* which ran across the battleship *Thuringen* at about 0010. The German battleship and her neighbours opened fire and scored numerous hits from the stern forward with shells of various calibres. *Black Prince* stood little chance and her magazines blew up; she scored two 6in hits on the battleship *Rheinland* before she went down.

The German battleships next ran across a group of destroyers from three separate British flotillas, the Ninth, Fourth and Thirteenth, which had joined up into a single line. The rear of this line was straight in the path of the German fleet and *Westfalen* had no choice but to choose two to bear down on. These were *Petard* and *Turbulent*; the former had no torpedoes and could make no reply to the 5.9in and 3.5in shells that set her on fire. She survived but *Turbulent* was less lucky. She was engaged by both *Westfalen* and *Thuringen* and disabled; she later sank, possibly as a result of a German torpedo-boat's coup de grace. The other British destroyers showed little enterprise and did not attack, despite possessing torpedoes.

The final barrier for Scheer to pass was the Twelfth Flotilla, led by Captain A. J. B. Stirling in the leader *Faulknor*. Two members of the flotilla were absent and there were thus fourteen destroyers and leaders in formation, the leader ahead, two divisions of four on each quarter and five boats astern led by *Marksman*. *Faulknor* spotted enemy ships on the starboard bow but in the misty confusion of the attack *Marksman*'s half flotilla lost contact. Another destroyer, *Mindful*, also separated to make a lone attack because of boiler trouble. The British destroyers were helped by the Germans' expecting their own flotillas to be about and they mounted a spirited attack, shortly after 0200, on the dreadnoughts of the German Fifth Division and the pre-dreadnoughts of the Second Squadron. *Faulknor*, *Obedient*, *Marvel* and *Onslaught* fired twelve torpedoes between them. One of *Obedient*'s torpedoes exploded in the wake of *Kronprinz*, but one of *Onslaught*'s found its mark on *Pommern*. Ships of the last German pre-dreadnought class had very vulnerable magazine arrangements and the 6.7in ammunition seems to have been ignited by the torpedo warhead's explosion. *Pommern* blew up and broke in two and sank with all hands (844 men). *Schleswig-Holstein* was able to get limited revenge with a 6.7in hit on *Onslaught*'s bridge which killed her captain. The Second Division of the Flotilla fired another seven torpedoes but none of these hit. *Champion*, and what was now only a portion of the Thirteenth Flotilla, showed their usual lack of enterprise by not following up this engagement, whose sounds they had overheard. *Moresby*, however, did put in a solo attack on the tail of the German line and fired a torpedo which passed ahead of *Von Der Tann*. This was effectively the last shot of the battle.

During the night several German cripples sank. The most notable was *Lützow*, Hipper's former flagship, which had suffered more hits in the last battlecruiser engagement. The flooding slowly got worse with all four compartments below the armour deck filled. As the forecastle sank, so water gushed in through shell holes in it. The battlecruiser's bows sank deeper and deeper and the water covered her fore turret. An attempt was made to go astern but this failed as the stricken ship could not be steered and the propellers were almost lifted out of the water. At 0055 the decision was taken to abandon *Lützow* and her crew was taken off by the escorting torpedo-boats *G37*, '*38*, '*40* and *V45*. *G38* inflicted the coup de grace at 0145 with a torpedo amidships. The torpedo-boats carrying the 1,250 survivors had a brief brush with the British destroyers *Garland* and *Contest* at about 0225 and, an hour later, with the cruiser *Champion* and destroyers *Obdurate*, *Moresby*, *Maenid* and *Marksman*. *G40* was hit by the one 6in shell fired by the cruiser and she had to be taken in tow.

The damaged German light cruisers also sank shortly after *Lützow* slipped beneath the waves. Only one survivor was picked up by a passing merchantman from the brave *Wiesbaden* which had fought virtually the entire Grand Fleet. *Elbing*, immobile with her collision damage, was scuttled when British destroyers appeared. The torpedoed *Rostock* got under way but her boilers had been damaged and she had to be taken in tow by the torpedo-boat *S54*. Eventually she had to be scuttled, shortly before 0400 when the British light cruiser *Dublin* hove into view.

These losses, however, were almost as nothing to Scheer's success in taking the High Sea Fleet across Jellicoe's rear and back to Germany. Jellicoe was given indications of Scheer's position by the Admiralty but an accurate piece of information received from London at 2305, based on Room 40's work on the High Sea Fleet's orders, was ignored because of the previous error in putting Scheer at his base and, ironically, another previous correct signal based on a erroneous piece of dead-reckoning by its German originator that Jellicoe clearly knew to be in error. The British C-in-C was not kept well informed by his fleet, and what signals he received gave him the impression that Scheer was still to the west.

The Admiralty did not help by failing to pass to Jellicoe all the signals intelligence they had received. Scheer had given orders for Zeppelins to reconnoitre the area of the Horn's Reef and the German destroyer commodore had also given orders for his flotillas to sail there. Neither of these messages, which clearly gave the destination of the High Sea Fleet, reached the C-in-C. Jellicoe later complained bitterly:

'It is impossible to understand this extraordinary omission on the part of the Admiralty Staff but there can be no doubt whatever that the escape of the High Sea Fleet from being engaged in daylight off the Horn's Reef was due to this neglect.'[5]

Jellicoe interpreted the flashes and bangs of the British flotilla action as probes by Scheer's own flotillas to find out whether the route eastwards was clear. No signal mentioning battleships got through to Jellicoe because of a mixture of oversight, preoccupation and defective wireless. British battleships clearly spotted and identified German capital ships but made no reports as they did not want to give away their position to the German flotillas by making numerous wireless transmissions. For the same reason they held their fire even when enemy ships were clearly identified. In any case, the impression on board the British battle line was that the High Sea Fleet was still to the west.

It was not, however. At 0300 on 1 June Scheer was at the Horn's Reef. Jellicoe had turned twenty-one minutes before but it was too late, as was confirmed by a signal received in *Iron Duke* at 0355 from the Admiralty that at 0230 placed Scheer 16 miles to the west of the Horn's Reef lightship. It was clear that the quarry had indeed slipped through the Grand Fleet's fingers and, after a sweep north to try to round up stragglers, the fleet turned for home late on the morning of 1 June. The damaged *Marlborough*, escorted by *Fearless*, had detached earlier and was attacked by *U46* at 1030am. Only one torpedo was fired, which missed. The other British straggler, *Warspite*, had also been attacked by a U-boat, but the two torpedoes fired by *U51* also failed to find the mark.

A Zeppelin, *L11*, spotted units of the British fleet shortly after 0300 on the 1st. She made several sighting reports. The airship was persistently engaged by British ships, sometimes with the main armament, and eventually lost contact at about 0420. *L11* was unable to calculate her position accurately but her reports reassured Scheer that the Grand Fleet was no longer a danger to him.

At 0520 the battleship *Ostfriesland* hit a mine laid by *Abdiel* some weeks earlier and this led to some firing at supposed submarines. Twenty minutes later the badly damaged *Seydlitz* rejoined and took station astern of the pre-dreadnoughts, but her forecastle was now so low in the water that she had to reduce speed to 7 knots. More and more water entered through holes made by previous hits and at 0900 *Seydlitz* went aground for half an hour. She was eventually reduced to crawling astern with over 5,000 tons of water on board. Various craft, including pumping steamers, came to her aid and she staggered back to the entrance to the Jade anchorage, which she reached on the morning of 2 June. Her return had been a major feat of wreck salvage. The rest of the dreadnoughts had passed the outer Jade lightship shortly after noon on 1 June. The Second Squadron anchored in the Elbe. A relieved Scheer ordered champagne for his companions on *Friedrich der Grosse*'s bridge.

RESULTS

The Germans had suffered considerable damage, but only one of their ships had been destroyed suddenly and this limited casualties. Some 2,115 German personnel had lost their lives (844 in *Pommern*, 589 in *Wiesbaden* and 320 in *Frauenlob*) and 80 were wounded. Materiel losses were the battlecruiser *Lützow*, battleship *Pommern*, light cruisers *Wiesbaden*, *Elbing*, *Rostock* and *Frauenlob*, and torpedo-boats *V4*, *V27*, *V29*, *S35* and *V48*. The British lost three battlecruisers, *Invincible*, *Indefatigable* and *Queen Mary*; three armoured cruisers, *Defence*, *Warrior* and *Black Prince*; the flotilla leader *Tipperary* and the destroyers *Ardent*, *Fortune*, *Nestor*, *Nomad*, *Shark*, *Sparrowhawk* and *Turbulent*. 5,672 men were killed (5,069 in the five large ships that blew up), 65 were wounded, and 177 taken prisoner (the latter mainly from the destroyers *Nestor* and *Nomad*).

The British could not fail to be displeased at the balance of casualties and the fact that they had failed to destroy the High Sea Fleet. Nevertheless, their fleet as a whole was able to declare itself ready for action on the morning of 2 June. The British had 24 undamaged dreadnoughts against Scheer's ten. The eight damaged British ships were repaired by the end of July. It was not until 18 August that the High Sea Fleet tried another sortie (still minus *Seydlitz* and *Derfflinger*). Scheer was lucky to escape annihilation when his Zeppelins caused him to alter course southwards in the mistaken belief that the Harwich Force were the detached group of capital ships he was seeking. He thus avoided being cut off by Jellicoe coming down from the north. Scheer had already written to the Kaiser that these attempted spoiling operations would not get Germany anywhere. Instead he put his weight behind using the German U-boats as the main German naval sword, to be employed in unrestricted warfare against British commerce. While they did so, the High Sea Fleet would tie down British naval strength at Scapa and Rosyth by its very existence as a fleet in being. Only the belated introduction of mercantile convoys prevented this strategy from bringing Britain to her knees in 1917.

No more could have been expected from the quantitively inferior High Sea Fleet. The two battlefleets continued to contain each other for the remainder of the war. Contrary to belief, the Germans were not entirely confined to port. Scheer came out again in October 1916 to support his flotillas in an offensive against North Sea shipping, and again in April 1918, but morale in his capital ships began to suffer and mutiny in the fleet played a significant role in Germany's eventual collapse at the end of 1918. Morale stayed higher in the Grand Fleet which passed under Beatty's leadership from November 1916.

The lessons of the battle were studied carefully in the Grand Fleet and applied to improve the chances of inflicting a rapid defeat on the High Sea Fleet should the chance ever again present itself. These improvements went on after the war and made the Royal Navy possibly the finest exponent of night surface action outside Japan. British long-range gunnery became second to none. New technologies began to have their impact also. After the August affair, in which two British light cruisers had been sunk by U-boats (and in which a British submarine torpedoed and damaged the accident-prone German battleship *West-falen*), the movements of the Grand Fleet in the southern North Sea were restricted. Fast British fleet submarines also made their appearance with the Grand Fleet, although their integration with surface ships proved a serious problem. The maturing of the Zeppelin as a reconnaissance asset also led to a major build-up in the Grand Fleet's air forces, both in carriers and individual capital ships and cruisers. By the time large main fleets would clash again, 28 years later, aeroplanes and submarines would not be simply necessary auxiliaries: they would be the main fleet striking forces.

5
THE POST-DREADNOUGHT
REVOLUTION

B ETWEEN 1919 AND 1939 naval warfare underwent a revolution even greater than that of the decade before 1914. This was
not so much a revolution in the existing weapons of the gun
and torpedo, although both did undergo considerable improvement. It was more a coming of age of the aeroplane and the submarine
as platforms that could be even more effective than the surface ship in
the delivery of ship-killing ordnance. This meant that decisive damage
could be inflicted on an enemy before the battlefleets came within gun
range.

Only in the late 1930s did the aeroplane reach this level of
development. For most of the inter-war period aircraft remained limited
to levels of performance not very different from those of the First World
War. Then, in the late 1930s, the development of the 1,000-horsepower
aero-engine transformed the potential of the aeroplane in terms of range,
speed and payload. Suddenly the aircraft developed a maritime striking
potential that took many of its owners somewhat by surprise. Both Japan
and the United States had the resources to develop their naval air arms
to the full, and demonstrate this potential well enough for it to be noted
in naval planning. Britain's Royal Navy was hamstrung by a different
strategic predicament and bureaucratic structure that followed from it.
The United Kingdom believed that it faced the threat of a 'knock-out
blow' from Continental strategic air forces. It therefore put its main air
effort into the development of a well equipped air force for strategic
attack and defence, organized as an independent Royal Air Force. The
conflict of this independent service with the Royal Navy did not create
a favourable environment in either service for the full development of
naval aviation.

Thus it was that by 1939 the Royal Navy had a small air arm still
devoted essentially to the roles of reconnaissance, gunnery spotting,
attacking the enemy battlefleet in harbour, slowing a fleeing enemy down,
putting his line into confusion at the outset of action, and contesting the
other side's similar uses of the air. These roles were not very different

from those accepted in the air doctrines of the US and Japanese Navies, but differences in resources allocated to naval aviation meant that by 1941 their air arms were of a quality and quantity that allowed them to take over much of the primary striking role also.

Both Pacific navies had good reason to emphasize the role of the aircraft in what would now be called precursor operations before the final clash of the battle line. Japan had accepted numerical inferiority in capital ships at the Washington Conference in 1922 and gave great thought to means of inflicting attrition on enemy battlefleets. She developed the 24in oxygen-fuelled 'Long Lance' torpedo which had a range of 21,900 yards at 48–50 knots and 43,700 yards at 36–38 knots with a 1,080lb warhead. The full-sized torpedoes were fitted to her cruisers and destroyers from 1935 onwards, and smaller 21in variants with a range of 13,100 yards at about 46 knots were developed for submarines; 17.7in versions were developed for midget submarines to be carried in ocean-going mother ships. Aircraft carrying 17.7in aerial torpedoes of more conventional design would add their weight to an offensive which, it was hoped, would deliver a decisively damaged and demoralized US battle line on to the guns of the Japanese battlefleet.

The Japanese also took their quest for quality to the battlefleet itself. As well as modernizing their older super-dreadnoughts, they built the largest battleships afloat, the 69,000-ton *Yamato* and *Musashi*, armed with nine 18.1in guns and with armour of 25.6in maximum thickness. Maximum speed was 27 knots. These vessels, laid down in 1937–38, took to an extreme the post-First World War attempt to combine gun power, speed and protection in one hull. Both, however, were to be sunk by aircraft in the last year of the coming war. Even aerial spotting putting the range of guns over the horizon could not counter a threat that could strike at 100 miles or more.

The Americans were faced with the challenge of countering the Japanese quest for technical superiority. Stimulated by the conversion into aircraft-carriers of two large battlecruisers, *Lexington* and *Saratoga*, as a result of the Washington Treaty, the US Navy solved the problems of operating very large numbers of aircraft from individual carriers. This encouraged the development of the concept of the use of carriers in separate 'Task Forces' for offensive purposes, fighting a battle for air-superiority with both the Japanese carriers and the land-based air forces flying from the island possessions with which Japan was well endowed in the Central Pacific. The Americans thus emphasized the development of dive-bombers and fighters for their carriers. Heavily armoured warships were to be left to surface ships, and the torpedo-bomber, the only weapon capable of sinking such vessels, almost died out in the US Navy. American aviators had little patience with its inevitably low performance, but the possibility of torpedo-bombers of more adequate capability resulting from the engine and airframe developments of the 1930s saved the concept. American torpedo-bombing forces were still very weak in 1942 and it is doubtful whether US carriers could actually have sunk Japanese battleships at the time of Midway. They could, and did, however easily sink the other fleet units without which the battleships could not operate, notably the carriers. By 1944 the Grumman Avenger torpedo-bomber was a more than adequate American battleship-killer if loaded accordingly and flown by an appropriately trained crew.

Given this lack of capability against large armoured ships, the Americans provided their carrier task forces with special fast battleships. In 1940 the first two units of the 'Iowa' class were laid down; of 57,540 tons full load displacement, these ships were capable of the exceptionally high speed of 32.5 knots, a similar maximum to that of the contemporary 'Yorktown'-class carriers. They combined this high speed with 12.1in belt armour, 17.3in barbette armour and 19.7in protection on the turret faces. The Japanese used their rebuilt battlecruisers of the 'Kongo' class as heavy gun support ships for their fast carrier task forces.

In April 1941, a few months before the outbreak of the Pacific War, the Japanese had decided to group their carriers together as a concentrated striking fleet to deal with enemy carriers and to strike shore targets. The Japanese emphasized the striking power of their ships with powerful torpedo-bombers (which could double in the level bombing role using heavy high-explosive or armour-piercing bombs), dive-bombers and fighters for the escort of strikes. All were of the highest possible performance, fully up to the standard of the best contemporary land-based aviation. It was the carrier-based torpedo-bombers and the torpedo-dropping long-range bombers of the shore-based 11th Air Fleet that gave the Japanese naval air arm its unique potential against the most heavily protected battleships in 1941. British carrier-based aviation could sink battleships in harbour but only cripple them at sea; Japanese naval aviation could sink them at sea also.

The key to successful torpedo attack was the delivery of sufficient weapons, quickly, to cause catastrophic damage and overwhelm both the enemy's protection and his damage control. This affected surface and sub-surface means of torpedo delivery, as well as airborne. The key development in torpedo warfare in the inter-war years was the recognition that only large numbers of torpedoes could be effective. Destroyer armament in most navies increased to at least eight, and sometimes sixteen, tubes. Two Japanese light cruisers were even given no fewer than 40 tubes in ten quadruple mountings; a more normal Japanese cruiser armament was eight to twelve 24in tubes.

Modern Japanese and American submarines also mounted up to eight multiple tubes in their forward battery to give a good chance of scoring hits on an enemy. US submarines were built to a large 2,410-ton design specially for trans-Pacific operations. They were known as 'fleet' boats, reflecting their role as forward pickets with the main fleet (although they were to achieve their greatest success as commerce raiders). Armed with six tubes forward and four aft, they were formidable boats and available in large numbers. Their only problem was the lack of a reliable torpedo; US torpedoes were defective in both depth-keeping and warhead fusing as late as 1943 and were not fully reliable even by 1944. Japanese submarines were more varied in design and were in two main groups, large fleet reconnaissance boats of 3,500-6,600 tons dived displacement numbered in an 'I' series, some of which carried seaplanes, and smaller boats of 1,350-1,500 tons numbered in the 'RO' series (and armed only with a bow salvo of four tubes). The former tended to be rather too big, the latter too small.

The emphasis on the air threat forced fleet units to improve their capacity to engage aircraft. Destroyers began to acquire dual-purpose main armaments of about 5in calibre and, in both the US and Japanese Navies, tachymetric computer-assisted fire control systems that measured the speed and height of hostile aircraft and worked out fire control solutions for the guns and fuse settings for the shells. These dual-purpose guns and fire control systems also became the secondary armament of cruisers and battleships. Radar was added as a sensor to the American system from 1941, but the Japanese were not to equip themselves with specialized fire control radar before the end of the war. When trade-offs had to be made in ships' weapon fits between dual-purpose guns and light anti-aircraft guns on the one hand and torpedo tubes on the other, it was the latter which were sacrificed.

Anti-submarine warfare (ASW) techniques also became priority activities and the capabilities required also ate into anti-surface weapon space. The main impetus to development in this sphere of naval activity was less the fleet actions but more the campaigns fought in the direct defence of shipping. The submarine gave much greater strength to the 'guerre de course', such extra power that in the Atlantic the U-boats almost neutralized Allied command of the sea gained by superior battlefleet strength. A range of sonar sensors and ASW weapons was developed and refined for this campaign which began to be applied elsewhere in support of the battlefleet. Specialized modern convoy escort types also began to be applied to battlefleet ASW operations – just as fleet destroyers were often used for convoy escort work.

The growing complexity of naval warfare and its expansion into a complex three-dimensional struggle on, above and below the waves led to the development of more sophisticated organization for integrating tactical data. Tactical plots had been developed during the First World War to allow commanders to acquire some idea of the complex events that were taking place around them in a modern fleet action. In the two most electronically advanced navies, the British and the American, spaces began to be set aside during the war where the sensor inputs and the plotting functions could be integrated. In US ships these spaces became known as Combat Information Centres (CIC); in British ships the surface and air plots were separated, the whole being known as 'action information organization'. The need to set aside precious volume for this vital task began to have an effect on the more obvious military capabilities of ships – i.e., their numbers of actual weapons – a tendency that would increase post-war, to the uninformed dismay of many.

Radar direction had a crucial impact on fleet air defence. Before radar the problem of directing fighters on to oncoming raids had seemed almost insuperable. Indeed, the British had, for a time, abandoned the fighter as an instrument of dealing with air attack; British Fleet Air Arm fighters were only intended to deny the enemy air reconnaissance and spotting. Visual warning by scout aircraft and standing fighter patrols offered some protection to those well equipped with aircraft to exploit these techniques, but such defences could be penetrated quite easily, as the Japanese found out at Midway when their fighters were totally wrong-footed by a mix of high-level torpedo-bombers and high-flying dive-bombers. Both the British and the Americans soon mastered radar techniques to direct fighters and control the air battle. This was not just a means of defence. It allowed carriers to use their fighters as effective offensive combat instruments to destroy the enemy's air forces in inherently stronger defensive forms of operations, applying the Clausewitzian advantages of the defensive form of war. Such was to be the path to victory in one of the largest three-dimensional fleet actions in naval history, the only time in fact that large fleets of carriers clashed in combat – the Battle of the Philippine Sea, fought on 19 and 20 June 1944.

6
THE POST-DREADNOUGHT ERA: PHILIPPINE SEA

BOTH THE USA AND JAPAN had long expected that if their rivalry for the control of East Asia and the Pacific came to blows, their essentially naval war would be decided by a fleet action. The Marianas were always a highly probable location for such a battle. These islands stood across the direct route between Pearl Harbor and the Philippines, America's major Asian possession. Most of the Marianas had been taken from Germany by Japan in 1914 and it seemed the natural place for the Japanese to make their main line of resistance to any American advance across the Pacific.

STRATEGIC BACKGROUND

In December 1941 the scale and suddenness of the Japanese attack, especially the carrier air strike as far east as Pearl Harbor, took the Americans by surprise; but once the new Japanese Empire, the 'Great East Asia Co-Prosperity Sphere', was in place the natural American strategic response was to put a version of the old 'Orange' plan into action, an advance across the Pacific from Hawaii, capturing bases in the Marshalls and Carolines, and then advancing to the Marianas. The fact that the latter islands were a vital part of the communications chain to the Japanese South Pacific bases at Truk and Rabaul added to the incentives to take this path. The 'Central Pacific Drive', controlled by Admiral

Nimitz at Pearl Harbor, did not begin until the end of 1943, while the Americans built up overwhelming strength and debated strategic options. The main focus of the Pacific War in the second half of 1942 and throughout 1943 had been in the south-western part of the Pacific theatre where the Japanese had been drawn into a debilitating campaign of attrition in the Solomons and New Guinea. General MacArthur, the local commander, wanted to make this the main axis of the advance against Japan but Admiral King, Chief of Naval Operations and overall US Fleet Commander, insisted on the basic 'Orange' scenario, part of whose rationale was drawing the Japanese Navy into a decisive battle. King had an ally in the head of the US Army Air Forces, General Arnold, who wanted a base for his Boeing B-29 bombers close enough to carry out a strategic air offensive against the Japanese home islands.

When the American Central Pacific drive opened with an attack on the Gilberts in November, the future direction of the American thrust had still not been settled. A two-pronged compromise, with combined Central Pacific and South-Western Pacific drives, was agreed in principle before the end of the year but it was not until March, when the Central Pacific forces moved on to the Marshalls, that it was finally decided to assault the Marianas in mid-June 1944.

With the Americans undecided about the direction of their own thrust, it was hardly surprising that the Japanese should be undecided as to where they should place their counter-blow. They did, however, plan to strike the next American thrust with the full strength of their still powerful battlefleet. At the beginning of March this was formed into a new structure, First Mobile Fleet, effectively placing the surface forces, including the battleships, under the command of Japan's carrier fleet commander, Vice-Admiral Jisaburo Ozawa. The Japanese toyed with the idea of unleashing this force on the US fleet at its advance base at Majuro in the Marshalls, but the death of Admiral Koga, Combined Fleet Commander and Ozawa's superior, threw these plans out of gear. The new Combined Fleet Commander was Admiral Soemu Toyoda, who hoisted his flag on 2 May 1944. The following day he issued Combined Fleet Order 76 that set out plan 'A-Go', a combined offensive by the First Mobile Fleet and the land-based First Air Fleet (as it had now become) when the Americans revealed their hand and moved further westward.

The Japanese were short of oil because of the depredations of American submarines against their tankers and relied on the Borneo oilfields of Tarakan and Balikpapan for their fleet. Refinery capacity was limited and this retricted Japanese activities. If the Americans assaulted the Marianas rather than take the southern route, they would have to be confronted by land-based air power and forced southwards into Ozawa's jaws. These plans were soon changed to allow the First Mobile Fleet to operate in a more forward defence of the Marianas. This was through the expedient of loading Tarakan crude oil direct into the tankers and then into the bunkers of the fleet at its advanced anchorage at Tawi-Tawi, at the western end of the Sulu Archipelago in the southern Philippines. Tawi-Tawi was a well placed base to cover the heart of Japan's 'Co-Prosperity Sphere' and it was less than 200 miles from the Tarakan oilfields. Yet it had serious disadvantages, notably the lack of an airfield to help train carrier air groups, and it was also in waters infested by US submarines. Nevertheless, First Mobile Fleet concentrated at Tawi-Tawi on 16 May 1944.

Both sides deployed their submarines to reconnoitre and, if possible, inflict attrition on the enemy. The USS *Lapon* spotted a powerful force of carriers off the west coast of Borneo on 13 May and the USS *Bonefish* was ordered to carry out a surveillance operation on Tawi-Tawi. On the way her captain fired five torpedoes at a small tanker convoy heading for Tawi-Tawi, and sank a tanker and a destroyer. On 16 May the submarine examined the anchorage and saw the majestic strength of Ozawa's fleet deployed there. Only having one torpedo left, *Bonefish* could do little but report their presence. More submarines were brought in, *Puffer* and *Bluefish*, which attacked units of the Mobile Fleet out on training exercises. *Puffer* fired six torpedoes at the carrier *Chitose*, but although one scored a hit none exploded. This and submarine sightings by the Japanese had the important effect of forcing the Japanese to stay in the protected anchorage, preventing the carriers from engaging in any flying. More demonstrations of the submarine danger kept occurring. *Puffer* had better luck on 5 June when she despatched the aircraft stores ships *Ashizuri* and *Takasaki* in the Sulu Sea. On 6/7 June near Tawi-Tawi, the USS *Harder* sank three Japanese detroyers around the anchorage, a clear demonstration of the powerlessness of the Japanese to do much about the American submarine threat.

Japanese submarine operations had less positive results; indeed, they were little short of disastrous. A patrol line of new 600-ton coastal submarines of the 'KS' class, code-named 'NA', was set up 120 miles south-east of the Admiralty Islands. Thanks to American signals intelligence, the position of these submarines became known and a small ad hoc hunter-killer group, made up of three destroyer escorts, was sent to deal with it: this consisted of the USS *George, Raby* and *England*. The first victim was not a member of the line but the large submarine *I16* on a supply mission to Bougainville. She was sunk on 19 May by at least two hits by *England*'s 'Hedgehog' ahead-throwing weapons. The first 'NA' boat, *R106*, was found on the surface by aircraft flying from Manus. The three DEs were guided in and the Japananese submarine was detected on radar very early on 22 May at 14–15,000 yards. *R106* dived when the

Americans switched on their searchlights, but *England* gained a sonar contact at 2,500 yards and sank her with her second 'Hedgehog' salvo. On the following day, 23 May, *Raby* detected *RO-104* on the surface with her radar. The little submarine outmanoeuvred *Raby* and *George* and used her own sonar to confuse the American DEs. The latter made a number of attacks but it was the lucky *England* which scored a hit with her first 'Hedgehog' salvo and sank *RO-104*. The group now systematically set about the rest of the line. Just after midnight on the 24th *George* spotted a target, *RO-116*, at 14,000 yards; it was caught by *England* on her sonar and was sunk by her third 'Hedgehog' salvo with three bomb hits. Later on the 25th, as the group headed for Manus to replenish, it found *RO-108;* again it was *England*'s Hedgehog' which sank the Japanese coastal submarine with its first salvo. One American destroyer escort had been responsible for the loss of one large and four small Japanese submarines.

At Seeadler Harbour at Manus, these three DEs became part of a larger hunter-killer group based around the escort carrier *Hoggatt Bay*. It consisted additionally of the 'Fletcher'-class fleet destroyers *Hazelwood, McCord, Hoel* and *Heerman* and the DE *Spangler*. This group returned to hunt the remnants of the 'NA' line. After a prolonged engagement with *RO-105* on 30–31 May, *England* eventually delivered the coup de grace with six 'Hedgehog' hits. It was the sixth kill in thirteen days for one ship, which received a well earned Presidential Unit Citation. Admiral King signalled: 'There'll always be an England in the United States Navy.' The remarkable achievement was due to good signals intelligence, ASW sensors and weapons well suited to the relatively shallow conditions, good team work with the rest of the ASW group and a well run ship with an excellent executive officer, Lieutenant J. A. Williamson of the USN Reserve.

Other members of the Japanese submarine picket line did little better. In all, eleven other Japanese submarines, including *RO-111* from the ill-fated 'NA' line, were sunk by American surface ships and aircraft in the area of 'A-Go' operations between 17 May and 19 June. It was a crushing vindication of the maturity of American ASW technique after three years' hard education in the Atlantic theatre.

With their submarine pickets demolished, the Japanese had even less idea where the American blow would fall. The focus of the submarine losses seemed still to indicate a southern drive. Toyoda placed his forces on six-hour alert on 20 May with the signal 'Start A-Go'. The following day Admiral Ozawa called his commanders to meet on board his flagship, the new carrier *Taiho*. He emphasized that the coming encounter was to be a decisive battle. All units, including gun- and torpedo-armed surface ships, were to press home attacks regardless of damage suffered. All ships were to be considered expendable.

On 27 May the South-West Pacific forces invaded the island of Biak off the north coast of New Guinea. This caused much uncertainty to the Japanese command, who moved forces, especially land-based air squadrons, southwards both to reinforce the defenders and to be ready if the attack presaged a movement of the US fleet. On 10 June Ozawa despatched a no lesser force than the *Yamato* and *Musashi* to the south: it was attacked, unsuccessfully, by the pugnacious submarine *Harder*.

On 11 June the American Fast Carrier Task Force 58 began its softening up of the Marianas with a sweep by Hellcat fighters (over 200 aircraft in all) against the Marianas airfields. This lost eleven aircraft but destroyed thirty-six Japanese in the air and on the ground and put out of action about a third of the available Japanese land-based aircraft upon which great hopes had been placed. Overnight Mitsubishi G4M 'Betty' torpedo-bombers from Truk attacked the northernmost of the American carrier task groups: no hits were scored and one 'Betty' was shot down. Attacks on Saipan, Guam, Tinian and Rota were repeated on the morning of the 12th, 468 sorties in all, directed against both airfields and shore installations. By 13 June there could be no doubt that the Marianas were the major target. At 0900 that day the First Mobile Fleet sailed on an already planned sortie to find better bases in the Philippines. This became a combat sortie as Ozawa made up his mind about American intentions. At 1727 he signalled 'Prepare for "A-Go" Decisive Operation'; the forces sent south were ordered to rendezvous with the rest of the fleet in the Philippine Sea. The main body of First Mobile Fleet, its departure noted by the US submarine *Redfin*, made first for the Guimaras anchorage between Panay and Negros, which it reached on the 14th to refuel.

At 0844 on 15 June, a week after the Normandy landings in Europe, US Marines hit the beach on Saipan. Eleven minutes later Admiral Toyoda sent First Mobile Fleet the following order: 'On the morning of the 15th a strong enemy force began landing operations in the Saipan-Tinian area. The Combined Fleet will attack the enemy in the Marianas area and annihilate the invasion force. Activate "A-Go" Operation for decisive battle.' Five minutes later he sent Togo's Nelsonic signal of just over thirty-nine years before: 'The rise and fall of Imperial Japan depends on this one battle. Every man shall do his utmost.'[1] The result of this battle would be as far removed from Tsushima as was the technology with which it was fought. It would, however, be equally decisive for the rise, and fall, of Japanese naval power.

THE JAPANESE FORCES

The core of First Mobile Fleet was made up of three carrier divisions. The Japanese were still suffering the effects of the losses – notably four carriers – at Midway two years earlier and it had been a struggle to fill the gap in their forces. Only the First Carrier Squadron, commanded by Admiral Ozawa himself, was made up of fully first-rate fleet carriers. Its flagship was the 37,720-ton (full load displacement) *Taiho*, completed only three months before. She was an excellent ship, modelled after British practice with a 3.1in armoured flight deck. Unlike the smaller British ships, however, she was built to carry a large air group of 75 aircraft, 27 A6M5 'Zero' fighters, 27 D4Y1 'Judy' dive-bombers, 3 D4Y1C 'Judy' reconnaissance aircraft and 18 B6N1 'Jill' torpedo-bombers. Defensive AA armament comprised twelve 3.9in and seventy-one 25mm guns. In support were the two veterans of Pearl Harbor and the Coral Sea that had missed the Battle of Midway, *Shokaku* and *Zuikaku*. These 32,105-ton carriers had armoured hulls but unprotected hangars and decks. Each carried an air group of the same composition as *Taiho*'s. Their defensive armament was sixteen 5in dual-purpose guns and seventy 25mm light AA. The carriers were screened by two 13,120-ton heavy cruisers, the sisters *Myoko* and *Haguro*, each armed with ten 8in guns, eight 5in dual-purpose secondary batteries and twenty-four 25mm light anti-aircraft guns. The rest of the screen was provided by the Tenth Destroyer Flotilla. This was led by the 8,500-ton, 6in-gun cruiser *Yahagi* and consisted of a mixed group of seven modern destroyers. Four, *Akitsuki*, *Wakatsuki*, *Hatsusuki* and *Shimotsuki*, were fine new 3,700-ton vessels built especially for carrier escort and each armed with four twin 3.9in rapid-firing dual-purpose guns and twenty-nine 25mm light AA guns. Torpedo armament was limited to four 24in tubes but 72 depth-charges were carried. The other three were of the slightly older 'Kagero' class, *Urakaze* and *Isokaze* and 'Asashio' class, *Asagumo*. These 2,330–2,450-ton ships had been originally built for surface action with eight 24in torpedo tubes and six 5in guns in three twin mounts, one forward and two aft. One of the after mountings was removed in 1943–44 to allow the addition of up to twenty-eight 25mm light AA guns. The number of depth-charges was also increased from 16 to 36. This had the effect of increasing displacement, the load displacement of a modified 'Asashio' reaching 2,635 tons. The more classical destroyers and the cruisers could make 35 knots, but the newer *Taiho* and the 'Akitsuki'-class destroyers were limited to about 33 knots; the two 'Shokakus' could make over 34 knots. The whole battle group was designated Force 'A'.

The Second Carrier Squadron was somewhat slower as it was made up of three carriers converted from non-combatant vessels. *Junyo* and *Hiyo* had both been laid down in 1939 as liners but they had been taken over while under construction in 1940 for conversion into carriers. They displaced over 28,000 tons full load and could carry 51 aircraft each; they were very vulnerable to both aerial and underwater attack, having virtually no armour and poor watertight subdivision. Their air groups were made up of 18 'Zero' fighters, 9 'Zero' fighter-bombers, 18 dive-bombers (9 'Judys' and nine older D3A 'Vals' in *Junyo*, 18 'Vals' in *Hiyo*) and 6 'Jill' torpedo-bombers. Defensive armament was twelve 5in dual-purpose guns and forty 25mm light AA guns. The third carrier was the 16,700-ton *Ryuho*, a small light carrier converted in 1941 from the submarine depot ship *Taigei*. The conversion was not considered successful and she was used mainly for training; her presence in the battle line was a sign of Japanese weakness. Her air group comprised only 33 aircraft, 18 'Zero' fighters, 9 'Zero' fighter-bombers and 6 'Jill' torpedo-bombers. Defensive armament was eight 5in dual-purpose guns and forty-two 25mm light AA weapons. Like her two larger companions, she was a weak ship and somewhat slow; although in theory capable of 25–26 knots, the true maximum speed of the group was only 22–23 knots.

The Second Carrier Squadron, commanded by Rear Admiral Joshima flying his flag in the carrier *Junyo*, was slow enough to be allocated a 25-knot battleship as part of its battle group: the 43,000-ton *Nagato*, completed in 1920 but rebuilt in the mid-1930s. She was armed with eight 16in and sixteen 5.5in guns, but more useful were the eight 5in dual-purpose guns and a recently enhanced armament of sixty-eight 25mm light AA weapons. Also assigned was the 13,670-ton heavy cruiser *Mogami*, rebuilt after the Battle of Midway with enhanced seaplane arrangements, six 8in guns, eight 5in dual-purpose and thirty 25mm light AA guns. The destroyer screen was made up of eight ships from two separate flotillas. The Fourth Destroyer Group of the Tenth Flotilla comprised two 'Asashios,' *Michishio* and *Yamagumo* and the 'Kagero' *Nowaki;* the Twenty-Seventh Destroyer Group of the Second Flotilla was a mix of two older 2,000-ton 'Shiratsyus', *Shigure* and *Samidare*, the 'Kagero' *Hamakaze*, and the new 2,500-ton 'Yugumo'-class fleet destroyers *Hayashimo* and *Akashimo*. All were armed with two twin 5in dual-purpose mountings and eight torpedo tubes for 'Long Lances'; up to twenty-eight 25mm light AA guns were carried. This battle group made up Force 'B'.

The weakest Japanese aircraft-carrier squadron was the Third, commanded by Rear Admiral Obayashi in the light carrier *Chitose*. She and her sister *Chiyoda*, the squadron's second unit, had been built in the 1930s as seaplane/midget submarine-carriers; they were converted into 15,000-ton light aircraft-carriers as an emergency measure after Midway.

They carried only 30 aircraft each, 6 'Zero' fighters and 15 'Zero' fighter-bombers, with 3 'Jill' and 6 older B5N 'Kate' torpedo-bombers. Defensive armament was eight 5in dual-purpose guns and forty-eight 25mm AA guns. The third member of the squadron was the slightly smaller 14,200-ton *Zuiho*, originally completed as the submarine support ship *Takasaki* and converted as part of pre-war mobilization. She was armed and equipped like *Chitose* and *Chiyoda*. These ships could all make 28 knots. They were grouped in a mixed carrier/surface battle group, Force 'C', under the command of Vice-Admiral Takeo Kurita flying his flag in the heavy cruiser *Atago*. The surface component, or 'Heavy Screen Group', was an extremely powerful combination of:

(a) *First Squadron*:[1] The pair of giant 71,659-ton (full load) battleships *Yamato* and *Musashi* armed with nine 18.1in guns and six 6in guns. *Yamato* had an anti-aircraft armament of twenty-four 5in and ninety-eight 25mm guns: her sister mounted only twelve 5in guns but 116 25mm weapons. Both super battleships had lost two triple 6in low-angle mountings on each beam to make space for more anti-aircraft weapons. Maximum speed was 27 knots.

(b) *Third Squadron*: The two surviving fast battleship rebuilds of the First World War 'Kongo'-class battlecruisers, *Kongo* and *Haruna*. These displaced about 35,000 tons and were armed with four twin 14in turrets, eight 6in guns with twelve 5in and thirty-four 25mm AA guns. Maximum speed was 30.5 knots.

(c) *Fourth Squadron*: The four powerful 35.5-knot 'Takao'-class cruisers, *Atago*, *Takao*, *Chokai* and *Maya*, built at the beginning of the 1930s and modernized between 1938 and 1942. *Takao* and *Atago* displaced 15,781 tons full load and carried five twin 8in gun mounts, five twin 5in dual-purpose gun mounts, twenty-six 25mm AA guns and sixteen 24in torpedo tubes; *Chokai* was less extensively modernized and only had eight 5in guns and eight torpedo tubes; *Maya*, badly damaged the previous year, carried only four main turrets but instead had six twin 5in AA mounts, thirty 25mm light AA guns and eight tubes.

(d) *Seventh Squadron*: The pair of 12,400-ton (standard) 'Mogami'-class cruisers, still armed with five twin 8in gun mountings, eight 5in dual-purpose guns and thirty 25mm AA guns; plus the pair of 11,215-ton 'Tone'-class cruisers built for scouting duties with carrier forces and armed with eight 8in guns forward, eight 5in dual-purpose guns, twelve 25mm light AA guns, twelve 24in torpedo tubes and five seaplanes; all members of the squadron were capable of 35 knots.

(e) *Destroyer Screen*: This was made up of most of the Second Destroyer Flotilla led by the cruiser *Noshiro*, a sister of *Yahagi*, and consisting of the 'Yugumo'-class ships *Asashimo*, *Kishinami*, *Okinami* and *Tamanami*, the earlier 'Kagero' *Hamakaze* and the 3,000-ton experimental 40-knot destroyer *Shimakaze* armed with eight 5in guns, twenty-five 25mm guns and fifteen 24in torpedo tubes.

In support of these three main battle groups were two Supply Forces. One comprised the newly built fleet tanker/seaplane-carrier *Hayasui* and three converted merchant tankers, *Nichei Maru, Kokuyo Maru* and *Seiyo Maru*. These were escorted by the older 1932–33 'Special Type' destroyers *Hibiki* and *Hatsushima,* the old 1920-vintage second-class destroyer *Tsuga* and the new 1,500-ton destroyer escort *Yunagi*. The Second Supply Force had two former merchant tankers, *Genyo Maru* and *Azusa Maru,* escorted by the 'Kagero'-class destroyer *Yukikaze* and the 1920s destroyer *Uzuki*.

THE AMERICAN FORCES

The extremely powerful main US fleet in the Central Pacific was numbered the Fifth when commanded by Admiral Raymond A. Spruance and his staff and the Third when commanded by Admiral Halsey. Spruance was in command for the Marianas operation and the Admiral flew his flag in the 12,755-ton (full load) heavy cruiser *Indianapolis,* specially fitted out as a flagship and armed with nine 8in guns. The main fighting component of the Fifth Fleet was Task Force 58, commanded by Vice-Admiral Marc A. Mitscher flying his flag in the carrier *Lexington*. TF58 was composed of four Carrier Task Groups and a Heavy Surface Strike Group. The main equipment of the carrier task group was the 35,000-ton 'Essex'-class fleet carrier and the 15,000-ton 'Independence'-class light fleet carrier.

The 'Essex' class were excellent carriers with a complement of up to 98 aircraft, making them the most powerful warships in the world. Their hangars were open and unprotected, allowing aircraft to be warmed up in the hangar for the rapid launch of large air strikes. The hulls were armoured with belts of 4in maximum thickness, hangar deck protection of 2.5in and internal armoured decks over the belt of 1.5in. Defensive armament was twelve 5in dual-purpose guns, sixty-eight 40mm AA guns and fifty-two 20mm AA guns. Maximum speed was 32.7 knots. The 'Essex' class had been laid down under the 1940 'Two-Ocean Navy' programme and the first, *Essex,* had been launched in July 1942. Six were available to Spruance by June 1944.

The 'Independence' light carriers were an emergency programme designed to provide additional carrier hulls rapidly. They were built on standard 11,000-ton 'Cleveland'-class light cruiser hulls and all nine were commissioned in 1943. Spruance had all but one of the class available off the Marianas. They could each carry up to 35 aircraft, mainly fighters, and allowed the fleet carriers greater concentration on the strike role. The ships were armed with twenty-six 40mm and forty 20mm AA guns and all but *Independence* and *Princeton* had 5in armoured belts. All ships had a 2in armoured main deck. They could make 31.6 knots.

Task Group 58.1 was composed of the 'Essexes' *Yorktown* (flagship of Rear Admiral Ralph E. Davison) and *Hornet* and the light carriers *Belleau Wood* and *Bataan*. *Yorktown* carried 42 F6F-3 Hellcat fighters, 40 SB2C-1C Helldiver dive-bombers, 4 SBD-5 Dauntless dive-bombers, 17 TBF/TBM-1C Avenger torpedo-bombers and 4 F6F-3N Hellcat night fighters; *Essex* had 37 Hellcats, 33 Helldivers, 18 Avengers and 4 Hellcat night fighters. *Belleau Wood* had 26 Hellcats and *Bataan* 24, while both light carriers carried 9 Avengers. In support of TG58.1 were the first three 17,031-ton (full load) heavy cruisers of the 'Baltimore' class, *Baltimore, Boston* and *Canberra*, all commissioned in 1943 and armed with nine 8in guns, twelve 5in dual-purpose, thirty-eight 40mm and twenty-four 20mm AA guns.

The Group Screen was headed by the 8,340-ton (full load) AA cruiser *Oakland* armed with twelve 5in dual-purpose, sixteen 40mm and sixteen 20mm AA guns and six 21in torpedo tubes; she led two Destroyer Squadrons (DesRons). DesRon 46 had both its divisions, Destroyer Division (DesDiv) 91 with *Izard, Charette, Conner, Bell* and *Burns*, and DesDiv 92 with *Boyd, Bradford, Brown* and *Cowell*. All were new and powerful 2,924-ton (full load) 'Fletcher'-class ships, probably the best destroyers of their time and armed with five single 5in dual-purpose guns, up to ten 40mm and seven 20mm AA guns and ten 21in torpedo tubes. DesRon 6, composed only of DesDiv 11, was made up of the four older 2,219-ton (full load) pre-war destroyers of the 'Gridley' class, *Maury, Craven, Gridley* and *McCall* and the 2,245-ton 'Bagley'-class destroyer *Helm*. These were primarily surface warfare vessels with high speed (38.5 knots) and heavy torpedo armaments of sixteen 21in tubes each. All mounted four 5in dual-purpose guns. The 'Gridleys' could mount no AA guns bigger than 20mm (up to eight), but *Helm* carried a twin 40mm AA mounting and six 20mm weapons.

Task Group 58.2, commanded by Rear Admiral Alfred E. Montgomery in the carrier *Bunker Hill*, consisted of two 'Essexes', *Bunker Hill* with 38 Hellcats, 33 Helldivers, 18 Avengers and 4 Hellcat night fighters, and *Wasp* with 35 Hellcats, 32 Helldivers, 18 Avengers and 4 Hellcat night fighters. The two CVLs were *Monterey* (21 Hellcats and 8 Avengers) and *Cabot* (24 Hellcats and 9 Avengers). In support were the 14,131-ton (full load) 'Cleveland'-class light cruisers *Santa Fe, Mobile* and *Biloxi*, armed with twelve 6in guns, twelve 5in dual-purpose, twenty-four to twenty-eight 40mm AA guns and twenty-one 20mm weapons. The screen was composed of the 'Atlanta'-class AA cruiser *San Juan*, one of the older units armed with sixteen 5in guns, a squadron (DesRon 52) of

'Fletchers', *Owen, Miller, Tingey, The Sullivans, Stephen Potter, Hickox, Hunt, Lewis Hancock* and *Marshall,* and a small DesRon 1 composed of three pre-war 'Farraguts', *MacDonough, Dewey* and *Hull,* 2,064-ton (full load) vessels armed with four 5in dual-purpose guns, two twin 40mm AA guns, five 20mm guns and eight 21in torpedo tubes.

Task Group 58.3, the nerve centre of TF58, contained the last remaining veteran of the original Pacific War battles, the 25,484-ton (full load) fleet carrier *Enterprise,* commissioned in 1938. She had a maximum speed of 32.5 knots, 4in armoured belt, and a 1.5in armoured main deck. Defensive armament was eight 5in guns, forty 40mm and forty 20mm guns and she carried 31 Hellcats, 21 Dauntlesses, 14 Avengers and 3 F4U-2 Corsair night fighters. She carried the flag of Rear Admiral John W. Reeves, Group Commander, and was accompanied by: *Lexington,* the Task Force flagship, with 37 Hellcats, 34 Dauntlesses, 18 Avengers and 4 Hellcat night fighters; and two CVLs, *San Jacinto* and *Princeton,* each with 24 Hellcats and, respectively, 8 and 9 Avengers. The cruiser support unit consisted of the 'Cleveland'-class light cruisers *Cleveland, Montpelier* and *Birmingham,* with Spruance's flagship *Indianapolis* attached. The destroyer squadron, led by the AA cruiser *Reno* (twelve 5in guns), was the entirely 'Fletcher'-equipped DesRon 50 with three Divisions: 90, *Anthony, Wadsworth, Terry* and *Braine;* 99, *Clarence K. Bronson, Cotten, Dortch, Gatling* and *Healey;* and 100, *Cogswell, Caperton, Ingersoll* and *Knapp.*

The weakest Task Group was 58.4 commanded by Rear Admiral William K. Harrill. This had only one 'Essex', *Essex* herself with 38 Hellcats, 36 Helldivers, 20 Avengers and 4 Hellcat night fighters. The two CVLs were *Langley* and *Cowpens,* each with 23 Hellcats and 9 Avengers. The cruisers of the support unit were the 'Cleveland'-class light cruisers *Vincennes, Houston* and *Miami.* The screen was made up of the AA cruiser *San Diego* (sixteen 5in guns) and two Destroyer Squadrons. DesRon 12 had two Divisions: 4 with the 'Fletchers' *Lang, Wilson, Sterrett* and *Ellet:* and 23 with the slightly older 2,515-ton (full load) 'Gleaves'-class *Lansdowne, McCalla* and *Lardner* with four 5in guns, four 40mm and six to seven 20mm AA guns and five 21in torpedo tubes, and the 2,100-ton pre-war 'Mahan'-class destroyer *Case* (four 5in guns, two twin 40mm and five 20mm guns, and twelve 21in torpedo tubes). DesRon 23 was composed of 'Fletchers', DesDiv 45 with *Charles F. Ausburne, Stanley* and *Dyson;* and DesDiv 46 with *Converse, Spence* and *Thatcher.*

The final Task Group was TG58.7, the Heavy Surface Strike Group, commanded by Vice-Admiral Willis A. Lee and including seven modern battleships, each armed with nine 16in guns. These ships were intended to support the carriers with both heavy gunfire, if required, and with AA protection. The ships were of three classes. *Washington* (flagship) and *North Carolina* were the first two US battleships of post-First World War conception, both commissioned in 1941. Displacing 44,377 tons full load, they had 12in belt and 16in turret armour and could make 28 knots. Secondary armament comprised twenty 5in dual-purpose guns, sixty 40mm guns and fifty-six 20mm weapons. Next came the 44,519-ton (full load) 'South Dakotas' completed in 1942, *South Dakota, Indiana* and *Alabama,* built shorter with heavier 13in belt and 18in turret protection. *South Dakota* had sixteen 5in and sixty-eight 40mm guns; the other two ships had twenty 5in dual-purpose guns and fifty-six 40mm. All carried forty 20mm guns. Speed was 27.5 knots. Finally, there were the first two of the fast 57,500-ton (full load) 'Iowas', specially built to support the carriers. *Iowa* and *New Jersey* were 200ft longer than the 'South Dakotas' and their 212,000shp engines (compared with 130,000shp in the earlier ships) could drive them at 32.5 knots. Armour was 13in thick on the belt and 19.7in on the turrets. Secondary armament comprised twenty 5in dual-purpose guns and, respectively, sixty and sixty-four 40mm light AA guns plus sixty 20mm weapons. The nine 16in guns of the main battery of these two ships were also more powerful 50-calibre weapons, compared with the 45-calibre tubes of the earlier vessels. Both had been completed in 1943.

The battleships were supported by four 33-knot heavy cruisers, each armed with nine 8in guns. *Wichita,* completed in 1939, was a unique ship of just over 13,000 tons full load displacement. As lighter armament she carried eight single 5in, twenty 40mm and twenty 20mm guns. The other three were most of the survivors of the 'New Orleans' class, *New Orleans, San Francisco* and *Minneapolis.* Their secondary armament comprised eight single 5in, sixteen 40mm and nineteen 20mm guns. All had been completed in 1934. The screen was made up of two Destroyer Squadrons. DesRon 45 had two divisions; DesDiv 24 of older destroyers, *Bagley, Mugford* and *Patterson* of the 'Bagley' class, *Conyngham* of the 'Mahan' class and *Selfridge,* a large 2,600-ton leader of the 'Porter' class (two twin and one single 5in mounts, two twin 40mm guns, six 20mm guns and eight 21in torpedo tubes); and DesDiv 89 with five 'Fletchers', *Halford, Guest, Bennett, Fullam* and *Hudson.* DesRon 53 had only one division, DesDiv 106 with four 'Fletchers', *Yarnall, Twining, Stockton* and *Monssen.*

TF58 was a naval force of awesome striking power with 902 carrier aircraft, double the 450 available to the Japanese. The US surface ships were also much better equipped for anti-air warfare. This was due partly to the fact that so many of them had been completed since 1941, an indication of the USA's extraordinary powers of production. In addition to the TF58 forces mentioned above, there were older battleships and escort carriers assigned to the direct support of the Marianas landings.

More directly concerned with the fleet action were the US submarines operating as a distant reconnaissance and striking line. There were four packs of these boats operating in support of Spruance: one, with *Gar*, *Archerfish*, *Plunger*, *Plaice* and *Salmon*, operating around the Bonins; another, with *Pintado*, *Pilotfish* and *Tunny* to the south-east and east of Formosa; a third, with *Albacore*, *Seawolf*, *Bang*, *Finback* and *Stingray*, was west and south-west of the Marianas; while a fourth, *Flying Fish*, *Muskallunge*, *Cavalla*, *Seahorse*, *Pipefish* and *Growler*, was operating near Ulithi in the Philippines. These were of a number of related classes of 'fleet submarine' of 2,000–2,400 tons submerged displacement, launched from 1936 onwards. The older boats had only four tubes fore and aft but the later boats, launched from 1939 onwards, had a six-tube forward salvo, significantly increasing their striking power. They could make about 20 knots on the surface and 8–9 knots submerged.

AIR AND ANTI-AIR WARFARE

The key to the Battle of the Philippine Sea would be less gunnery and torpedo work per se, but much more general proficiency in air and anti-air warfare. This had three dimensions: (a) the quality of the two sides' aircraft and pilots; (b) the techniques of fighter control used; and (c) the quality of the anti-aircraft gun defence systems on both sides. These will be discussed in turn. One important point, however, ought to be reiterated. Often anti-air warfare is seen purely in terms of 'air defence'. In fact, the capacity of a fleet to destroy the aircraft attacking it is an important part of its *offensive* fighting capability. Drawing the enemy into making air attacks is like drawing out his surface units. If they expose themselves by attacking, they make themselves subject to engagement, engagement moreover where the Clausewitzian advantages of the defender are on the side of the forces being attacked. The destruction of an attacking air fleet is an offensive fleet engagement like any other.

Quality of Aircraft and Pilots

The Americans were in a much better situation than the Japanese with respect to both aircraft and pilot quality. The standard US Navy fighter, the F6F-3 Hellcat, was slightly faster than the 'Zero' in its latest A6M5 version at 375mph against 350. The F6F was heavier and more robust with an engine of almost twice the power. Its six 0.5in heavy machine-guns could inflict terrible damage on the lightly built Japanese machines. The 'Zero' was quite well armed with two 20mm cannon and three machine-guns but lacked both armour and self-sealing fuel tanks. Only the latest A6M5b versions carried by *Chitose*, *Chiyoda* and *Zuiho* had armoured glass windscreens and automatic fire-extinguishers. Japanese fighter advantages were in manoeuvrability and rate of climb, but the Japanese fighter pilots were in no position to exploit these characteristics. Japanese training had suffered badly through fuel shortages and the need to replace the heavy casualties of 1942–44. During the winter of 1943–44 advanced combat training had been abandoned for the best pilots coming out of elementary/intermediate training, and although this decision was reversed in the spring of 1944, the damage had been done. Many potentially good pilots had been killed prematurely on operations. A very large proportion of the Japanese pilots in First Mobile Fleet were fresh out of training school with little, if any, combat experience. The average Japanese naval pilot had only 275 hours of flying time compared with 525 for an American.

A major reorganization of Japanese air groups had been undertaken in February 1944. Air groups had been formed for groups of carriers. Air Group 601 covered the fleet carriers *Taiho*, *Shokaku* and *Zuikaku*. It consisted of skilled survivors of previous battles, seaplane pilots and freshly trained personnel. It had been able to carry out training at Singapore but the inability to carry out flight operations around the Tawi-Tawi base caused a degradation of flying skills. Air Group 652 covered *Junyo*, *Hiyo* and *Ryuho* and had suffered serious attrition in the fighting around Rabaul in early 1944. The replacements for these losses were hastily gathered together in Japan where fuel was short. The 'Zero' fighter-bombers were flown by bomber pilots with little, or no, air combat experience. The combat capability of the group was considered to be 'modest'. Again, deployment to Tawi-Tawi prevented any further training in the period just prior to the battle. Air Group 653 (*Chitose*, *Chiyoda* and *Zuiho*) was in almost as bad shape. The majority of its pilots were of the September 1943 or January 1944 graduating classes, probably mainly the less able members of these groups who had received advanced training but who had had no combat experience. Average pilot training times for each group were six months for 601, two months for 652 and three months for 653. Before the war pilots had averaged forty-two months of training!

All this was bad enough, but the Japanese aircraft depended on the *superior* pilot skill that had been displayed by the first generation of Japanese pilots in the months after December 1941. Both the new Yokosuka D4Y-1 Suisei ('Comet') dive-bomber (Allied code-name 'Judy') and the Nakajima B6N-1 Tenzan ('Heavenly Mountain') torpedo-bomber ('Jill') were fast and manoeuvrable, being significantly lighter than their US counterparts. The 'Judy' had a loaded weight to power ratio of only 6.9lb/hp and the 'Jill' only 6 compared with their American counterparts' 7.4 and 8.6. Their range was also significantly better, but they were also harder to fly. The Japanese were also still using a higher proportion of older aircraft of the first war generation, both the 'Val' dive-bomber and 'Kate' torpedo-bomber. The latter in particular combined poor protection and performance by 1944 standards.

The American air groups were combat-hardened veterans who had emerged from a richly endowed training programme back in the USA. US pilots had 300 hours of flying before carrier assignment and 24 months or so of training before entering combat. Many had been in combat for ten months and their aircraft were suffering, being in need of overhaul and with fuel consumption higher than normal. This exacerbated the Americans' disadvantage in combat range. The Avenger torpedo-bomber was, however, relatively fast and well armed and armoured. The Helldiver dive-bomber was even faster than the Avenger and could absorb much punishment, but it was not as manoeuvrable as its slower but well liked predecessor, the SBD-5 Dauntless, which was still in service in TG58.3 and in small numbers in *Yorktown*. Given the Japanese inability to exploit the good features of their aircraft, for which their designers had sacrificed other desirable qualities, they were outmatched both qualitatively and quantitatively in the air. American problems were marginal by comparison.

Fighter Control

By June 1944 the Americans had a well established system of Combat Information Centres (CICs) where radar operators plotted enemy raids on cathode-ray tubes with range and bearing indicators. They then passed this information to plotters who put the target on a plexiglass display. Raids were numbered and the position of friendly fighters shown. The status of all the fighters being controlled by a particular ship was placed on another display. The fighter direction officer observed both boards and allocated fighters to intercept the incoming raids, guiding them into position by VHF radio. There was a Task Force fighter director (FD) officer in the TF58 flagship in touch with the five Task Group fighter director officers. These in turn were in touch with the FD officers in each carrier. The director allocated raids to the TGs and the latter raids to individual ships. The system was an advanced and integrated one and worked remarkably well. The electronic hardware on which it was based comprised SC or SK search radars which worked at a frequency of 400mHz; range was 60-100 miles respectively and bearing error was 2° at 100 miles (7 miles). SM fighter control radar, carried in carriers, gave height information and also indications of the composition and vertical formation of the attackers. High-frequency SG surface search radar (3,000mHz) could give warning of low-altitude torpedo-bomber attacks.

The Japanese were much less well equipped in this vital regard. Their fighter director officers seem to have worked more or less straight from the radar consoles, giving instruction by radio. The main Japanese air warning radar was the Type 2 with a frequency of 200mHz. It was of low power, which limited range to 50 miles at best. Bearing error was 5° at such ranges. A still lower frequency radar of higher power, similar range but lower accuracy, the Type 3, was also used.

Anti-Aircraft Gun Defence Systems

The Americans were also ahead in shipborne air defence. They had pioneered tachymetric fire control systems for their 5in dual-purpose guns as early as the late 1920s. Originally, these systems had been fed by optical instruments but in the Mk 37 system, developed just before the war, provision for radar was included in the design. An electro-mechanical computer, capable of dealing with 400-knot targets, was located below deck; rate of change of range control was fully automatic. It is generally considered the best heavy anti-aircraft system of the war. Mk 4 radar was installed in the Mk 37 from September 1941, but by mid-1944 it was being replaced by a more accurate Mk 12 with Mk 22 height-finder. What made this system, combined with the 5in gun, so formidable was the development of the radar-activated VT proximity fuse, which caused the shell to explode as it passed lethally close to a target.

Japanese dual-purpose guns lacked both these fuses and radar director control: their 5in gun also had a lower muzzle velocity, range, shell weight and rate of fire and was regarded as an inferior AA weapon to the 20–24rpm 4in gun mounted in the latest Japanese ships. Tachymetric directors were fitted for heavy AA guns and the smoke used to aid fire control made Japanese AA barrages kaleidoscopes of colour. Their director systems, however, tended to be heavy, complicated and slow. The Japanese relied on time fuses for their AA shells, which included large 'incendiary shrapnel' shells for big guns of up to 18.1in calibre.

The Japanese lacked an equivalent of the 40mm Bofors gun carried in virtually all US ships. Mounted in twin or quadruple mounts, it could fire 900gm shells at 160 rounds per minute per barrel. These effective weapons were supplemented by 450rpm 20mm Oerlikons, although the latter's effectiveness was limited by 123gm shells. The Japanese only had 25mm light AA guns, often in triple mounts. These were quite good guns as far as they went, with a rate of fire of about 220rpm, but they also suffered from low shell weight (about 250gm), slowness in elevation and training, inadequate sights, excessive vibration, small magazines and excessive muzzle blast. They were large and unwieldy for their limited hitting power. Some were director fired. The Japanese, however, even more than the Americans, had to rely on a sheer hail of shot to protect their ships from aircraft.

Overall, the US forces were much better equipped for anti-air warfare at all ranges than their Japanese opponents. The latter were as much behind their enemies as they had been ahead of the Russians in surface gunnery thirty-nine years before.

ANTI-SURFACE WEAPONS

The only anti-surface ship weapons used in this battle were torpedoes and bombs. The main potential ship-killers were torpedoes. US submarines carried three types of 21in torpedo. The Mk 18 was an electrically propelled 'trackless' weapon with a 575lb warhead and a range of 4,000 yards at 29 knots. The other two weapons were more conventional 'heater' torpedoes, the very similar Mk 14 and the Mk 23. Both carried a 643lb Torpex warhead 4,500 yards at 46 knots. All three weighed over 3,000lb, which was too much for aerial delivery. Aircraft carried the 22.4in Mk 13, a short 'heater' weapon which combined a heavy explosive charge (600lb of Torpex) with a weight of just over 2,200lb. It had a range of 6,300 yards at 33.5 knots. By 1944 it had been modified with a detachable wooden air tail and a false head to allow dropping at high speed from 1,000ft. Original dropping conditions had been 50ft at 110 knots, which helps explain the continued antipathy in the US naval air arm towards torpedo operations. In June 1944 US Navy strike squadrons continued to rely primarily on bombs. Armour-piercing bombs were available in two weights, 1,600lb (only about 20 per carrier for delivery by Avenger torpedo-bombers) and 1,000lb. The latter weapons were best delivered by dive-bombers which could carry one each, with which the aircraft could penetrate a 5in armoured deck from 6,500ft in a 60deg dive. The most commonly used weapons by both dive- and torpedo-bombers were however 1,000lb and 500lb General-Purpose (50 per cent burster) and SAP (semi-armour piercing, 30 per cent burster) bombs that could wreak havoc on and beneath unprotected decks, but which could do little to damage the watertight integrity of armoured warships.

The Japanese used a small-calibre 17.7in torpedo of conventional 'heater' propulsion as their standard anti-ship weapon for carrier- and land-based attack aircraft. This could deliver a charge of a 450–530lb 2,200 yards at about 42 knots. Later versions could be launched at 300–350 knots. Alternatively bombs converted from 16in armour-piercing shells could be carried. The 'Judy' dive-bomber could carry a 1,082lb SAP bomb internally that could penetrate over 3in of armour plate. The 'Zero' fighter-bomber and 'Val' dive-bomber both relied on the 551lb weapon, although with its dive brakes the latter could deliver its load, usually supplemented by two small 66lb bombs, more accurately. With the lesson of their own fire problems at Midway, the Japanese had also developed phosphorus cluster munitions for anti-carrier incendiary work. The effectiveness of all these weapons depended on enough being delivered to their targets – something the Japanese were unable to achieve.

TACTICS

Both the concept of inflicting decisive attrition on a numerically superior enemy before the final engagement and outranging the enemy were traditional features of Japanese doctrine. Essential to the 'A-Go' plan were preliminary attacks by land-based aircraft on the US fleet. Then the carriers would conduct strikes, exploiting the superior range of their aircraft to which the Americans could make no reply. Shuttle bombing between carriers, flying to and from land bases, was also to be utilized if possible. The carriers would be split into three forces to be deployed in 'straight line thrust' or 'vertical depth disposition'. This placed Force 'C' of battleships and cruisers ahead, supported by its light carrier squadron. This was to act as a shield for the main carrier battle groups, as a scouting force and early warning picket, as well as being a tempting lure for the enemy to attack. Splitting the carriers into separate groups made them vulnerable to defeat in detail, but after the experience of the Battle of Midway – when three out of the four carriers of a concentrated force were sunk virtually at one blow – it was considered the lesser of the two evils. It also gave scope for 'encirclement', enveloping the enemy in the pincer-like movements so beloved of Japanese operational planners.

By mid-1944, however, fuel shortages inhibited ambitious ship manoeuvres. Forces 'A' and 'B', the carrier battle groups, had one carrier as formation guide at the centre. The other ships were on each quarter at 1,500 metres. Battleships and heavy cruisers in the formation where also placed on this 1,500-metre circle, while light cruisers and destroyers were at 2,000 metres. Japanese ships were supposed to manoeuvre in conformity to the guide carrier, but they tended to manoeuvre independently when under air attack and paid little regard to the requirements of mutual defence. The weakness in the scale of Japanese AA weapons meant that they were forced to put greater emphasis on desperate individual manoeuvres to protect themselves from air attack.

Japanese air attack tactics showed little sophistication, being direct thrusts with little or no attempt at evasion. The strike aircraft, in massed formation led by pathfinders, were covered by escort fighters above, behind and on the flanks. The idea was that the enemy's combat air patrol would be defeated by a sufficient number of aircraft to inflict decisive damage on the lightly protected decks and hangars of the US carriers. Some attempt was made to disrupt American radars by the use of air-dropped 'chaff', but it was relatively easy for American radar operators to identify the correct targets.

The Americans had adopted the task group method of deployment as their answer to solving the conundrum of concentration versus dispersion. Two fleet and two light fleet carriers seemed the maximum dispersion congruent with adequate screening by the available numbers of cruisers and destroyers. The structure was a flexible one and essentially TF58 was composed of five separate fleets, one of battleships and four of carriers, able to operate as one concentrated force or independently as required. Even when operating at some distance from each other, the range of carrier aircraft allowed mutual support.

One of the carrier groups, the weakest, was allocated to support the battle line. If the air battles led to command of the air, then it was intended that the cruiser support groups of the carrier groups, plus some of their destroyers, were also to be released to supplement the surface action group, usually known as the 'battle line'. When the fleet formed into a concentrated force, three carrier groups were to operate 12 miles apart on a north-south axis: the battle line would operate 15 miles ahead of TG58.3 with the battle line carrier group (TG58.4) 12 miles ahead of the northernmost carrier group. Two picket destroyers were disposed 20 miles ahead of the battle line.

The battle line was in fact a misnomer. It was deployed in anti-air formation with the flagship in the centre and the other vessels in a 6,000-yard circle around it. The carrier groups were formed with one ship in the centre and the others on a 2,000-yard circle; cruisers and destroyers were 2,000 yards further out. This formation was kept strictly and manoeuvres were based on the movement of the guide except in emergency, notably torpedo attack. The powerful task groups could rely on effective fighter and AA protection and mutual support, rather than individual manoeuvre, to give them sufficient protection.

The keys to such protection were the fighter direction teams mentioned previously. Each Task Group kept two eight-aircraft divisions as a strong combat air patrol (CAP). As the fighter director officers (FDOs) in the CIC observed and evaluated raids, they would vector the CAP, usually of eight Hellcats, on to the interception point, giving estimates of the size of raid, altitude, course and speed. When the CAP made visual contact, its commander advised the FDO as to the raid's actual course, speed and composition – and then attacked. A CAP committed to intercept a raid would be replaced by another group of fighters to provide an immediate reserve. This technique meant that enemy raids were engaged out to 60 miles. Attackers had to face 15 minutes of air combat, which meant that not many would reach their targets.

American offensive carrier tactics were less well developed as there had been no major carrier versus warship engagements for some time. The specialized scout squadrons had been integrated with the dive-bomber squadrons, and this had serious effects on American abilities to find moving targets. One critic has argued that '. . . it is perplexing to read the aggressive pronouncements of the American carrier admirals when discussing the Japanese carrier force . . . and their failure to develop an effective doctrine for finding that force . . . When one remembers the numerical superiority of the Japaneses force the scale of American air searches borders on negligence'.[1]

Even when the enemy had been found, another problem was the lack of expertise of the US bomber units in their primary role. They had had more experience in bombing in support of the island offensive than in attacking ships with torpedoes. The tendency to overestimate the bomb as a weapon against heavy warships was a natural response to the Midway success, but it underestimated the special conditions of that battle. Avengers, therefore, tended to be used as bombers to supplement the dive-bombers rather than as the basic anti-ship strike systems that they really were. Only half the Avengers in any strike were torpedo-armed. A 'deck load' strike of a fleet carrier comprised 16 Hellcats, 12 dive-bombers (50 per cent with GP bombs, 50 per cent with SAP bombs) and 9 Avengers. Armour-piercing bombs were to be used as targets offered themselves.

Spruance, an essentially surface sailor, did not overestimate the striking power of his carriers. His plan was for his aircraft to knock out enemy carriers and then attack cruisers and battleships 'to slow or disable them'. The surface striking force of battleships and cruisers would then inflict the coup de grace: Lee was 'to destroy the enemy fleet either by fleet action if enemy elects to fight or by sinking slowed or crippled ships if enemy retreats'.[2] It was hoped to pursue a retreating enemy to destruction.

THE ENCOUNTER

On the evening of 15 June, Ozawa's carrier fleet was spotted by the submarine *Flying Fish* coming out of San Bernadino Strait in the Philippines. Shortly afterwards the submarine *Seahorse* spotted the battleship group coming northwards 200 miles ESE of Surigao Strait. Because of Japanese jamming, this sighting report was not received until early the following morning, the 16th. Spruance, knowing the enemy fleet was out, postponed the invasion of Guam, timed for two days later. He reinforced his fleet from forces assigned to shore bombardment duties and ordered the concentration of his carrier groups 180 miles west of

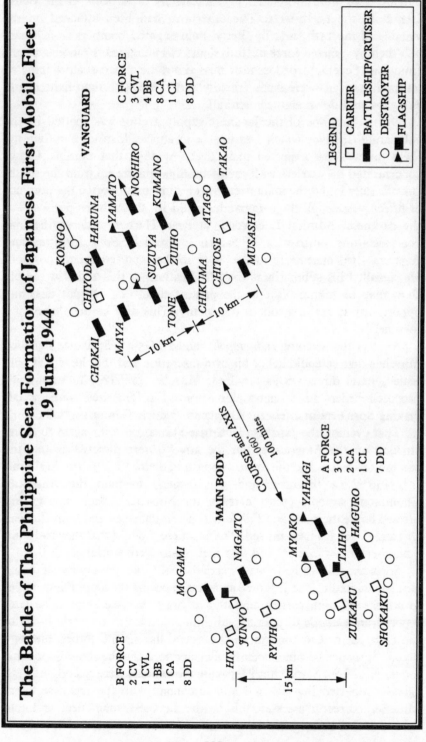

The Battle of The Philippine Sea: Formation of Japanese First Mobile Fleet
19 June 1944

LEGEND

CARRIER

BATTLESHIP/CRUISER

DESTROYER

FLAGSHIP

VANGUARD

C FORCE
3 CVL
4 BB
8 CA
1 CL
8 DD

KONGO
CHIYODA
HARUNA
YAMATO
NOSHIRO
SUZUYA
KUMANO
ZUIHO
ATAGO
TAKAO
CHIKUMA
CHITOSE
MUSASHI
CHOKAI
MAYA
TONE

10 km

10 km

MAIN BODY

COURSE and AXIS
060°

100 miles

A FORCE
3 CV
2 CA
1 CL
7 DD

MOGAMI
NAGATO
MYOKO
YAHAGI
TAIHO
HAGURO
HIYO
JUNYO
RYUHO
ZUIKAKU
SHOKAKU

B FORCE
2 CV
1 CVL
1 BB
1 CA
8 DD

15 km

Tinian. Two were away striking successfully at airfields in the Bonin Islands to the north-west. The other two had been attacked on the evening of the 15th, first by 'Betty' twin-engined bombers from Guam and then by a mixed force of 'Judys' and twin-engined 'Frances' aircraft from Yap. Several torpedoes near-missed but the only casualties inflicted on the Americans were from 'friendly' AA fire. CAP, night fighters and AA guns shot down eighteen aircraft.

On 17 June one of the Japanese supply groups was spotted by the submarine *Cavalla*, which was unable to attack. Instead, she followed them towards the expected main fleet. At 1650 that evening Ozawa concentrated his carriers with the battleships coming up from the south. *Cavalla* duly found the main fleet that evening and reported the presence of fifteen vessels, all the commander could see through his periscope in the darkness. Admiral Lockwood, at Pearl Harbor, ordered the four boats scouting north-west of Saipan – *Finback, Bang, Stingray* and *Albacore* – to concentrate to the south in the reported enemy position. He signalled his submariners that: 'Indications at this end that the big show may be taking place at the present time . . . Do not miss any opportunity to get in a shot at the enemy. This may be the chance of a lifetime.'[1]

At 1741 that evening *Indianapolis* joined TG58.3. Spruance signalled Mitscher that he could act at his own discretion and that he would only issue general directives as required. Mitscher preferred to submit his proposed orders to Spruance for approval before they were issued, making Spruance in effect the Officer in Tactical Command (OTC)

That evening the Japanese land-based air forces tried again to inflict attrition on the Americans, but the attacks were directed against the amphibious forces and the forces supporting them. Fifty Japanese aircraft (17 'Judys', 2 'Frances' and 31 'Zeroes') mistook the American amphibious support escort carriers for Mitscher's fleet carriers and pressed home their attacks: *Fanshaw Bay* was damaged and both *Gambier Bay* and *Coral Sea* near-missed. The Japanese thought that they had sunk a number of fast carriers and that their plans were working.

Spruance, unscathed, was worried about the possibility of being outmanoeuvred by the Japanese and thus exposing the amphibious forces to attacks by both carrier aircraft and heavy surface ships. The later report from *Cavalla* of only fifteen ships, received in the early hours of the 18th, seemed to confirm an attempt to use several forces, one as a decoy. Spruance became increasingly convinced that he should not come too far west from Saipan until Japanese movements were clearer. At 0730 *Cavalla* reported that she was still in contact with the Japanese force. Mitscher correctly assessed this as the Japanese main fleet and told Spruance that he intended to close the Japanese at high speed, locate it

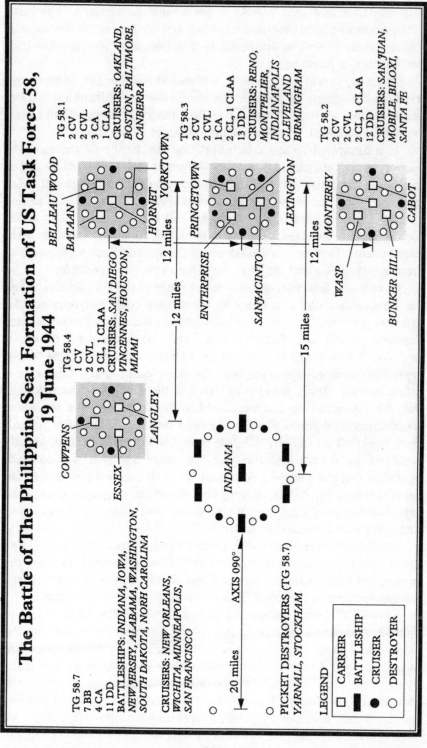

The Battle of The Philippine Sea: Formation of US Task Force 58, 19 June 1944

TG 58.1
2 CV
2 CVL
3 CA
1 CLAA
CRUISERS: *OAKLAND, BOSTON, BALTIMORE, CANBERRA*

TG 58.3
2 CV
2 CVL
1 CA
2 CL, 1 CLAA
13 DD
CRUISERS: *RENO, MONTPELIER, INDIANAPOLIS CLEVELAND BIRMINGHAM*

TG 58.2
2 CV
2 CVL
2 CL, 1 CLAA
12 DD
CRUISERS: *SAN JUAN, MOBILE, BILOXI, SANTA FE*

TG 58.4
1 CV
2 CVL
3 CL, 1 CLAA
CRUISERS: *SAN DIEGO VINCENNES, HOUSTON, MIAMI*

TG 58.7
7 BB
4 CA
11 DD
BATTLESHIPS: *INDIANA, IOWA, NEW JERSEY, ALABAMA, WASHINGTON, SOUTH DAKOTA, NORTH CAROLINA*
CRUISERS: *NEW ORLEANS, WICHITA, MINNEAPOLIS, SAN FRANCISCO*

PICKET DESTROYERS (TG 58.7)
YARNALL, STOCKHAM

BELLEAU WOOD
BATAAN
YORKTOWN
HORNET
PRINCETON
LEXINGTON
ENTERPRISE
SAN JACINTO
MONTEREY
WASP
BUNKER HILL
CABOT
COWPENS
LANGLEY
ESSEX
INDIANA

AXIS 090°

12 miles
12 miles
12 miles
15 miles
20 miles

LEGEND
□ CARRIER
■ BATTLESHIP
● CRUISER
○ DESTROYER

133

that afternoon and send TG58.7 in for a night engagement. The battle line commander, however, had too much respect for Japanese abilities in night actions to feel secure about such a prospect. He signalled back to Mitscher in direct terms:

'Do not (repeat *not*) believe we should seek night engagement. Possible advantages of radar more than offset by difficulties of communications and lack of training in fleet tactics at night. Would press pursuit of damaged or fleeing enemy, however at any time.'[2]

This confirmed Spruance in his opinion that he should remain in the vicinity of Saipan, moving eastwards by night and westwards by day as far as the wind allowed: US carriers had to turn to the east into wind whenever they wished to operate aircraft. Spruance agreed with Lee that given US general superiority, the balance of advantage in a night action would go to the Japanese. He would not therefore seek a night engagement. The carriers would cover the islands from surface attack from any direction and strike at the enemy as soon as possible.

Ozawa was, however, cruising out of range of the US carriers, biding his time for a strike at a range at which they could not respond. Air searches were sent out by both sides, which came into contact. Three Japanese aircraft, two 'Judys' and an E13A 'Jake' floatplane, were lost, one of each type to US fighters. At 1525 Ozawa received the first of four reports of carrier groups to the east. The Americans found nothing except a few aircraft. Ozawa decided to strike at the Americans the following day. This decision was communicated to the fleet just as the aggressive Rear Admiral Obayashi was sending off a deckload strike of 67 aircraft from his CVLs, *Chitose*, *Chiyoda* and *Zuiho*. *Chiyoda* had already launched 22 aircraft and one was lost when the raid was recalled. Spruance thought a strike might occur at dusk and had his carriers sail into the setting sun so that the attackers would show up more easily. The Japanese had tried attacks with land-based aircraft during the day, but none ever found Spruance's battlefleet.

Shore-based direction-finders picked up the Japanese fleet as TF58 sailed east-north-east during the night. Mischer wished to turn the carriers to be within strike range at dawn. Spruance, misled by overheard submarine reports, preferred however to keep the current course.

Kurita's 'C' Force was spotted on radar by a US Navy PBM Mariner flying-boat at 0115 on the 19th, close to the direction-finding fix, but the flying-boat's radio signal was not picked up. *Enterprise* launched her radar-equipped Avengers, whose pilots were specially trained in night flying. They flew together for 100 miles and then split up to search individually, missing the Japanese force by 45 miles. Ozawa also sent out search aircraft, a mix of 19 'Jake' floatplanes from his surface ships, 13 'Kates' and 11 'Judys'. All 43 aircraft were in the air by 0600 and the

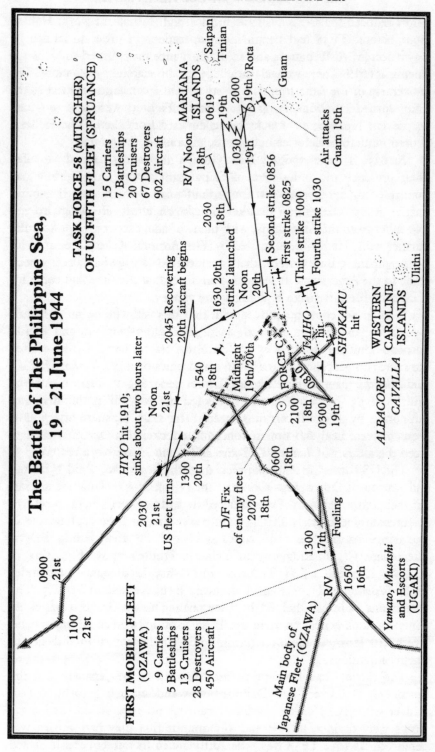

The Battle of The Philippine Sea, 19 – 21 June 1944

TASK FORCE 58 (MITSCHER)
OF US FIFTH FLEET (SPRUANCE)

15 Carriers
7 Battleships
20 Cruisers
67 Destroyers
902 Aircraft

MARIANA ISLANDS

Saipan
Tinian
Rota
Guam

R/V Noon 18th

0619 19th
2000 19th
1030 19th

Air attacks Guam 19th

Second strike 0856
First strike 0825
Third strike 1000
Fourth strike 1030

SHOKAKU hit
TAIHO hit

WESTERN CAROLINE ISLANDS

Ulithi

ALBACORE
CAVALLA

FORCE C
0810
0300

2030 18th
1630 20th strike launched
Noon 20th
2045 Recovering 20th aircraft begins

1540 18th
Midnight 19th/20th
2100 18th
0300 19th
0600 18th

HIYO hit 1910; sinks about two hours later

Noon 21st
2030 21st
US fleet turns
1300 20th

D/F Fix of enemy fleet 2020 18th

Fueling
1300 17th

R/V 1650 16th

Main body of Japanese Fleet (OZAWA)

Yamato, Musashi and Escorts (UGAKI)

0900 21st
1100 21st

FIRST MOBILE FLEET
(OZAWA)

9 Carriers
5 Battleships
13 Cruisers
28 Destroyers
450 Aircraft

effort reduced the assets available for fleet anti-submarine work. Half an hour before, TF58 had begun flight operations in order to launch its dawn search, ASW patrols and CAP. Spruance only turned towards the enemy at 0619. There were clashes between the searchers once more. The movement of the American fleet westwards was constantly slowed as the ships turned into wind to operate aircraft. Fighters were sent to Guam to prevent Japanese air attacks being directed from there. The Hellcats scored numerous victories both in the air and on the ground.

At 0730 a 'Jake' spotted Task Groups 58.7 and 58.4 and signalled their presence 160 miles west of Saipan to Ozawa. This sighting was confirmed by another aircraft four minutes later which spotted another carrier group. Ozawa now decided to make his effort. His vanguard was 300 miles from the Americans, with the two main carrier groups 80 miles further west. He had been misled by Vice-Admiral Kakuta, commander of the Japanese Base Forces, that considerable damage had already been done to the Americans. It seemed, therefore, that the time had come for a maximum-effort strike to confirm the victory.

It could not come quickly enough for Obayashi who began to launch two 'Kate' pathfinders at 0800, 45 'Zero' fighter-bombers and 8 'Jill' torpedo-bombers escorted by 17 'Zero' fighters at 0825. Ozawa waited for more contact reports but at 0856 could wait no longer. *Taiho*, *Shokaku* and *Zuikaku* together launched 48 'Zeroes' escorting 27 torpedo-carrying 'Jills' and 53 'Judys'. The strike was led by two 'Jill' pathfinders and supported by a 'chaff'-carrying 'Judy'. The main Japanese attack thus went in piecemeal and not in concentrated strength; Ozawa wished to keep the aircraft of Force 'B' (*Junyo*, *Hiyo* and *Ryuho*) as a reserve.

The US battleship *Alabama* picked up the first wave, 'Raid 1', at 140 miles at 0957. Other ships soon had the two groups of Japanese aircraft on their radar. At 1005 TF58 ordered its fighters over Guam to return. Lieutenant Joe Eggert, TF58's fighter director, had the leading role in the entire battle. His main colleagues were the Task Group FDOs, Lieutenant C. D. Ridgeway in TG58.1, Lieutenant R. F. Myers in TG58.2, Lieutenant J. H. Trousdale in TG58.3, Lieutenant-Commander F. L. Winston in TG58.4 and Lieutenant E. F. Kendall in TG58.7. The Americans were also helped by Lieutenant (Junior Grade) Charles A. Sims, an intelligence officer in the TF58 flagship, who could understand overheard Japanese radio chatter and hence gain tactical intelligence of enemy intentions.

The carriers had been preparing to strike at the Japanese and the Avengers, Helldivers and Dauntlesses were launched to orbit out of danger while the Hellcats were put into the air. Aircraft on the hangar decks were drained of fuel and any ammunition they had aboard was removed. At 1019 TF58 was ordered to launch its fighters and it turned eastwards into wind. The task groups had lost their tight formation. TG58.1 was due east of TG58.3 and TG58.2 was a little ahead of station to the south-east. Groups were 12 to 15 miles apart. Between 1023 and 1038, 140 Hellcats were launched and the 82 already on CAP moved west to intercept the attackers. The inexperienced Japanese had begun to orbit while waiting to be assigned targets by the group leader. This gave Sims the opportunity to listen in to the Japanese plans and also gave the Americans time to launch all their fighters. When the Japanese moved in to attack, they ran straight into the well-directed Hellcats. The Japanese were at 18,000ft; the Americans at 17,000–24,000ft. The American fighters scored numerous successes. *Essex*'s Hellcats claimed 20 kills; *Cabot*'s 15 and *Monterey*'s 11. Several pilots scored four victories each. Only about 40 Japanese aircraft broke through the outer air defences, to be attacked by more fighters. Some Japanese attacked the picket destroyers, but more closed in to attack the battleships of TG58.7. *South Dakota* was hit by a bomb, the only hit on a US ship that day, although *Minneapolis* was near-missed. At 1057 'Raid 1' was declared over. Only 8 'Zero' fighters, 13 fighter-bombers and 6 'Jills' were still in the air to return to their carriers.

At 1107 Eggert saw another strike approaching, the 601st Air Group from the three Japanese fleet carriers. As the aircraft flew over the Japanese Force 'C', Kurita's over-enthusiastic gunners engaged them, shooting down two and causing eight aircraft to abandon their mission. Again the strike leader tried briefing his crews in the air, allowing the US fighters to move to optimum altitude for an interception. Commander David McCampbell, of *Essex*, claimed five 'Judy' dive-bombers and one 'probable'; the rest of his squadron another 15½ kills. Other fighters joined in, the Japanese aircraft demonstrating a tendency to blow up after a few hits. One pilot, Lieutenant (JG) Vraciu from *Lexington*, claimed six 'Judys'. About twenty Japanese broke through the fighter cordon, pursued by more US fighters. No hits were scored, although one crashing 'Jill' hit *Indiana*'s armoured belt. The US AA fire came into its own, clawing the Japanese aircraft out of the sky. One 'Judy' near-missed *Wasp* and another *Bunker Hill*, both causing some damage, albeit limited. It was poor recompense for the 97 aircraft destroyed in this raid; only 16 'Zeroes', 11 'Judys' and 4 'Jills' returned to the carriers.

The carnage inflicted on the two strikes was not the only problem facing Ozawa. The US submarine *Albacore* had been allocated a patrol square in the path of the Japanese fleet. Her captain, Commander J. W. Blanchard, first saw one carrier and then another in a more favourable position to be attacked. It was *Taiho*, which Blanchard planned to attack at 2,000 yards with a full salvo of six torpedoes. Blanchard's fire control computer malfunctioned and *Albacore* was forced to fire by eye at

0909.32. One of *Taiho*'s aircraft, a 'Jill', observed one of the torpedoes and crashed into it to protect the carrier, but one of the six scored a hit on *Taiho*'s starboard side forward. The forward lift was jammed and fuel lines broken, but the carrier had been slowed by only one knot and damage seemed limited. Atrocious damage control, however, soon exacerbated the problem. As aviation spirit was pumped out of the damaged fuel tanks, a large amount was spilled on to the hangar deck. Then it was decided to open the ventilating ducts and blow the fumes away. This had the effect of spreading a dangerous and volatile mix of petrol and crude oil through the ship.

As *Taiho*'s damage control officers did the Americans' work for them, the Japanese Force 'B' launched its strike of 7 'Jill' torpedo-bombers and 25 'Zero' fighter-bombers, escorted by 15 'Zero' fighters. The strike had been sent out on the basis of erroneous sighting reports and was redirected while in flight to a more accurately reported spot further south. Not all the aircraft got the message and some continued to their original destination, where they found nothing. Twenty 'Zeroes' did turn south, where they were engaged by Hellcats, twelve from *Hornet* and four night fighters from *Yorktown*. Six 'Zeroes' were shot down. Only one 'Zero' attacked a ship, missing *Essex* by 600 yards with its bomb. It was shot down by a *Langley* Hellcat. The 40 remaining Japanese aircraft made it back to their carriers.

At 1030 Force 'B' sent out another strike of 10 'Zero' fighter-bombers, 9 'Judys', 2 'Jills' and 27 'Vals', escorted by 26 'Zeroes'. This was supplemented by 4 'Zeroes' and 4 'Jills' from *Zuikaku*. It took an hour to launch and was again directed at a spurious contact. When it found nothing, the formation split up. Most aircraft went to land at Guam while the 8 *Zuikaku* fighters and the 8 'Zero' fighter-bombers turned back to the carriers. Some Guam-bound aircraft found TG58.2. The carrier *Monterey* picked up the first part of 'Raid 4' at 1330 at 134 miles. The aircraft had closed to 53 miles, however, before they were positively identified as enemy and *Monterey* had communications problems that prevented her from controlling the engagement properly. *Wasp*'s FDO was put in control and his own fighters made the first interception, but they overlooked the need to confirm the height of the enemy themselves. This allowed 'Judys' to come in under the CAP to attack with bombs, including incendiary clusters. *Wasp* was near-missed but shot down three aircraft. Another 'Judy' attacked *Bunker Hill* but missed with its three bombs, which blew a Hellcat into the water. The Japanese aircraft was shot down, as was another, by the light carrier *Cabot*.

The Japanese aircraft heading back for the carriers found an American search group of two Avengers and a Hellcat, but the superior US pilots more than held their own, even in the torpedo-bombers. The first American group was supported by a second and shot down six 'Zeroes'. Another American search team was less lucky with its opponents. A Helldiver and Hellcat were both brought down by the 'Zeroes' they engaged.

As the rest of the Guam-bound Japanese aircraft approached their destination, they were attacked by about sixty Hellcats and Corsairs from *Cowpens*, *Essex*, *Hornet*, *Enterprise*, *San Jacinto* and *Princeton*. McCampbell shot down another two aircraft. A strike from *Hornet* cratered the airfield at Orote on Guam and the fighters tore into the aircraft in the air. Thirty of the 49 Japanese aircraft were shot down and the rest were so badly damaged either in flight or on landing that they were effective losses. Two American fighters were lost in the fighting.

While the doomed 'Raid 4' was in the air, nemesis struck the main Japanese carrier force. At 1152 *Cavalla* found Force 'A' and easily avoided the weak and badly trained and equipped ASW screen. (Japanese sonar was useless at much above 10–12 knots). The submarine fired a six-torpedo salvo at *Shokaku*, four of which hit. *Cavalla* was then depth-charged by the escorting destroyers but managed to escape. The Japanese carrier was very badly damaged by the four hits and was set on fire, the flames being fed by aviation spirit and the fumes of Tarakan crude oil. Just after 1500, as she settled in the water as a result of serious flooding, *Shokaku* exploded and sank, taking 1,263 out of her complement of 2,000 to their doom. Half an hour later *Taiho* suddenly exploded as the volatile fuel fumes were accidentally ignited. Holes were blown in the bottom of the ship, the flight deck bulged and split and the sides were blown out of the hangar deck. Ozawa and his staff were transferred to the destroyer *Wakatsuki* and later to the cruiser *Haguro*. Attempts to control the conflagration on board the carrier were futile and, after another explosion just before 1830, the ship capsized and went down stern first; 1,650 of her 2,150 crew lost their lives.

The day had proved to be an unmitigated disaster for the Japanese. The First Mobile Fleet had lost its major striking power. Of the 374 aircraft committed to raids by the three carrier groups, 244 had been lost, plus another 50 land-based aircraft. Nineteen of these were shot down by AA gunfire; the rest by fighters. Twenty-two more aircraft went down with *Taiho* and *Shokaku*, bringing the one day's aircraft losses to over 300. On the American side, only 31 aircraft had been lost, 22 fighters in air combat or by AA fire over Guam, three on search missions and six in operational accidents. One of *Lexington*'s fighter pilots had earlier compared the day's events to 'an old-time turkey shoot'; the day's combat soon became known as 'The Great Marianas Turkey Shoot'.

The US carriers had done exceptionally well in battle against the Japanese strike waves, but their own strike forces had been disrupted.

Attempts were made to send strike aircraft in the air westwards to look for the Japanese carriers, but it proved impossible to communicate with the strike squadrons because of congested radio channels. TG58.1 sent some of its Helldivers to attack Guam at about noon and an hour later, on his own initiative, the commander of *Lexington*'s Dauntlesses organized a strike against Orote field on Guam supported by Dauntlesses and Avengers from *Enterprise*. The armour-piercing bombs of the dive-bombers did little damage, but the delayed-action high-explosive bombs dropped by the Avengers did crater the runway. Serious damage to the airfield had to await the mid-afternoon strike mentioned previously.

The US strike squadrons had suffered minimal casualties in the operations of the 19th and were ready to strike at Ozawa's fleet, if it could be found and brought within range. The need to recover aircraft delayed TF58 heading west until 2000. TG58.4 had to be left behind because of its need to refuel. As the rest of TF58 closed the expected enemy position, there was little information as to Ozawa's precise location. The two submarines' attack reports were helpful, as was a sighting report by a US Navy Liberator long-range reconnaissance aircraft. Less so was an HF direction-finding report which erroneously put First Mobile Fleet further to the south than it in fact was. Night searches with night fighters and radar-equipped Avengers were considered but rejected as both types of aircraft had been used heavily the previous day and the pilots were tired. Operating them would also mean turning back to the east. At 2207 Mitscher changed course to 260° and increased speed to 23 knots, the best economical speed for his destroyer screen.

The Japanese were, in fact, moving away during the night to the north-west. They were not as downcast as they should have been because of erroneous messages of heavy damage inflicted on the US carriers. Ozawa intended that the three groups would rendezvous to replenish on the 21st. Admiral Toyoda signalled more detailed orders in the early hours of 20 June. Mobile Fleet was to reorganize and replenish; disabled ships should proceed to Japan and some carriers back to Lingga for further training. On the 22nd the surface ships and remaining carriers would continue to attack the US Task Force, in co-operation with land-based aircraft; the carrier aircraft would then be transferred to these bases to continue operations and the carriers would join the others at Lingga. The surface ships would then 'mop up' around Saipan.

On the 20th Kurita sent off fifteen search aircraft to the east and when four failed to return and US aircraft were reported, the cautious Force 'C' commander recommended withdrawal to the west. Ozawa, however, shared Toyoda's optimism and said that the fleet would remain, as ordered, to fight again the following day. The Americans also sent out searches, although only to the normal 325-mile range. During the middle of the day, at the instigation of his air officer, Mitscher decided to send out a special search/strike force of twelve bomb-laden Hellcats from *Lexington*, escorted by eight other fighters from *San Jacinto*, to search for the enemy out to 475 miles. As the aircraft made their way westwards, the First Mobile Fleet milled around in some confusion at its rendezvous point: Ozawa was suffering communications problems from the cruiser *Haguro*. The threat of an attack delayed fuelling and when it was finally decided upon, a false sighting of supposed American aircraft delayed it once more. Only at 1300 was Ozawa able to get on board a suitable flagship, the carrier *Zuikaku*, and reassert control. He found out for the first time the extent of the previous day's losses but still thought the sacrifice had been worth it because of the erroneous reports of damage inflicted on the Americans. As Ozawa went on board *Zuikaku*, *Chitose* and *Zuiho* launched three 'Kates' on a scouting mission, but these did not find the Americans until 1715 that evening.

The Americans finally won the race to find the enemy at 1540 that afternoon. At 1330 eight Avengers and two Helldivers, with Hellcat escort, took off from *Enterprise* and *Wasp*. At 1538, as he approached the end of his outward leg, Lieutenant Robert Nelson spotted something on the horizon: two minutes later he clearly identified Force 'A' with its surviving carrier and caught a glimpse of Force 'B' with its carriers. Joined by two other Avengers, Nelson shadowed the Japanese for half an hour and one of the other pilots, Lieutenant (JG) James S. Moore, corrected the fix for longitude. The enemy was now placed at 134°30′E, 15°34′N, over 275 miles from TF58. Any strike would therefore have to be at extreme range. At 1542 another search aircraft spotted Force 'C'.

At 1548 Mitscher ordered a deckload strike, despite the risks of striking at maximum range. 'The decision to launch strikes,' he later wrote, 'was based on so damaging and slowing enemy carriers and other ships that our battle line could close during the night and at daylight sink all ships that our battle line could.'[3] He recognized the likelihood of heavy losses with a night recovery of pilots untrained in flying after dark. Nevertheless, Mitscher told Spruance that he was launching everything he had; a second deckload strike was to be prepared to follow the first. All but one carrier launched in the first wave: it took ten minutes for the eleven ships to launch 240 aircraft, 95 Hellcats (some with 500lb bombs), 54 Avengers (many equipped with four 500lb bombs), 51 Helldivers and 26 Dauntlesses. As the news came in that the Japanese were 60 miles further away than expected, Mitscher decided to hold back his second wave until the morning. The American aircraft already in the air throttled back to conserve fuel, which was even more important when they received the news that they had to fly even further.

Based on his 1715 sighting report, Ozawa gamely launched a night strike from Force 'C' with seven 'Kate' torpedo-bombers led by three radar-equipped 'Jills'. These were to land on Guam after the attack. Force 'A', with the flagship, was 18 miles north-west of the intact Force 'B'. Force 'C', with its powerful surface ships, was to the south of 'B' but at a distance of 8 miles was unable to give much support to the carriers. The three light carriers of Force 'C' were in a line north to south with *Chitose* covered by *Musashi, Atago* and *Takao; Zuiho* by *Yamato, Chikuma, Kumano, Suzuya* and *Tone;* and *Chiyoda* by *Kongo, Haruna, Chokai* and *Maya.* To the east and south were the oilers of the supply groups with their destroyer escorts.

As the sun set, the desperate American aviators threw themselves into the attack. First to be assaulted was the supply group, which was attacked by twelve Helldivers and seven Avengers from *Wasp*, escorted by sixteen Hellcats. The Helldivers attacked each of four tankers; the fifth was attacked by four Avengers. The Hellcats strafed the escorts and gave cover from Japanese fighters. Two auxiliaries, *Seiyo Maru* and *Genyo Maru*, were hit so severely that they had to be scuttled that evening: *Hayasui* was hit be a single bomb, but not fatally. The attackers were engaged by six of the 68 'Zeroes' (including 28 fighter-bombers) launched in defence of the fleet by Ozawa's carriers. One US bomber and one fighter were lost.

The attacks on the carriers were put in as rapidly as possible. Commander Arnold, TG58.1's strike leader, ordered his aircraft to attack *Zuikaku*, which was screened by *Myoko* and *Haguro*, 1,600 yards on each bow, and *Yahagi* and the seven destroyers in a 2,200-yard circle all round the fleet carrier. Two groups of Helldivers from *Hornet* attacked *Zuikaku*, followed by twelve more of these aircraft from *Yorktown*. Then six Avengers from *Hornet* attacked the carrier but only four had torpedoes and two of these attacked cruisers; due to other mistakes or malfunctions, and no torpedo hits were scored. Finally, ten Hellcat fighter-bombers from *Bataan* attacked in two divisions. Attacks were made on *Zuikaku* and one of the cruisers and Hellcats got entangled with *Zuikaku's* CAP. *Zuikaku* was hit several times and near-missed five times by the American bombers. Her aviation fuel was set on fire and it looked as if she might have to be abandoned. Orders were in fact given to do so, but her experienced damage control officers got the fires under control and the ship was saved.

Force 'B' was disposed with the carrier *Junyo* in the centre, *Hiyo* 1,500 metres away on her port quarter and *Ryuho* the same distance on *Junyo's* starboard quarter. The battleship *Nagato* was ahead to starboard and the cruiser *Mogami* to port. The destroyers were spread out in a 2,000-metre circle. Lieutenant-Commander Weymouth, *Lexington's* dive-bomber commander and group leader, saw that *Zuikaku* was under attack and concentrated on the carriers of Force 'B'. The Avengers accompanying his Dauntlesses were all armed with bombs rather than torpedoes. *Junyo* was hit twice and near-missed six times. The attackers were engaged by 'Zeroes' on the way in and out but were protected by the escorting Hellcats. One Hellcat, one Avenger and one Dauntless were hit. *Ryuho* was attacked by four Avengers from *Enterprise* as the escorting Hellcats drove off defending fighters. The US aircraft were engaged by guns of all calibres, including *Nagato*'s main armament, as they made their glide-bombing attacks. All survived but *Ryuho* was only near-missed. *Hiyo* next came under attack by three Avengers from *Belleau Wood*. These were torpedo-carrying aircraft and, thanks to the heroism of Lieutenant (JG) George Brown, the flight leader, who deliberately drew down Japanese fire, two hits were scored. The converted liner was badly damaged and listed to port, heavily on fire. The carrier sank before the eyes of Brown's two crew men, who had been told to bale out; Brown himself was badly wounded and crashed on the way back to the carrier.

As the Americans attacked Force 'C' it was recovering a strike launched at 1600 against a false contact. The hapless Japanese aircraft were shot down as they circled their carriers. *Chiyoda* seemed the largest target to the attackers and was dive-bombed by *Bunker Hill*'s Helldivers, all of which missed. Then came bomb-carrying Avengers from *Monterey* and *Cabot* and Avenger torpedo aircraft from *Bunker Hill*. The *Monterey* Avengers scored two hits on the carrier's stern which destroyed two aircraft on the hangar deck. The four Avenger bombers from *Cabot* split themselves between *Chiyoda* and the battleship *Haruna*. The latter was hit three times aft and near-missed twice forward, but continued moving at 27 knots. The Avenger torpedo-bombers carried out a high-speed, high-altitude attack on *Chiyoda* but all five torpedoes dropped missed. The Americans thought that they had scored hits, however, and the last three Avengers attacked a cruiser and a battleship. Again no hits were obtained.

Hiyo finally sank two hours after being hit. She was the only Japanese warship actually sunk, although four other carriers had been damaged, one heavily, along with the battleship *Haruna*, the cruiser *Maya* and the destroyer *Shigure*. The main losses were Ozawa's airmen. Despite a skilful defence by some fighter pilots that contributed to the seventeen US aircraft lost in combat during this phase, the day's events saw the loss of a further 65 Japanese carrier aircraft. By the evening of 20 June First Mobile Fleet was down to 35 carrier aircraft plus 12 floatplanes. Japanese carriers would never put to sea with fully operational air groups again. It was the end of the Japanese carrier force as an effective unit.

The main losses to the Americans were yet to come. As the US aircraft tried to fly back to their carriers they began to ditch in the sea as they ran out of fuel. Some pilots, unused to flying at night, got lost and had to be guided in by an *Enterprise* night fighter. First, Admiral Clark of TG58.1, followed by Mitscher, ordered their ships to turn on their lights. Aircraft landed wherever they could; some trying to land on cruisers and destroyers. Many crashed on landing or collided with other aircraft on deck; others ditched in the sea. No fewer than 17 fighters, 42 dive-bombers and 23 Avengers were lost in deck crashes, bringing total losses to 99. Excellent rescue work the following day kept aircrew deaths down to sixteen pilots and thirty-three crewmen; two officers and men were also killed on board the carriers.

Recovery had begun at about 2045 and lasted until 2252, when the carriers turned westward to retrace their path over the downed airmen. Ozawa ordered Kurita'a powerful surface force eastward for a night attack, but no enemy ships could be found and at 2205 Kurita was ordered to turn to the north-west and retire with the rest of First Mobile Fleet. Mitscher had suggested that Lee's battleships be sent ahead as the carriers rescued aircraft, but Spruance preferred to keep his assets concentrated; in any case, Lee was too far away to catch the enemy by the following morning. It seemed better in the circumstances to keep the surface action force to deal with any cripples encountered. The Japanese fleet was tracked overnight by a US Navy Mariner flying-boat and Avengers with long-range tanks, but the need to sail eastwards to operate aircraft held back the pursuit. At 0545 and 0615, TF58 launched two strikes of Hellcat fighter-bombers to search and strike out to 270 miles in case any enemy ships could be found: nothing was. At 0743 TF58's Avengers finally broke contact with First Mobile Fleet at a range of 360 miles from TF58. The greatest encounter between carrier fleets in history was over.

RESULTS

At 1920 on 21 June Spruance issued orders that if nothing was spotted that day Task Force 58 was to retire to the east. The fleet duly reversed course at 2030 with Lee's battleships in the area where the American aircraft had made their attacks the previous evening. Ozawa ordered his fleet to enter Nakagasuki Bay, Okinawa, the same evening and offered his resignation to Admiral Toyoda; it was refused. He had, indeed, handled his forces well, only being let down by his inferior air groups. There were more recriminations on the American side about Spruance's overly defensive tactics. The fleet commander himself clearly recognized 'that going out after the Japanese and knocking their carriers out would have been much better and more satisfactory than waiting for them to attack us; but we were at the start of a very important and large amphibious operation and we could not afford to gamble and place it in jeopardy. The way Togo waited at Tsushima for the Russian fleet has always been on my mind. We had somewhat the same basic situation; only it was modified by the long-range striking power of the carriers'.[1]

Yet on balance it is hard to fault Spruance too much. Indeed, alternative, more obviously aggressive tactics might have been counter-productive. For, adopting the apparently cautious tactics that he did, allowed Spruance to concentrate all his fighters on knocking the Japanese naval air arm out of the sky. The enemy's 'fleet' had been drawn out and annihilated; this loss of the Japanese carrier aircraft was the most decisive immediate result of the battle. As a signal that appeared in Japanese Naval Headquarters after the fall of Saipan made clear: 'Our Imperial Combined Fleet is now powerless.'[2] It was clear that nothing more could be done to defend the Japanese Empire using conventional forces and tactics. The Tojo Government resigned and any nation other than Japan might have sought peace. But Japan in 1944 was culturally incapable of making peace. She embarked on an increasingly desperate policy of making the Allied advance too expensive to continue.

When the US fleets converged on the Philippines, Japan expended *Zuikaku*, *Chiyoda* and *Ryuho* with virtually no aircraft as decoys in a desperate multi-pronged pincer manoeuvre to exploit the residual striking power of the Japanese surface fleet. After coming disturbingly close to success, it eventually failed, with heavy losses, in the Battle of Leyte Gulf. After that it was the turn of the suicide pilots and other units, including the surviving battleship *Yamato*, which was overwhelmed by TF58 aircraft on a one-way mission to Okinawa. It took the awesome suddeness of two nuclear weapons dropped by USAAF Marianas-based B-29 bombers to shake the Imperial Government into seeing reason in surrendering. Not only had Spruance's victory of 19/20 June 1944 destroyed the main fighting power of the Japanese fleet, it had also secured the bases from which the most significant strategic air attacks in military history were flown. The Philippine Sea must, therefore, be regarded as one of the most decisive fleet actions of all time.

7
EPILOGUE:
THE POST-WAR ERA

THE BATTLE OF THE PHILIPPINE SEA demonstrated that in future the main striking platforms of battlefleets would be those that operated above the waves at great speed and at great distance or below the waves with great stealth. The operations of these two new and fast-maturing forms of naval technology made it very difficult for gun-armed warships, even the most powerful examples of the genre ever seen, to get into direct contact. After the Second World War the battleship was retained only by the US Navy, which found in its existing 'Iowa' class a useful means of shore bombardment and also a tough weapons platform suitable for longer-range surface-to-surface land-attack and anti-shipping cruise missile systems, when these were eventually developed. It was clear, however, that the main surface ships of the post-war battlefleets were the aircraft-carriers. Fleet carriers were the main units of the Atlantic Striking Fleet formed by NATO's Atlantic Command when it was set up in 1952 with a 'role . . . analogous to that of the Grand Fleet of World War I and the British Home Fleet of World War II, namely the offensive force for Atlantic and Northern waters and the essential cover under which defensive forces, protecting our shipping from attack by aircraft, submarine and mine can do their work.'[1]

This striking fleet deployed forward would both attack the enemy's forces at source, so reducing the direct threat to sea communications, and give cover from larger surface units that could otherwise overwhelm convoy escorts. The importance of the escorts had been re-emphasized during the Second World War. In the Atlantic the British Home Fleet, reinforced from time to time by American battleships and carriers, had been able to do nothing directly to defeat the formidable U-boat threat. This had to be confronted around the merchantmen themselves. Yet the escorts that eventually won the Battle of the Atlantic would have been able to do little against the powerful German capital ships if the latter had not been confronted and dealt with at their own level.

The requirement to deal with the most potent enemy naval striking units remains the fundamental raison d'être of the modern 'battlefleet'. During the 1950s the development of the nuclear-powered submarine finally gave submerged torpedo-carrying platforms sufficient mobility to play a full part as main fleet striking assets, albeit still as individual hunters rather than as a concentrated force unit. Already the final generation of conventional submarines had raised doubts about the ability of numerous but individually relatively weak and slow convoy escorts to cope with their threat. From the mid-1950s onwards the nuclear-powered submarine outclassed smaller surface escorts in a way that powerful surface warships once had. This was a threat, therefore, that would have to be addressed in more traditional 'main fleet' terms. Nuclear-powered submarines were also most potent assets for repeating the successes of the US submarines in the Philippine Sea battle against major surface ships.

A completely new element in the post-war naval equation was the impact of nuclear and thermonuclear weapons. Mutal deterrence enforced by nuclear-tipped ballistic missiles – for which the nuclear-powered submarine provided the best launching platform – maintained peace in the intense 'Cold War' atmosphere. The advent of the ballistic missile submarine, however, had a considerable impact on more narrowly naval strategy also. It first drew the Soviet Navy's forces out into the oceans, both to pose nuclear threats and to protect against them; and then it gave the Soviets a vital form of sea use that had to be defeated – i.e., the maintenance of the Soviet SSBNs with their long-range missiles on patrol in their defended bastions in the North and Far East. On the American side, the SSBN replaced the carrier as the primary means of making long-range nuclear strikes against shore targets, a 'strategic' role that had come to dominate US carrier operations and doctrine in the 1950s. This freed US carriers for more limited operations against the shore, and also for use in a more traditional role as naval battlefleet units against the other side's naval forces.

As Soviet maritime capabilities improved in the 1960s and 1970s, their 'battlefleet' began to emerge. It was composed of forces designed to deal with the main American naval threats to the homeland and the SSBN bastions. Against this the Soviets deployed primarily submarines, many equipped with anti-ship missiles of long and short range, and land-based anti-ship aircraft. In order to support these forces, a surface fleet of 'missile cruisers', 'anti-submarine ships' and even 'large aircraft-carrying cruisers' was also built up. Although constructed primarily for defensive purposes, this fleet of submarines and aircraft posed a potent threat to vital Western shipping, both military and civilian, that required not only direct defence but also the latest evolution of battlefleet doctrine.

This was done from the late 1970s onwards, when strategic theorists in both NATO and the US Naval Staff began to re-articulate traditional naval concepts to contain and, if necessary, defeat the Soviet Navy. By taking the initiative and deploying main battle forces of carriers and SSNs forward, the Soviets would be forced on to the defensive and the direct threat to Western shipping would be greatly reduced as forces were deployed on defensive missions. The trend in naval technology had been to make the forces designed for guerre de course and commerce protection even less distinguisable from battlefleet units than previously. This made drawing down the direct threat to shipping by absorbing it in main fleet operations somewhat easier. Submarines and aircraft, and even surface ships, engaged in combating the Western 'battlefleet' could not be in two places at once.

There were many echoes of the Philippine Sea battle in these concepts. The aim was clearly to draw out Soviet air and submarine forces into a battle they would lose, perhaps catastrophically. In these circumstances, further enhancing the AAW and ASW strength of the carrier striking force was of paramount importance. From the mid-1980s, therefore, the NATO Striking Fleet began to work out techniques of operating its carriers in large Norwegian fjords, a mode of operation that would greatly complicate an attacker's problems. Aircraft and submarines would have to approach on more predictable axes, allowing a concentration of anti-air and anti-submarine assets against them. The mountainous walls of the fjords would also make it difficult to produce fire control solutions for anti-ship missiles. In addition, friendly shore-based aircraft could add their weight to the anti-air and anti-submarine battle. While this was going on, forward deployed Anglo-American SSNs would be prowling northwards into the Soviet 'bastions', forcing the Soviets to commit their own SSNs (and other ASW forces) in their SSBNs' defence. The force requirements of this slow-moving submarine battle, combined with that of committing forces to try conclusions with the carriers, would reduce the assets the Soviets might commit to any guerre de course to reasonable, and more easily dealt with, proportions.

Such is the essence of the 'forward maritime strategy' to which Western navies are currently committed. It is the latest variant of an old concept, the use of one's main naval units as a mobile striking force to be manoeuvred to neutralize and/or destroy the enemy's main and most dangerous naval force. The likelihood of an actual encounter between the battlefleets of East and West seems even more remote that it did in the 1980s. Indeed, there will probably never be an encounter between mature carrier/air/submarine battlefleets. Instead, the two main fleets of the world, with the Royal Navy adding its not insignificant weight to that of the US Navy, will act as fleets in being, complicating the options of the other side and helping maintain the peace of the world. The fleet-to-fleet encounters that do not actually take place are often more important than those that do.

NOTES

1. INTRODUCTION

1. Sir Julian Corbett, *Some Principles of Maritime Strategy* (new edition edited by E. J. Grove, Annapolis & London, 1988), p. 167.
2. 'Final Note' of *Strategical Terms and Definitions Used in Lectures on Naval History,* reproduced as Appendix to above, pp. 324–5.

2. TSUSHIMA

Gunnery

1. From table in Nicolas Klado, *The Battle of the Sea of Japan* (London, 1906), p. 32.
2. 'Order of the Commander in Chief of the Second Pacific Squadron No. 29, Jan 23 1905' in *The Russo-Japanese War Reports from Naval Attaches, etc.,* Vol IV (Admiralty Intelligence Dept, August 1907) pp. 215–6.
3. *ibid.*
4. *Reports from Naval Attaches, etc.,* Vol I (December 1904), p. 162.

Tactics

1. J. S. Corbett in concert with Rear Admiral Sir Edmond Slade, *Maritime Operations in the Russo-Japanese War 1904–5,* Vol II (Admiralty War Staff Intelligence Division, October 1915), p. 242.

Encounter

1. Quoted Corbett, Staff History, Vol II, p. 239.
2. Rozhestvensky, *Last Days,* quoted *ibid.,* p. 249.

3. Semonov, *Battle of Tsushima*, *ibid.*
4. Admiral Kamimura, quoted *ibid.*, p. 265.
5. Report by Captain W. C. Pakenham dated November 1905, *Reports from Attaches*, Vol IV, p. 14.
6. Report of the Japanese First Division, quoted *ibid.*, p. 286.
7. *ibid.*, p. 292.
8. Quoted *ibid.*, pp. 290–1.
9. Japanese Official history, quoted *ibid*, p. 319.
10. Evidence at Nebogatov's court-martial, *ibid.*, p. 319.
11. *ibid.*
12. Russian Officer quoted *ibid.*, pp. 320–1.

Results
1. Corbett, Staff History, pp. 332–3.
2. *ibid.* p. 344.
3. *ibid.*
4. *ibid.*, p. 383.
5. J. N. Westwood, *Russia Against Japan 1904–5, A New Look at the Russo-Japanese War* (London, 1986), p. 163.

3. THE DREADNOUGHT REVOLUTION

1. For a full account, see J. Sumida, *In Defence of Naval Supremacy* (London, 1989).
2. Quoted A. Marder, *From the Dreadnought to Scapa Flow*, Vol I (Oxford, 1961), p. 334. By this was meant traditional *close* blockade off the enemy's coast.

4. JUTLAND

The Forces
1. Marder, *ibid.*, Vol. III, pp. 113–4.

Encounter
1. Unpublished work by Dr Andrew Gordon makes this controversial point clear.
2. H. H. Frost, *The Battle of Jutland* (Annapolis, 1936 and 1964), p. 241.
3. *ibid.*, p. 243.
4. Jellicoe to First Lord, quoted Marder, *Dreadnought to Scapa Flow*, Vol III, p. 110.
5. Jellicoe, quoted *ibid.*, p. 175.

6. PHILIPPINE SEA

Background
1. Quoted in W. T. Y'Blood, *Red Sun Setting: The Battle of The Philippine Sea* (Annapolis, 1981), p. 66.

Tactics

1. W. D. Dickson, *The Battle of The Philippine Sea* (London, 1975), pp. 31–2.
2. Quoted S. E. Morison, *New Guinea & the Marianas* (History of US Naval Operations in World War Two, Vol VIII, 1953), p. 243.

Encounter

1. Quoted Y'Blood, *Red Sun Setting*, p. 85.
2. Quoted Morison, *New Guinea and the Marianas*, p. 244.
3. TF 58 Action Report, quoted Y'Blood, *Red Sun Setting*, p. 151.

Results

1. Letter to S. E. Morison, quoted in *New Guinea and the Marianas*, p. 135.
2. Dickson, *Battle of The Philippine Sea*, p. 168.

7. EPILOGUE

1. *The Role of Aircraft-Carriers*, Memorandum by First Lord, 9 November 1953, Public Record Office, ADM1/24695.

THE JAPANESE FORCES

1. The Japanese surface squadrons were numbered in continuous order, reflecting the tendency of Pacific navies after 1922 to regard the new 10,000-ton heavy cruisers developed as a result of the Washington Treaty as light capital ships. There were also echoes of Togo's use of cruisers as capital ships at Tsushima. Of course, the heavy cruisers of this period were no match for battleships in gun power or range, although the long-range Japanese torpedoes did give the cruisers carrying them some long-distance potential against heavy ships.

INDEX

A6M5 'Zero' fighters, see 'Zero' fighters
Abdiel, 60, 104
Acasta, 90
Acheron, 63
Active, 59, 63
Action information organization, 110
Admiral Nakhimov, 15, 27, 39, 41
Admiral Seniavin, 15, 27, 39
Admiral Ushakov, 15, 27, 39, 42, 43
Adzuma, 18, 19, 25
Agincourt, 57, 96
aircraft, 81, 105, 106–10, 117, 123–30, 146,
   148
aircraft carriers, 107, 116, 146–7
airships, 51, 79, see also Zeppelins
Ajax, 56, 95
Akashi, 19, 38, 44
Akashimo, 117
Akebono, 19
Akitsuki (Tsushima), 19
Akitsuki (Philippine Sea), 116
Akitsushima, 38
Alabama, 122, 136
Albacore, 123, 132, 137
Alexander III, see Imperator Alexander III
Almaz, 16, 27, 39, 45
Ambuscade, 100–1
AMCs, see also Shinano Maru, Ural
ammunition, 23, 25, 33, 71, 83–4, 108–9
Anadir, 39, 45
Anthony, 121
anti-aircraft warfare, 123–4, 126–8
anti-submarine warfare (ASW), 109, 114
Apraksin, see General Admiral Graf Apraksin
Arbuthnot, Sir R., 90, 93
Archerfish, 123
Ardent, 101, 104
Argo Clock, 72, 74, 86
Ariake, 42
Ariel, 63
armament, 87, 108–9, 116–23, 126–8
Arnold, Cdr., 142
Asagumo, 116
Asahi, 17, 23, 24, 25, 33
Asama, 18, 23, 35, 36
Asashimo, 118

Asashio (Tsushima), 19
'Asashio'-class destroyers (Philippine Sea),
   118
Atago, 118, 142
'Atlanta'-class cruisers, 120
Attack, 63
Audacious, 56
Aurora, 11, 16, 27, 39, 44
Ausburne, see Charles F Ausburne
Australia, HMAS, 62
'Avenger' torpedo-bombers, 120–1, 125, 130,
   134, 136, 140–4
Azusa Maru, 119

B5N 'Kate' torpedo-bombers, see 'Kate'
   torpedo-bombers
B6N-1 'Jill' torpedo-bombers, see 'Jill'
   torpedo-bombers
B97, 69
B98, 69
B109, 69, 81
B110, 69, 81
B111, 69
B112, 69
Badger, 94
Bagley, 122
'Bagley'-class destroyers, 120
'Baltimore'-class heavy cruisers, 120
Bang, 123, 132
Barham, 62, 85, 87–8
Barr & Stroud rangefinders, 22, 74
Bataan, 120, 142
'Battlefleet', 147–8
battleship design, 47–8
Bayern, 65
Beatty, Adml., 54, 68, 70, 76, 80–105
Beaver, 63
Bell, 120
Belleau Wood, 120, 143
Bellerophon, 57, 96
Bellona, 59
Benbow, 57, 91
Benett, 122
'Betty' torpedo-bombers, 115, 132
Bezuprechni, 42
Biloxi, 42

Birkenhad, 63
Birmingham (Tsushima), 63
Birmingham (Philippine Sea), 121
Black Prince, 58, 91, 101, 104
Blanchard, Cdr., 137
Blanche, 59
Blestyashtchi, 44
Blohm & Voss, 69, *see also* 'B'-boats
Blücher, 48, 53
Boadicea, 59, 79
Bodri, 44
Bofors guns, 126
'Boiki'-class destroyers, 16
bombs, 127, 130
Borodino, 13, 27, 36, 39, 40
'Borodino'-class battlships, 11, 13, 21
Botha, 63
Boyd, 120
Bradford, 120
Braine, 121
Bravi, 27, 44
Broke, 60, 100–1
Bronson, see Clarence K Bronson
Brown, 120
Brown, Ltd., 143
Brummer, 77
Buini, 27, 39, 44
Buistri, 27, 42
Bukhvostov, Capt., 36
Bunker Hill, 120, 137, 138, 143
Burns, 120
Byedovi, 27, 43, 44

Cabot, 120, 137, 138, 143
Calliope, 59
Cammell Laird, 60
Campania, 61
Canada, 57
Canterbury, 59
Caperton, 121
Caquot kite balloon, 61
Caroline, 59, 98
carriers, 108
Case, 121
Castor, 60, 98–9, 101
Cavalla, 123, 132, 139
Centurion, 56
Champion, 63, 101–2
Charette, 120
Charles F Ausburne, 121
Chatfield, Capt., 83–5
Chemulpo, 10
Chester, 59, 63, 89, 91
Chihaya, 36, 37
Chikuma, 142
Chin Yen, 20
Chitose (Tsushima), 19, 38, 42
Chitose (Philippine Sea), 117–18, 123, 134, 141–2
Chiyoda (Tsushima), 20
Chiyoda (Philippine Sea), 117–18, 123, 134, 142–3, 145

Chokai, 118, 142
Clarence K Bronson, 121
Clark, Adml., 144
Cleveland, 121
'Cleveland'-class light cruisers, 120–1
Coastal Motor Boat No 4, 44
Cochrane, 58
Codes, 79–80
Cogswell, 121
Collingwood, 57, 96
Colossus, 57, 96
Combat Information Centres (CIC), 110, 125
Comus, 59
Conner, 120
Conqueror, 56
Constance, 59
Contest, 98, 100, 102
continuous aim, 21, 23, 25, 33
Converse, 121
convoys, 105, 109
Conyngham, 122
Coral Sea, 132
Coral Sea, Battle of the, 116
Corbett, J., 28, 45
Cordelia, 62
cordite propellant, gunnery, 70
Cornwell, Boy 1st Class J., 89
'Corsair' night fighters, 121, 139
Cotten, 121
Cowell, 120
Cowpens, 121, 139
Craven, 120
Cromarty Firth, 61
cruisers, 128–30

D3A 'Val' dive-bombers, *see* 'Val' dive-bombers
D4Y-1 'Judy' dive-bombers, *see* 'Judy' dive-bombers
D4Y-1C 'Judy' reconnaissance aircraft, *see* 'Judy' reconnaissance aircraft
'Dauntless' dive-bombers, 120–1, 125, 136, 140–1, 143
Defence, 58, 90, 93, 104
depth charges, 116
Derfflinger, 67, 75, 83–6, 88–9, 94–8, 105
Deutschland, 66
Dewa, Adml., 29, 31
Dewey, 121
director firing, 50, 78
dive-bombers, 110
Dmitri Donskoi, 16, 22, 27, 39, 42, 44
Dniepr, 16, 27
Dogger Bank, Battle of the, 53, 61
Donskoi, see Dmitri Donskoi
Dortch, 121
Dotter simulators, 25
Dreadnough, 56
'Dreadnought' battleships, 48
Dreyer fire control system, 49, 71–2, 77, 86–7
Dreyer-Elphinstone Clock, 72

Dublin, 63, 103
Duke of Edinburgh, 58
Dumaresq instruments, 24, 49, 72, *see also*
  Entfernungs Unterscheid Peilschreiber
Dyson, 121

Eggert, Lt., 136–7
Elbing, 68, 81, 98–100, 102
Ellet, 121
Elphinstone, Keith, 72
Emden, 44
Engadine, 64, 81, 93
England, 114
Enkvist, Adml., 44
Enterprise, 121, 134, 139, 140–41, 143–4
Entfernungs Unterscheid Peilschreiber, 75
Erin, 56
Essex, 119–21, 137–9
'Essex'-class carriers, 119
Evan-Thomas, Adml., 81, 85, 87–9, 93

F4U-2 'Corsair' night-fighters, *see* 'Corsair'
  night fighters
F6F-3 'Hellcat' fighters, *see* 'Hellcat' fighters
F6F-3N 'Hellcat' night fighters, *see* 'Hellcat'
  night fighters
Falmouth, 63, 91
Fanshaw Bay, 132
'Farragut'-class destroyers, 121
Faulknor, 60, 101–2
Fearless, 63, 103
Felkerzam, Adml., 27
Ferzen, Capt., 43
Fighter control, 123–4, 128–30
Finback, 123, 132
Fire control, 25, 47, 49, 71, 86, 109, 126, 137
Fisher, Adml. J., 47
'Five-Minute Ships', 66
Fleet Air Arm, 110
'Fleet' submarines, 109
'Fletcher'-class destroyers, 120–22
Flying Fish, 123, 130
Fortune, 98, 100, 104
'Forward maritime strategy', 148
'Frances' bombers, 132
Frankfurt, 68, 81, 90
Frauenlob, 69, 99, 104
Friedrich der Grosse, 65, 104
Fuji, 18, 24, 25, 39
Fullam, 122

G7, 70
G8, 70
G9, 70
G10, 70
G11, 70
G37, 69, 102
G38, 102
G39, 70
G40, 70, 102
G41, 69
G42, 70

G86, 69, 96
G87, 69
G88, 70
G101, 69
G102, 69
G103, 69
G104, 69
Galatea, 62, 79, 81, 83
Gambier Bay, 132
Garland, 98, 101–2
Gatling, 121
Gefechtskehrwendung, 78, 95
General Admiral Graf Apraksin, 15, 27, 39
Genyo Maru, 119, 142
George, 114
Germaniawerft, Kiel, 69, *see also* 'G'-boats
'Gleaves'-class destroyers, 121
Gloucester, 63
Goeben, (*Yavuz*), 67
Goodenough, Cdre., 88–9, 91, 99
Grant, Warrant Officer, 71, 84
'Great Marianas Turkey Shoot', 139
Gridley, 120
'Gridley'-class destroyers, 120
Gromki, 41
Grosser Kurfürst, 65, 89, 96
Growler, 123
Grozni, 43, 44
Grumman Avenger torpedo-bomber, 108
Guam, 130, 132, 136, 138–40, 142
Guest, 122
gunnery, 20–6, 38, 49, 70–5

Haguro, 116, 139, 141–2
Halford, 122
Halsey, Adml., 119
Hamakaze, 117–18
Hamburg, 68, 98–100
Hancock, *see Lewis Hancock*
Hannover, 67, 97–8
Hardcastle torpedoes, 49
Harder, 115
Harding, E., 47
Harrill, Adml., 121
Hartog, Capt., 95
Haruna, 118, 142–3
Harusame, 40
'Harusame'-class destroyers, 19
Harvey, Maj. (RM), 83
Harwich Force, 54, 105
Hatsuki, 116
Hatsuse, 18
Hatsushima, 119
Hawksley, Commodore, 98
Hayashimo, 117
Hayasui, 119, 142
Hazelwood, 114
Healey, 121
'Hedgehog' weapons, 114
Heerman, 114
Heinrich, Commodore, 69
Helgoland, 66, 96

'Hellcat' fighters, 115, 120–1, 123, 129–30, 136–44
'Hellcat' night fighters, 120–1
'Helldiver' dive-bombers, 120–1, 125, 139–43
Hercules, 57, 72, 96
Hessen, 66, 67, 97–8
Hibiki, 119
Hickox, 121
Hipper, Adml., 54–5, 67–8, 80, 88–90, 93–5, 98, 102
Hiyo, 117, 124, 136, 142–3
Hoel, 114
Hoggatt Bay, 114
Hood, Hon. H., 89–93
Hornet, 120, 138–9, 142
Horn's Reef, 98, 103
Houston, 121
Howaldtswerke, Kiel, 69, *see also* 'H'-boats
Hudson, 122
Hull, 121
Hunt, 121

Idzumo, 18, 19, 23, 29, 38
'Ikazuchi'-class destroyers, 19
Imperator Alexander III, 12, 27, 36, 39
Imperator Nikolai I, 15, 27, 33, 36, 39
Inconstant, 62
Indefatigable, 62, 68, 79, 83, 85, 104
Independence, 120
'Independence'-class light carriers, 119–20
independent fire, 25
Indiana, 122, 137
Indianapolis, 119, 121, 132
Indomitable, 58, 90, 97–8
Inflexible, 58, 93, 97
Ingersoll, 121
Invincible, 58, 89–90, 93–4, 104
'Invincible'-class battle cruisers, 48, 58
Iowa, 122
'Iowa'-class battleships, 108, 122, 146
Iron Duke, 55, 57, 71, 94, 96, 103
Irtish, 39, 45
Izokaze, 116
Iwate, 18, 19, 23, 33, 35, 43
Izumrud, 16, 26, 27, 29, 39, 43

Jackson, Capt., 80
'Jake' floatplanes, 134, 136
Jellicoe, Adml., 54, 70–2, 76–8, 80–105
Jemtchug, 16, 21, 26, 27, 29, 39, 44
Jerram, Adml., 97–8
'Jill' torpedo-bombers, 116–18, 124, 136–8, 142
Joshima, Adml., 117
'Judy' dive-bombers, 116–17, 124, 127, 132, 134, 136–7
'Judy' reconnaissance aircraft, 116, 134
Junyo, 117, 124, 136, 142–3

Kagero (Tsushima), 43
'Kagero'-class destroyers (Philippine Sea), 116, 119

Kaiser, 65, 96
Kaiserin, 65
Kakuta, Adml., 136
Kamchatka, 16, 45
Kamimura, Adml., 18, 37, 39
Kasagi, 19, 38
Kasuga, 18, 25, 43, 44
'Kasuga'-class cruisers, 18
Kasumi, 19
Kataoka, Adml., 20, 40
'Kate' pathfinders, 134, 136, 141
'Kate' torpedo-bombers, 118, 125, 142
Kempenfelt, 60
Kendall, Lt., 136
King, Adml., 114
King George V, 56, 97
Kishinami, 118
Klado, Cdr., 12
Knapp, 121
Kniaz Suvorov, see Suvorov
Kokuyo Maru, 119
Kongo, 118, 142
'Kongo'-class battlecruisers, 108, 118
König, 65, 88, 94, 96
König Albert, 65
Korea, 39, 45
Kostroma, 16, 27, 45
Kronprinz, 65, 102
Kronstadt (1919), 44
Kuban, 16, 27
Kumano, 142
Kurita, Adml., 118, 134, 137, 140, 144

Ladybird, 63
Lang, 121
Langley, 121, 138
Lansdowne, 121
Lardner, 121
Lebedev, Capt., 44
Lee, Adml., 121, 130, 134, 144
Lewis Hancock, 121
Lexington, 107, 119, 121, 137, 139–42
Leyte Gulf, Battle of, 145
Libau, 11
'Liberator' reconnaissance aircraft, 140
Liberty, 63
Lichtenfels, Adml., 67
Lion, 61, 71, 83–6, 89, 91, 97
'Lion'-class super dreadnoughts, 49–50
Lockwood, Adml., 132
'Long Lance' torpedo, 107, 117
Lowestoft Raid 1916, 54
Lugeol rangefinder, 22
Lützow, 67, 77, 83–6, 88–9, 93–4, 102, 104

McCall, 120
McCalla, 121
McCampbell, Cdr., 137, 139
McCord, 114
MacDonough, 121
Mackensen, 65
Maenid, 102

'Mahan'-class destroyers, 121
Malaya, 62, 87–9
Margrave, 65
'Mariner' flying-boats, 134
Markgraf, 89, 94, 96
Marksman, 60, 102
Marlborough, 57, 72, 91, 94, 96, 103
Marne, 99
Marshall, 121
Marvel, 102
Matsushima, 38
'Matsushima'-class cruisers, 20
Maury, 120
Mauve, Adml., 66
Maya, 118, 142–3
Miami, 121
Michelsen, Commodore, 69
Michishio, 117
midget submarines, 107, 117
Midway, Battle of, 108, 110, 116–17, 127–8
Mikasa, 17, 23, 24, 25, 33, 37, 39
Miklukha, Capt., 43
Miller, 121
Mindful, 102
Mines, 50, 77
Minneapolis, 122, 137
Minotaur, 58
Mitscher, Adml., 119, 132, 134, 141, 144
Mitsubishi G4M 'Betty' torpedo-bombers, see
    'Betty' torpedo-bombers
Mobile, 120
Mogami, 117, 142
'Mogami'-class cruisers, 118
Moltke, 67, 83–4, 86–7, 95, 97–8
Monarch, 56
Monomakh, see Vladimir Monomakh
Monssen, 122
Monterey, 120, 137–8, 143
Montgomery, Adml., 120
Montpelier, 121
Moore, Lt., 141
Moorsum, 88
Moresby, 102
Mosampo Bay, 12
Mugford, 122
München, 68, 99
Munster, 60
Murakumo, 42
'Murakumo'-class destroyers, 19
Murasame, 38
Musashi, 107, 115, 118, 142
Muskallunge, 123
Myakishev rangefinder, 22
Myers, Lt., 136
Myoko, 116, 142

Nagato, 117, 142–3
Nakajima B6N-1 Tenzan torpedo-bombers
    ('Jill'), see 'Jill' torpedo-bombers
Naniwa, 19, 38, 44
Nassau, 66, 99–100
Natal, 58

Navarin, 15, 27, 39
Nebogatov, Adml., 12, 27, 36–46
Nelson, Ltd., 141
Neptune, 57
Nerissa, 88
Nestor, 87–8, 104
New Jersey, 122
New Orleans, 122
'New Orleans'-class heavy cruisers, 122
New Zealand, 62, 79, 83, 97
Nicator, 87–8
Nichel Maru, 119
Niitaka, 19, 42, 44
Nikolai I, see Imperator Nikolai I
Nisshin, 18, 23, 25, 35, 39
Nomad, 87, 104
North Carolina, 122
Noshiro, 118
Nottingham, 63
Nowaki, 117
nuclear weapons, 147

Oak, 60
Oakland, 120
Obayashi, Adml., 117, 134, 136
Obdurate, 97, 102
Obedient, 102
Oerlikon guns, 125
Okinami, 118
Okinawa, 144–5
Oldenburg, 66, 101
Oleg, 16, 27, 39, 44
Onslaught, 102
Ophelia, 60
Orel (battleship), 13, 14, 22, 27, 36, 39, 43
Orel (hospital ship), 16, 27, 29, 45
Orion, 56, 72, 74, 94
Orote airfield, see Guam
Osliabia, 14, 27, 33–6, 44
Ostfriesland, 66, 104
Otowa, 19, 42, 44
Owen, 121
Ozawa, Adml., 114–16, 130–45

Pakenham, Capt., 24
Parsons' Specials, 63
Patterson, 122
Pearl Harbor, 116
Petard, 87–8, 101
Petrograd (1917), 44
Phaeton, 62, 79, 81
Pillau, 68, 81, 90
Pilotfish, 123
Pintado, 123
Pipefish, 123
Plaice, 123
Plunger, 123
Pohl, Adml., 53
Pollen fire control system, 49, 71
Pollen's Argo Clock, see Argo Clock
Pommern, 66, 98, 102, 104
Porpoise, 101

Port Arthur, 10, 12, 18
'Porter'-class destroyers, 122
Posen, 66, 97
Potter, see Stephen Potter
Princess Royal, 61, 83–6, 89, 91, 94, 97
Princeton, 120–1, 139
Prinzregent Luitpold, 65

Queen Mary, 61, 72, 83–6, 104

RO-104, 114
RO-105, 114
RO-108, 114
RO-111, 114
RO-116, 114
Raby, 114
Radar, 109–10, 125–6, 134
rangefinders, 22–4, 33, 87, 125
Redfin, 115
Reeves, Adml., 121
Regensburg, 69, 87–8, 90
Reno, 121
'Repeat Ms', 60
Revenge, 57, 95–6
Rheinland, 66, 101
Ridgeway, Ltd., 136
Rion, 16, 27
Rishitelny, see Akitsuki
Rossia, 45
Rostock, 69, 99–100, 102, 104
Rosyth, 54, 58, 61, 105
Royal Air Force, 106
Royal Navy, air arm, 106, *see also* Fleet Air
    Arm
Royal Oak, 57, 96
Royalist, 59, 98
Rozhestvensky, Adml., 11, 21, 27–39
Rus, 38
Rutland, Flt. Lieut., 81
Ryuho (ex-Taigei), 117, 124, 136, 142–3, 145

S15, 70, 98
S16, 70, 98
S17, 70
S18, 70, 98
S19, 70
S20, 70
S23, 70
S24, 70, 98
S32, 100
S33, 69
S34, 69
S35, 69, 96, 104
S36, 69
S50, 69
S51, 69
S52, 70, 101
S53, 70
S54, 70, 103
SB2C-C 'Hellcat' dive-bombers, *see* 'Hellcat'
    five-bombers
SBD-5 'Dauntless' dive-bombers, *see*

'Dauntless dive-bombers'
Sado Maru, 41
St Vincent, 57, 94, 96
Saipan, 115, 145
Sakhalin, 46
Salmon, 123
Samidare, 117
San Diego, 121
San Francisco, 122
San Jacinto, 121, 139, 141
San Juan, 120
Santa Fé, 120
Saratoga, 107
Sasebo naval dockyard, 12
Sazanami, 43
Scapa Flow, 54, 58, 61, 87, 105
Scheer, Adml., 53–6, 65–7, 69–70, 78, 80,
    88–104
Schichau, Elbing, 69, *see also* 'S'-boats
Schlesien, 66, 98
Schleswig-Holstein, 66, 97–8, 102
Schutz-Thornycroft boilers, 67
Schwartzkopf torpedoes, 26
Scott, Percy, 21, 50
Seahorse, 123, 130
Seaplanes, 109, 117–18
Seawolf, 123
Seiyo Maru, 119, 142
Slfridge, 122
Semenov, Cdr., 33
Seniavin, see Admiral Seniavin
Seydlitz, 54, 67, 83–6, 88–9, 94–8, 104–5
Shannon, 58
Shark, 90, 104
Sheerness, 56
Shells, 71
Shigure, 117, 143
Shikishima, 17, 23, 25, 37, 39
Shimakaze, 119
Shimose compound, 26, 33
Shimotsuki, 116
Shinano Maru, 29
Shirakumo'-class destroyers, 19
Shiranui, 41
'Shiratsyu'-class destroyers, 118
Shokaku, 116, 123, 136, 139
Short seaplanes, 61, 64
signalling, 78, 81, 91, 103
signals intelligence, 79–80, 114
Sims, Lt., 136–7
Sissoi Veliki, 14, 27, 39, 41
sonar, 109, 139
Sopwith float fighters, 61, 64
Southampton, 63, 88, 91, 99
South Dakota, 122, 137
'South Dakota'-class battleships, 122
Spandler, 114
Sparrowhawk, 100, 104
Spence, 121
Spitfire, 100
Spruance, Adml., 119, 130–45
Stanley, 121

Stephen Potter, 121
Sterrett, 121
Stettin, 68, 99
Stingray, 123, 132
Stirling, Capt., 101
Stockton, 122
Stuttgart, 68
Submarines, 78, 105, 108–9, 123, 127, 139, 146–8; development, 50
The Sullivans, 121
Sumida, J., 49
Superb, 57
Sussex, 54
Suvorov, 22, 27, 33–40
Suzuya, 142
Svietlana, 16, 39, 42
Svir, 45

TBF/TBM-1C 'Avenger' torpedo-bombers, *see* 'Avenger' torpedo-bombers
tactics, 26–9, 77–8, 128–30
Taiho, 114, 116, 124, 136–7, 139
Takachiho, 19, 44
Takao, 118, 142
'Takao'-class cruisers, 118
Tamanami, 118
Tawi-Tawi base, 124
Temeraine, 57
Terek, 16, 27
Termagent, 63
Terry, 121
Thatcher, 121
'Thornycroft Specials', 60, 63
Thunderer, 50, 56, 98
Thuringen, 66, 101
Tiger, 62, 84, 86, 97
Tingey, 121
Tipperary, 60, 99–101, 104
Tirpitz, Adml., 68
Togo, Adml., 12, 28–42, 115, 145
Tojo government, 145
Tokiwa, 18, 23
Tone, 142
Torpedo-Boat No 63, 41
torpedo-bombers, 107–8, 110
torpedoes, 26, 47–9, 75–7, 87–90, 94–102, 105, 107–8, 116, 118–21, 123, 127, 137, 142
Tovey, Lt. Cdr., 90
Toyoda, Adml., 114–15, 140, 144
Trousdale, Lt., 136
Tsessarevitch, 13
Tsuga, 119
Tsushima, 19, 44
Tunny, 123
Turbulent, 63, 88–9, 101, 104
Twining, 122
Tyrwhitt, Comm., 54

U-boats, 54–6, 79, 105; development, 51
U1, 50
U32, 79
U46, 103
U51, 104
U56, 79
U67, 79
U70, 79
UB22, 79
Uji, 20
Unity, 98
Urakaze, 116
Ural, 16, 27, 29, 38, 39, 45
Ushakov, see Admiral Ushakov
Uzuki, 119

V1, 70
V2, 70
V3, 70
V4, 70, 104
V5, 70
V6, 70
V26, 69
V27, 69, 87, 104
V28, 69
V29, 69, 87, 104
V30, 69
V44, 69
V45, 69, 102
V46, 69
V48, 70, 95, 97, 104
V71, 70
V73, 70
V186, 70
V189, 70
'Val' dive-bombers, 117, 125, 127, 138
Valiant, 62, 87–8
Vanguard, 57
Vickers rangefinders, 23, 72
Vincennes, 121
Vladimir Monomakh, 16, 27, 39, 41, 42
Von Der Tann, 48, 68, 83–8, 95–8, 102
Vraciu, Lt., 137
Vulcan, Stettin, 69: *see also* 'V' boats

Wadsworth, 121
Wakatsuki, 116, 139
Warrior, 58, 90, 93, 104
Warspite, 62, 87–8, 93, 103
Washington, 122
Washington Conference, 107
Wasp, 120, 137–8, 141–2
Westfalen, 66, 97–101, 105
Weymouth, Lt. Cdr., 142
Whitehead torpedoes, 26, 49
Wichita, 122
Wiesbaden, 68, 90, 94, 102, 104
Wilhelm II, Kaiser, 53
Williamson, Lt., 114
Wilson, 121
Winston, Lt. Cdr., 136

'Yagumo'-class cruisers, 118
Yahagi, 116, 118, 142
Yakumo, 18, 19, 23, 43

Yamagumo, 117
Yamato, 107, 115, 118, 142, 145
Yarmouth Raid 1916, 54
Yarmouth, 63
Yarnell, 122
'Yarrow Specials', 60, 63
Yellow Sea, Battle of the, 10, 19, 24
Yeo, Stoker, 84
Yokosuka D4Y-1 Suisei (Comet) dive-
  bomber ('Judy'), *see* 'Judy' dive-bomber
Yorktown, 120, 125, 138, 142
'Yorktown'-class carriers, 108

Yugiri, 40
Yugumo, 117, 118
'Yugumo'-class fleet destroyers, 118
Yukikaze, 119
Yunagi, 119

Zeiss rangefinders, 74
Zeppelin airships, 54, 103, 104–5
'Zero' fighters, 116–18, 123–4, 127, 132,
  136–8, 142
Zuiho (ex-*Takasaki*), 118, 123, 134, 141–2
Zuikaku, 116, 124, 136, 138, 141–2, 145